BETWEEN MUSLIMS

Stanford Studies *in* Middle Eastern
and Islamic Societies *and* Cultures

BETWEEN MUSLIMS

Religious Difference in Iraqi Kurdistan

J. Andrew Bush

STANFORD UNIVERSITY PRESS
Stanford, California

Stanford University Press
Stanford, California

© 2020 by the Board of Trustees of the Leland Stanford Junior University.
All rights reserved.

No part of this book may be reproduced or transmitted in any form or by any means, electronic or mechanical, including photocopying and recording, or in any information storage or retrieval system without the prior written permission of Stanford University Press.

Printed in the United States of America on acid-free, archival-quality paper

Library of Congress Cataloging-in-Publication Data

Names: Bush, J. Andrew, author.
Title: Between Muslims : religious difference in Iraqi Kurdistan / J. Andrew Bush.
Other titles: Stanford studies in Middle Eastern and Islamic societies and cultures.
Description: Stanford, California : Stanford University Press, 2020. | Series: Stanford studies in Middle Eastern and Islamic societies and cultures | Includes bibliographical references and index.
Identifiers: LCCN 2020008442 (print) | LCCN 2020008443 (ebook) | ISBN 9781503611436 (cloth) | ISBN 9781503614581 (paperback) | ISBN 9781503614598 (ebook)
Subjects: LCSH: Muslims—Religious life—Iraq—Kurdistān. | Islam—Iraq—Kurdistān—Customs and practices. | Irreligion—Iraq—Kurdistān. | Islamic ethics—Iraq—Kurdistān. | Kurds—Iraq—Kurdistān—Religion. | Kurdistān (Iraq)—Religious life and customs.
Classification: LCC BP63.I72 B87 2020 (print) | LCC BP63.I72 (ebook) | DDC 297.09567/2—dc23
LC record available at https://lccn.loc.gov/2020008442
LC ebook record available at https://lccn.loc.gov/2020008443

Cover art: Bahram Hajou, *Untitled*, 2018.
Cover design: Angela Moody

Contents

Acknowledgments vii
Notes on Transliteration xi
Preface xiii

INTRODUCTION
Fieldwork in Kurdistan: Islamic Traditions, Ordinary Relationships, and a Paradox   1

1 QURAN AND ZOROASTER
Attraction and Authority in Muslim Ethics   29

2 CHRISTIANS, *KAFIR*S, AND NATIONALISTS IN KURDISH POETRY   55

3 MYSTICAL DESIRE, ORDINARY DESIRE
Love, Friendship, and Kinship   87

4 SEPARATING FAITH AND *KUFIR* IN AN ISLAMIC SOCIETY   112

5 PLEASURE BEYOND PIETY
Religious Difference in Domestic Space   141

EPILOGUE
"Dear Reader!" 167

Notes 175
Bibliography 195
Index 209

Acknowledgments

IN THE FINAL DAYS OF WRITING MY FIRST ETHNOGRAPHY, I TRIED to remember the first ethnography I read as an undergraduate student. My memories of it had faded, and my thoughts rested on the teacher of the class who brought the ethnography to life. Jennifer E. Coffman first invited me to think about the relationship between ethnography and my own life. It was a life-changing invitation, and I thank her for it. My highest hope for this book is that the conversations it sparks include teachers with the passions, rigors, and care that she brought to the classroom.

This book began at Johns Hopkins University, where I had the privilege of working with Veena Das, Naveeda Khan, and Niloofar Haeri. Their contributions to my research have taken different shapes over the course of my study and beyond. They showed patience, demanded acumen, pushed me toward broader literatures, and pulled me deeper into the literature I thought I knew. If I have come to think of reading and writing as an act of care that happens in relationships, then it is in part due to the care they demonstrated in critique and experiment. Also at Johns Hopkins, I learned from Jane Guyer, Pamela Reynolds, and Aaron Goodfellow. Beyond anthropology my engagement with Bill Connolly, Jane Bennett, and their students shaped my thinking in many ways. Special thanks also go to Yitzhak Melamed and Jean McGarry.

Institutional support for this project dates to 2004 when an Andrew W. Mellon Fellowship in Humanistic Studies supported the start of my research at Johns Hopkins. I also had the good fortune of receiving fieldwork support from the Institute of Global Studies, the Department of Anthropology, and the Center for the Study of Women, Gender, and Sexuality (WGS) for the summers of 2005 and 2006. WGS and the Dean's Teaching Fellowship also supported my teaching, which became essential to the trajectory of my research. Fieldwork in 2008 and 2009 was funded by the National Science Foundation's Doctoral Dissertation Research Improvement Grant in Cultural Anthropology and the Wenner-Gren Foundation for Anthropological Research. In Kurdistan, support from the University of Silêmanî was indispensable to my research. Dr. Nzar Amin was extraordinarily gracious to me during many years of research.

The people in Kurdistan who welcomed me and supported my research in a variety of ways are too many to count. Dozens of people who shared their lives with me in support of my research have challenged and inspired me. While I wrote about many more individuals in the course of drafting the book, the three at the center of these chapters have become particularly significant. My gratitude to them has grown deeper with each draft. While conducting research for this book in Silêmanî, I was also inspired by the work of many other researchers, such as Shenah Abdullah, Schluwa Sama, Miran Emin, Sheikh 'Eli Qeredaxî, and 'Eta Qeredaxî.

At the New York University Abu Dhabi Institute (NYUAD), I held a Humanities Research Fellowship for three semesters and a summer that allowed me time for the research and writing of Chapters 2 and 4. The workshop I hosted there in 2015, "Islamism and Intimacy," was crucial for the development of Chapter 4. I thank Pascal Menoret, Sylvain Perdigon, Noah Salomon, and Rose Wellman for their participation and feedback there. Before and after the workshop, both Sylvain and Noah have continued to inspire me with their writing and thinking and generously responded to my writing in various formats. I thank Reindert Falkenburg for his support throughout my time at NYUAD, as well as Toral Gajarawala and Nathalie Peutz, who read individual chapters. Serra Okumuş and Alexandra Urbanikova both read the entire manuscript as undergraduate students. Their feedback was pivotal in the final stages of revision. During my time at NYUAD, many students inspired me as a writer with their readiness to tackle texts or ideas that initially appeared far from their own experience.

For friendship, support, and advice at various stages of my writing and teaching in Abu Dhabi, I also thank Marzia Balzani, Jonardon Ganeri, Jan Loop, Dale Stahl,

Corinne Stokes, Mark Swislocki, Deepak Unnikrishnan, and Luke Yarbrough. In addition to their support and friendship, Yousef Casewit and Mohammed Rustom helped me sort out many references to the Quran, hadith, and stories of Sufis. Conversations with Jill Magi kept me anchored in the perpetual movement of writing. At every stage, from book proposal to indexing, Marilyn Booth's advice was plentiful and reliable.

I thank Steve Caton for his generous engagement with this project since 2006, both in writing and in consultation. Suad Joseph provided crucial feedback on multiple chapters on different occasions. Previous versions of Chapters 3 and 5 were published in the *Journal of Middle East Women's Studies* and *American Ethnologist*, respectively; some feedback from reviewers and editors there has been incorporated into the revised versions of those articles for this book. Others who offered feedback on the original manuscript, draft papers, and occasional papers or presentations that stem from the project include Mohammed Fatih, Dahlia Gubara, Michiel Leezenburg, Sara Pursley, Edith Szanto, Marlene Schäfers, and Martin van Bruinessen. I am grateful for Mariwan Wrya Kanie's feedback in the last stages of writing, and Metin Atmaca was exceptionally kind to read multiple drafts of parts of this work.

Among many venues where I presented portions of the work, I was particularly challenged by questions and responses at the following institutions: American University of Beirut's Center for Middle Eastern Studies, Department of Anthropology, and Anthropological Society of Lebanon; the Department of Anthropology at University of California, Davis; Humanistic Studies at the Maryland Institute and College of Art; the Program in Arab Crossroads Studies at NYUAD; the Department of Iranian Studies at Jagellonian University; and the conference "Siting Pluralism" at the University of Göttingen. I thank my hosts and these audiences for their engagement.

Other colleagues further afield who have offered feedback on writing, correspondence on research questions, or support of other kinds are Alda Benjamen, Joanna Bocheńska, Tarek Dika, Maura Finkelstein, Khaled Furani, Laura-Zoë Humphreys, Amrita Ibrahim, Bridget Kustin, Laura A. Lewis, Neena Mahadev, Sidharthan Maunaguru, Urmila Nair, Anand Pandian, Vaibhav Saria, Nils Schott, and Jeremy Walton. Hitomi Koyama redefined for me what it means to be a comrade in academia.

The reviewers from Stanford University Press offered valuable feedback and suggestions that have reshaped the manuscript in important ways, and I thank them for their careful reading. Kate Wahl at Stanford has seen many versions of this project and offered crucial insight as she pushed it on to the next stage.

In the last days before the book went to press, I received advice and encouragement from my colleagues in the Program on Law and Society in the Muslim World at Harvard Law School; I thank Peri Bearman, Farzin Vejdani, and Nurul Huda Mohd Razif. In addition to his encouragement since we met in 2004, Michael Chyet advised me on transliteration of the Kurdish for this book. While I alone am responsible for any mistakes, I thank him for his advice. Cynthia Lindlof did a superb job copyediting. I am also grateful to Bahram Hajou for permission to use his art for the cover.

Finally, beyond academia, the book benefited from the inspiration offered by dozens of baristas in Abu Dhabi, Baltimore, Beirut, and San Jose; by the music of Makaya McCraven; by the love and support of my parents, Joe and Nina, my sisters, Ellen and Linda, and my friends Anna, Anne-Marie, Christine, Hossein, and Joe. Writing the book has been an adventure and a pleasure, but nothing compares to the adventure and pleasure of sharing life with Sakar Mohammed.

Notes on Transliteration

FOR KURDISH WORDS AND TERMS, THIS TEXT FOLLOWS THE ROMAN-ization guide set by the Library of Congress, with some exceptions. Diacritical marks have been removed wherever possible, and special characters have been omitted. But diacritical marks have been retained on four letters because their exclusion would lead to confusion: ê, î, ç, and ş. Following is a guide to help readers distinguish between these letters and the letters or sounds they closely resemble.

Vowels

a is a long vowel like the *a* in cap
e is a short vowel like the *e* in den
ê is like the vowel sound *eah* in yeah

î is a long vowel like the *ee* in teen
i is a short vowel like the *i* in tin

Consonants

ç is like the *ch* in chop
c is like the *j* in Jill
j is like the *j* in Jacques

ş is like the *sh* in shop
s is like the *s* in sap

Exceptions are the proper names used frequently in the text: Pexshan (rather than Pexşan), pronounced Pekhshan; Shadman (rather than Şadman); and words like Islamî (rather than Îslamî). When words of Persian, Arabic, Turkish, or English origin are used, this text opts for Kurdish transliteration reflecting the absorption of those words in Kurdish usage. When the text refers to texts or key terms from those languages, or when Kurdish speakers mark a word *as foreign*, the text follows the transliteration standards of the *International Journal of Middle East Studies*, except that diacritical marks have been removed. Their origin is indicated by (P.) for Persian and (Ar.) for Arabic. All translations are by the author unless otherwise noted.

Preface

IN CONTEMPORARY IRAQ, MANY PEOPLE CONSIDER THE VALUE OF understanding some kinds of religious difference to be self-evident. Researchers, politicians, investors, citizens, mothers, cousins, and children all seem to agree that understanding the relationship between Sunni Muslims and Shi'i Muslims is an essential task today. So, too, is the difference between Muslims, Christians, and Yezidis in Iraq. And so might be any difference between so-called extremist and moderate Muslims. These kinds of religious difference are politicized in familiar ways.

Of course, when scholars examine the situation, they find that these differences are not what they seem. Thus, we have learned that the difference between Sunni and Shi'i Muslims in Iraq has not precluded conviviality in the distant past or the more contentious present. When the so-called sectarian violence seemed to drag on and on in Baghdad in 2015, a social media campaign circulated an image that appeared to present a husband, wife, and their daughter. The parents held different signs that identified them, in English, as Sunni and Shia. The child held a sign with the portmanteau "Sushi." In this example, the obvious categories of religious difference do not line up with ordinary experience in everyday life.

Yet there are other kinds of religious difference that saturate everyday life. For example, many Muslims in the Kurdistan region of Iraq regard prayer and fasting as basic requirements of being a Muslim. However, many Muslims in that region do not pray or fast. Call this a difference between those who seek piety and those who turn away from it. It is a difference between those who take up what they consider to be the duties and attitudes that God asks of all humans and those who take other attitudes to those duties—brushing them aside, not listening to them, or finding themselves averse to them. Does this kind of religious difference make a difference?

This book argues that from the perspective of everyday life, the difference between those who seek piety and those who turn away from it *does* make a difference. Taking up piety or turning from it is not only an individual choice but also a tendency that is palpable in many kinds of relationships. If a child learns to pray and fast from her parents but abandons these practices early in life, how does she relate to Islam or to others? When a man does not pray and does not aspire to teach prayer to his children, yet his wife does aspire to those things, how does he explain this to his children? If the man's brother steps in to encourage the children toward prayer, how can he react to his brother? And how do individuals who are averse to prayer or fasting respond to the public invitations to piety that they encounter at public events, cafés, or family gatherings?

In responding to those questions, this book attends to small details of everyday life in the Kurdistan region of Iraq. While many studies of Kurdistan revolve around Kurds' aspiration to separation from their neighbors, this book's attention to small details has required greater acknowledgment of how Kurdistan is connected. These details include the words people choose, the gestures they make toward one another, and the way that relationships shift across time. An examination of those details reveals a range of ideas, practices, and social movements that links Kurdish Muslims to other Muslims, but it also reveals feelings, sensibilities, and relational dynamics that connect them to non-Muslims within or beyond the region—including the readers of this book.

In attending to everyday life and the ordinary relationships that make everyday life, this book asks for curiosity—curiosity about what Islamic traditions may be or become in everyday life and curiosity about how the less commonly acknowledged forms of religious difference become politicized. So this book does not take the obvious political stakes of sectarian identity in Iraq as its own stakes, and it does not take the obvious relevance of texts like the Quran as the measure of its relevance. Rather, it takes everyday relationships as a perspective from which to learn about Islamic traditions, and it asks for curiosity and uncertainty about how the "large" questions of divine texts and political identities appear in relationships between Kurdish Muslims.

Consequently, instead of assuming that the best knowledge offers the most certainty about the broad categories of religious difference just described, this book attends to the uncertainty that those broad categories acquire in everyday life. What does a perceived difference between Sunni and Shi'i tendencies mean for a Muslim who does not pray? What role has "extremist" violence played in the development of their attitudes? And given that many who do not identify as pious still identify as Muslims, how do they imagine relations with Christians or Jews?

Responding to these questions, this book suggests that acknowledging the uncertainty that surrounds *this* form of religious difference is a valuable endeavor. It is not a form of difference that has garnered much scholarly attention, but it has preoccupied many kinds of relationships. Not only Kurdish Muslims but Muslims worldwide encounter these differences. And Christians, Jews, and others have thought about those differences in their own traditions, albeit in different ways with different stakes. The book does not say anything about how these differences might translate, or not, to non-Islamic traditions. But it does invite readers to think comparatively by assuming that, in their own everyday lives, readers relate to others across lines of religious difference.

So whether readers approach the book as Muslims with a commitment to Islam, as Muslims who are ambivalent or disappointed with Islam, or as non-Muslims who bear their own forms of certainty or ambivalence about Islam, it will open to the door to thinking about the relationship between commitment and ambivalence in Islamic traditions.

BETWEEN MUSLIMS

Introduction

FIELDWORK IN KURDISTAN

Islamic Traditions, Ordinary Relationships, and a Paradox

CONSIDER THESE THREE CLAIMS: *NOTHING CAN BE TAKEN FOR granted about how Muslims relate to Islamic traditions.* Many Muslims aspire to be the best Muslims they can be, and they seek to live out Islam in the best way they can. Yet many forgo the effort to become pious Muslims. *In doing so, they do not cease to be Muslims.* Some may suppose that these Muslims are therefore secular rather than religious. But that opposition fails to describe their religious orientations. *Descriptions of the relationships they share with other Muslims, however, reveal the dynamism of their orientations to Islam.*

These claims set out the paradox that this book seeks to describe in the lives of Muslims who turn away from piety yet remain within Islam, but the book does not seek to resolve or explain away the paradox. Description here means to examine the ways that the paradox comes to thrive, to discover the conditions that allow it to come about, and to forge—or borrow—a language for talking about it. In this sense, even though these three claims rely on evidence and a form of analytical reasoning, they are just a beginning.

The claims result from three years of ethnographic and archival research I conducted in the Kurdistan region of Iraq between 2004 and 2013. The research took shape through a project of further archival research, writing, and rewriting that has expanded across another six years. The following chapters present evidence by connecting small details of everyday life in Kurdistan to the large questions of Islam and secularism that connect Kurdistan to the region and the world. The evidence alternates between ethnographic accounts of the everyday lives of Muslims who turn away from pious striving and analytical accounts of the discourses of Sufism and Islamism in Kurdistan.

While many conventions of anthropological writing suggest that ethnography should begin with anecdotal evidence that presents a puzzle to be solved, this Introduction takes a different path. It describes the methods that guided my fieldwork and my writing, and it introduces both the broader context in which the evidence of my fieldwork appeared and the "me" to whom that evidence appeared. Its goal is to cultivate a sense of curiosity and even uncertainty about what might count as evidence for these claims. The chapters that follow examine how Iraqi Kurdish Muslims themselves account for the role of claims, descriptions, evidence, and experience in their relations to Islamic traditions. In the Epilogue, I return to the question of how claims relate to lived experience.

A PARADOX

First, I must clarify a few things about the claims presented earlier. What does it mean that a Muslim forgoes the effort to become a pious Muslim? Islam provides a wide range of disciplines, practices, and institutions by which Muslims can bring virtue to their souls and their lives. Most famously in the anthropology of Islam, these include an ongoing engagement with the founding texts of the Islamic tradition, the Quran and the hadith—the speech events attributed to the Prophet Muhammad. Many Muslims regard the Quran as flawless and eternal and the hadith as companion texts that are authoritative insofar as they have been accurately preserved. Those texts prescribe practices such as prayer and fasting as two of the pillars on which to build a Muslim life in a community of Muslims. Building such a life requires ongoing striving. Even if Muslims do not *arrive* at perfection, the aspiration to move ever closer to the model of the Prophet's life is widespread.[1] This aspiration is a kernel from which grow many different ways of life and many kinds of piety. The terms "pious Muslims" or "proper Muslims" thus describe those who express one from a wide range of aspirations to be a "good Muslim."

Of course, not all Muslims share that aspiration. Many do not pray or fast as required. They do not seek to inculcate the texts into their hearts and lives and do not describe their moral lives as an effort to resemble the Prophet. They forgo piety, pass it up, or turn away from it.

There are at least three ways to describe that turning, which correspond to different (if not always discrete) orientations toward Islam. One is that they regret it and wish that they could strive more diligently. This orientation could appear in expressions such as, "I know I should pray, I would like to pray, but I cannot manage." I heard similar expressions from a young man who was plagued with intellectual doubts about his faith in 2008. Although he intensely felt the inability to pray, he still considered it a temporary state that he sought to overcome. An expression of that type is the beginning of repentance: it acknowledges that *this* is the way to become a good person and keeps the goal before one's eyes and the path beneath one's feet.[2]

A second way to describe a turn away from piety is to suggest that the practice is only contingently, or superficially, related to the true goal of piety. This could appear in expressions such as, "True prayer is that one always be conscious of divinity; ritual prayer is just a formality." It could also appear when Muslims do not fast during Ramadan but insist that they want to cultivate a virtuous attitude toward the suffering of the poor (which is often described as one goal of fasting) in the rest of their life. I heard a similar expression during an interview with a poet who described his own practice of fasting: sometimes when there are only a few minutes left before the end of the fast, he decides to drink a cup of tea. According to many Muslim scholars in Kurdistan, that would mean that the entire day of fasting was invalidated and he would have to make it up later in the year. Yet the poet did not plan to make it up. He saw himself as fulfilling the higher purpose of ritual activity and did not expect to endure God's wrath for his choice. That kind of orientation is the beginning of reform: it takes the goal provided by the Islamic tradition as given and seeks to transform the path to get there.

Those two orientations are quite different, but they are both examples of a pietistic orientation to Islam. Such orientations have been the subject of most studies of Islam in anthropology, religion, and history. Those studies demonstrate that piety is not a single thing but a moral aspiration that varies in different contexts. The scholarly focus on pietistic orientations is salutary since they are crucial components of ethical life for all Muslims.

However, this book is concerned with a third kind of orientation to explain why one may not seek to pray, fast, or absorb the Quran. "I have never had the feeling that 'right now, I should go pray.'" This expression belongs to one of my interlocutors in Kurdistan whose life I explore at length in Chapter 5. It is typical of an orientation to Islamic traditions that has received too little attention. It acknowledges that Islam provides a goal and a path for moral striving, but it does not explicitly take up that goal or path. It does not deny that Islam requires prayer but simply admits to habitually not praying.[3] The expression takes up the paradoxical posture of turning away from the path to piety laid out in Islamic traditions but without departing from Islam altogether. These expressions belong to Muslims who do not definitively claim to be non-Muslims—either atheists or adherents of another path such as Christianity or Zoroastrianism. They may insist that they have still have faith (*îman*), or they may be ambivalent about faith, but they are not ambivalent about turning away from piety. They are Muslims, but they do not aspire to the path of moral reform that they consider Islam to lay out for them. In this condition, to simply acknowledge that they remain Muslim does not describe much about their ethical orientation to Islam or to other Muslims.

I use the term "orientation" throughout the book to accommodate the multifarious and dynamic dimensions of how individual Muslims relate to Islamic traditions. Discussions of belief, faith, practice, participation, and identity often have to fight against the tendency to think of those concepts as static or binary. (Thus, one is or is not a Muslim, one has or does not have faith, one believes or one doubts, or one practices or does not practice.) Rather than argue against those binaries, I use "orientation" to describe how individuals relate to a tradition by referring to some of these concepts and by putting those concepts in motion in their everyday lives in relation to others. Thus, "turning away from piety" is a distinctive orientation to Islam that cannot be reduced to propositional claims about an individual's faith, belief, or practice.

From a certain normative view of Islam, found in a range of texts reaching across centuries of historical change in Kurdistan, including speculative theology, law, and epistolary correspondence of religious scholars, such an orientation can be considered an abandonment of Islam altogether. By turning away from the forms of moral striving that Islamic traditions offer, Muslims turn away from Islam itself and even from the effort to become good people. Some of those texts make dramatic prescriptions for addressing such Muslims: they should know that they stand in danger of being executed for apostasy; they should not be allowed to contract marriages or inherit from relatives; if they die in that state, they should not be buried in a Muslim cemetery; above all, perhaps, they should know that they are preparing themselves for the fire after death and squandering their chance at paradise. I heard such views on a daily basis in Kurdistan.

Yet this view does not determine the course of social life, for alongside it stands another normative view that Muslims who turn away from piety should be invited to return. They should be shown kindness, mercy, and patience in the hope that they discover an aspiration to become pious. This view can also summon an impressive array of texts, including the Quran, hadith, and texts in law and poetry, to support itself.[4] Even more important for the purposes of this study, it also has the authority of being embodied in a set of relations in which being a proper Muslim means demonstrating kindness to not-so-proper Muslims. I witnessed this on a daily basis in Kurdistan, where pious Muslims engaged other, not especially pious, Muslims in a spirit of kindness and generosity.

Thus, at least two norms compete with one another *within* Islam concerning how one should respond to Muslims who turn away from piety.[5] As a number of scholars have pointed out, Islam is not only a single normative view of the world, life, ethics, or the cosmos (even if some regard it that way). It is rather a field of debate, competition, ongoing struggle, contestation, and experimentation. What Islam looks like in the life of a Muslim who turns away from piety cannot be known in advance by reference to any text, doctrine, or even the precedent of practice. Rather than a given, one's relationship to those texts, and to Islam writ large, is an open question to which Muslims respond in many different contexts.

The competition of norms takes place within the big picture of public debate about Islam, as well as in the relationships that make up everyday life. The three orientations described previously often intersect one another in the lives of friends, family, neighbors, and the intimacy of strangers that crops up in public space. While some families are renowned for their piety, most pious families have a few members who break the mold. Conversely, in families where religion may seem to be absent, there are often some who become devout. In the encounters at school, teashops, corner stores, bakeries, cafés, and other public spaces through which Iraqi Kurds pass on a daily basis, they meet Muslims of different orientations. These meetings also make up a kind of relationship. "Relationship" is a broad, inclusive term as it appears in this book. It indicates a broad field on which different religious orientations—and different norms in approaching those orientations—are played out in diverse ways. In relationships between Muslims, religious orientations are sometimes the object of explicit verbal debate and disagreement, but they are also frequently worked out at the level of affective dispositions, subtle gestures, implications, and unstated assumptions.[6]

Many studies of Islam approach the work of moral striving by examining the range of what Muslims call "Islamic" practices. This approach opens up a field of practice that is rich with debate, contradiction, and paradox. Scholars have asked how practices that may appear to some as *un*-Islamic or *non*-Islamic become an integral part of an Islamic tradition. Topics such as spirit possession, which many observers consider self-evidently "un-Islamic," have been fruitful sites to inquire how it is that practices of citation and disputation subject a broad range of practices to the authority of Islamic traditions.[7] However, to date there are no book-length studies of Muslims who do not reject their Muslim identity or whose Muslim identity is not stripped from them but do not try to describe their ethical lives as pious.[8] This book explores that religious orientation as it appears in the lives of Kurdish Muslims in the Kurdistan region of Iraq.

This religious orientation is above all dynamic. Muslims who turn away from piety may nonetheless find themselves attracted to the lives or practices of pious Muslims—either prominent figures such as poets and saints or ordinary people such as kin and neighbors. Furthermore, this orientation is dynamic because many Muslims who turn away from piety do so after many years of pious commitment, and many Muslims who give up on piety at one stage in life may return to it later. Yet to insist that turning away from piety is only an exception within a broadly consistent pattern of Muslim piety or that the teleology of Muslim ethics ensures that Muslims remain oriented to piety as the inevitable end to a dramatic story is to ignore the paradox sketched out here: Without rejecting Islam, many Muslims do turn away from piety and sustain relations with other (pious) Muslims while doing so.

The religious orientation of Muslims who turn away from piety is internal to Islamic traditions in the sense that it cannot simply be attributed solely to non-Islamic influences. But it is not therefore separable from non-Islamic influences. Since its inception, Islam has been deeply engaged with other religious traditions, including Zoroastrianism, Christianity, Judaism, and Hinduism. More recently, "secularism" emerged as a new approach to governing religious difference. Secularism emerged from Europe alongside the formation of the modern state and in the midst of a colonial effort to govern populations beyond Europe. It now sets the predominant normative framework for thinking about politics anywhere.

This leads to the terms of the second claim mentioned earlier. Some may find it easy to describe those who turn away from piety as secular and attribute their attitude to the rise of secularism. The problem is not that this description is wrong. The term "secular" has been absorbed in the common vocabulary of all the languages that converge in this book: English, Kurdish, Persian, and Arabic. Kurdish borrows the Arabic neologism *'almaniyya*, which is used in different ways in ordinary conversation. It can refer to a political party in which the secular parties may (or may not) be opposed to the Islamist parties; to a high order of political theory in which the state seeks to confine religion to private life and exclude religion from the public life of politics; to another kind of political theory in which the state seeks to give equal voice to all religions in public space; and to a person who is not pious or is even an atheist.⁹

Yet describing those who turn away from piety as secular is not precise, accurate, or informative. It is not precise because it confuses historical conditions and personal dispositions rather than interrogates the linkage between them. It is not accurate because many Muslims practice piety in private life and remain firmly committed to a secular ethos in public debate. And it is not informative if it is taken at face value and not grounded in an account of the world in which it makes sense.¹⁰

This book provides an account of how that religious orientation appears in everyday life, when broad histories of religious discourse converge or diverge in ordinary relationships. It seeks to describe the world in which this religious orientation makes sense. Having a single Kurdish concept or key term might have made the work much easier (at least at first). If it were possible to make this book an elucidation of a fully formed or emergent concept, the analytical task might be more straightforward. But Kurdish offers a shifting set of terms whose denotation and connotation can differ dramatically, referring to different things and evoking different sensibilities.

One example is the term *bêdîn*. This word combines a negating prefix *bê-* with the complex term *dîn*—which can denote religion, Islam, a moral path, and/or Judgment Day. A literal English translation of *bêdîn* is "nonreligious" or "irreligious." But usage of the term varies widely in Kurdish. It can be used with the connotation of condemnation, for example, of someone who appears to behave toward others in a consistently vicious way, without any moral sensibility at all. It can also be used much more lightly to describe someone who does not practice religion (interestingly, either Islam, Christianity, or other religions). It could describe a self-declared atheist who claims to reject religion altogether, who is also called a *mulhîd*. Or it can describe someone who claims to be religious in speech but behaves differently—a hypocrite or *munafîq*. As if these variations were not enough, the term appears in poetic discourse as the condition of love-struck poets whose passion for their beloved has so consumed them that their commitment to *dîn* has been completely plundered or looted. Thus, *bêdîn* is flexible, appearing sometimes as an insult, sometimes as a disavowal, sometimes as a simple descriptor, sometimes as literary hyperbole. As this book is not specifically about hypocrites, atheists, or insults—although it touches on each—it is also not specifically about being *bêdîn*. To fulfill the descriptive task of this book, one cannot simply identify a local term and have its subject immediately clarified.

The book seeks to describe a religious orientation for which there is no ready-made name or category of thought. The kind of religious orientation it seeks to describe is not a process of change or a consequence of a historical event or social movement. It is not visible in a pattern of rituals or defined in a collection of texts. It is not a theological category, nor is it an object of state governance. In comparison to those subjects, the religious orientation described here is an analytically unstable subject. The phrase "turning away from piety" is not a stable object but a placeholder in English for a dynamic, distinctive orientation to Islamic traditions.

Even if this religious orientation is unstable, it is not unreal. It simply requires a different approach, a different manner of description, a different way of coming to understand what precisely it *is*. This book approaches religious orientation from the perspective of ordinary relations. Its approach is to write from ordinary relations to demonstrate how Kurdish Muslims themselves encounter different orientations to piety in Islamic traditions. But what are ordinary relations? And how does one write from them?

WRITING FROM ORDINARY RELATIONSHIPS

Describing relationships as *ordinary* has two aspects. First, it describes a loose group of common relationships. As anthropologist Veena Das put it, the ordinary is a part of everyday life where "the life of the other is engaged."[11] There are many kinds of "others" in everyday life, and ordinary relationships encompass all of them, including kinship relations between father and daughter, siblings, husband and wife, or grandchildren and grandparents. But these "others" also include relationships of friendship and the intimacy that crops up in public when one encounters strangers. Ordinary relationships are thus not only *close* relations but ones that fluctuate between the prospect of estrangement from a sibling or a spouse and an enduring intimacy, between the indifference one may feel toward a stranger on the street and the realization that this stranger is concerned with one's fate on Judgment Day. Ordinary relationships are not limited to those of the nuclear family, nor are they the preserve of a private rather than public domain. In fact, ordinary relationships are interesting precisely for the ways that they absorb and transform public discourses: they bring out a different, underappreciated aspect of a text or idea that is widely available by placing it in a new relationship. For example, in public discourse a "spy" might be a threat to national security, deserving trial or imprisonment. But in the context of a hospitable invitation to dinner, one can joke that the guest is a spy without deciding whether the person is really a spy or not. This relates to the second aspect of the ordinary described in this book.

The ordinary offers an analytic for thinking about relationships. Here again, the emphasis is on inclusion rather than exclusion. Examining relationships from the perspective of the ordinary does not mean flattening out the history of religious discourse in Kurdistan or ignoring the work of religious institutions, the state, and histories of literature and politics. Quite the contrary, it means attending to the difference between the way texts and ideas appear in broader public discourse and the way they appear in relationships. In addition to asking how a government regulates marriage practices, the ordinary as an analytic asks how a husband and wife absorb government regulations in their lives together; in addition to asking how grand theological ideas shape the pursuit of piety in the household, the ordinary perspective asks how a pious individual receives and reshapes grand theological ideas in their engagement with others in a house full of religious differences; in addition to asking how literary history has produced an imagination of Kurdish Muslims, the ordinary perspective asks how a Kurdish Muslim makes that imagination relevant to their own lives. In this sense, the difference between the ordinary and the grand narratives of politics or history may initially appear slight, but it grows more significant the closer one looks.

From the perspective of the grand narrative of Islamic history, the difference between those who are pious and those who turn away from piety appears slight and insignificant. But when one looks closely at ordinary relationships—how they unfold in an individual's life over a period of months, years, and decades—one can see the importance of the difference. One could say that taking the ordinary as an analytic emphasizes the human capacity to make history, to transform big ideas through small acts. But the ordinary does not valorize human agency, nor does it sacralize human action, because history may be remade as much by passivity as by activity, as much by suffering as by triumph. One may discover a new aspect of a text not in a moment of sovereign autonomy but in a moment of vulnerability or loss. (For example, the importance of the Quran may dawn on someone who is not seeking it, or an insight about the idea of God's love may only appear when one suffers from lost friendships.) For this reason, one needs to study the history of religious discourse on its own terms to then appreciate the work that ordinary Kurdish Muslims perform in making texts and ideas relevant to their own everyday lives. The analysis thus moves back and forth between the texts of religious discourse and the ordinary relationships where those texts are absorbed and transformed.

In her book on Muslim ethical life in Pakistan, where the rubrics of sectarianism cast a daunting shadow over any attempt to analyze religious difference, anthropologist Naveeda Khan proposed a study of how texts, religious differences, and ordinary life intertwine with the following question: "What if we ... think of the potential lines of movement among entrenched differences, cited texts, and possible positions generated by selves encountering others in the world?"[12] In Khan's view, the complex relationship between people's ordinary interactions with one another, the texts that appear in those interactions, and the more abstract ideas about religious difference is not a stable object to be located or categorized. It is rather a field of *movements* where the analytical task is to track the movement across lines of difference. This book examines similar movements in the lives of Kurdish Muslims by analyzing the intersection of ordinary language, poetic discourse, sacred texts of the Quran and the hadith, and the language of Islamist discourse available in sermons.

Chapter 1 begins with the definitive texts of Islamic tradition: the Quran and the hadith. It approaches those texts through the experience of a woman who encounters them in several types of relationships, including the memory of her father's instruction when she was a child and public audition of the Quran at a restaurant where she ate with her daughter. It also addresses the practices of prayer and fasting that form a primary nexus through which Kurdish Muslims relate to Islamic traditions and major events from early Islamic history that are a routine matter of contest in everyday conversations about Islam. In the search for a mode of description for this woman's relationship to Islamic traditions, the chapter closes with the evocation of poetry as a language for describing paradoxical orientations to Islamic traditions.

Chapter 2 investigates major themes from the texts of Kurdish poetry available to Kurdish Muslims. In taking up the history of religious discourse, it foregrounds the relationship between the Muslim poet as "lover" and the figure of the beloved, who is commonly a non-Muslim and commonly a *kafir* (that is, an apostate, who somehow denies the truth of divinity or divine revelation). The chapter historicizes this relationship between lover and beloved in Kurdistan, showing how the imagination of that relationship was differently politicized in the early nineteenth and early to mid-twentieth centuries. Through a close reading of poetic texts, it tells the story of how the poetic imagination shifted alongside the increasing incursion of foreign non-Muslims and a new politicization of religious identity in the beginning of the twentieth century.

Chapter 3 then shows how ideas of the relation between lover and beloved are transformed when absorbed by ordinary relationships. It reports conversations with a Kurdish Muslim man who engaged Kurdish poetry, as well as the Quran, and thought about figures of early Islamic history in his everyday life. It shows how ordinary relationships modify the broad discourses of religious difference between Muslims and Christians and between Sunni and Shi'i Muslims. Finally, it introduces the fragments of discourse from Islamist movements that appear in ordinary relationships of a Kurdish Muslim man who contemplates the intertwining of love, marriage, friendship, and local politics as one turns away from piety.

Chapter 4 explores the project of transforming ordinary relationships as proposed by a prominent leader of an Islamist movement in Kurdistan. By examining sermons and interviews of Mela Krêkar, the chapter demonstrates how his call for radical transformation asked Kurdish Muslims to focus their attention precisely on ordinary relationships. He sought to purge ordinary relationships of the influences of non-Muslim imperialism and to purge the imagination of a Muslim society from the influence of modern states and political parties. If the study of Islamist movements in the Middle East has commonly assumed that the goal of those movements is to capture and transform state institutions, Mela Krêkar shows how transformative ordinary relations can be.

Chapter 5 turns to the household, to the relation of a father with his family. In this household, the father is anxious about the influence of Islamist ideas like those of Mela Krêkar. If this father does not pursue piety, many there do, and this sets the stage for potential conflicts. Yet if the study of religious difference has commonly taken public acts of violence as its point of departure, this chapter asks how pleasure and enjoyment can be understood to facilitate ordinary relationships when different orientations to Islamic traditions meet in a single household. The chapter argues that beyond explicit claims, sometimes silent gestures and modes of description are important for sustaining relationships. Thus it demonstrates that the problem of how to describe a Muslim's relation to Islamic traditions is not only a problem for anthropologists but also a problem that Kurdish Muslims engage in everyday life.

The Epilogue turns an analytical eye toward the work of description and argument carried out in previous chapters, which argue that Kurdish Muslims' relations to Islamic traditions can be better described by the ordinary relationships they sustain than through the claims of the texts they engage. The Epilogue asks how ordinary relationships receive ethnographic texts. If the ethnography of Muslim societies is commonly addressed to readers who are imagined as independently reasoning, autonomous, secular, and liberal, then the Epilogue articulates the effort in this book to address a slightly different reader. While readers may have or even celebrate many of those features, readers of this book may also foreground other features of themselves. Readers may be *as* relational, *as* religious, or *as* orthogonally related to ideas of secularism and liberalism as are the Kurdish Muslims whom the book describes.

Each of these chapters revolves around a single figure: a mother, a beloved, a husband, a preacher, a father, a reader. Inevitably, some readers will be suspicious that the conclusions and arguments cannot be "general" if the evidence revolves around a relatively small number of individuals. In a sense, that suspicion misses the point that individuals are never only individuals, but they are always in relationships with one another. Every individual appears in this book within a nexus of relationships that make up the possibilities from which the individual draws. (One is a mother or father to children, a beloved to a lover, a preacher to an audience.) Yet at the same time, the suspicion is well founded because the results of this approach are indeed not general; they do not aim to make general statements about Kurdish Muslims as such. The result of focusing on individuals is not *general* knowledge but rather *connective* knowledge—knowledge that sharpens one's ability to follow the twists and turns of a text as it acquires a texture in different kinds of relationships and knowledge that deepens one's patience to see what lengths of transformation are possible in those twists and turns. In a sense, it is not a book about Muslims as much as a book about the kinds of love, mistrust, pleasure, and uncertainty that appear *between Muslims*.

Writing *from* relationships thus means taking ordinary relationships as a loose grouping of different kinds of relationships, none of which are necessarily given, natural, or fixed. And it means taking the ordinary as a perspective from which to examine how publicly available texts are absorbed and transformed in everyday relationships. Writing from ordinary relationships means following the twists and turns of texts as they are transformed in relationships—not waiting for dramatic events to show the truth of a relationship but waiting for dramatic events, grand ideas, or complex texts to be absorbed into relationships through small gestures, subtle words, or accommodating attitudes in everyday life.

IRAQI KURDISTAN

I learned about these relationships in a discrete stretch of time, within a relatively discrete geographical space. My research took place between 2004 and 2013 around an axis of two cities, occasionally extending to other cities, villages, and towns in Kurdistan. The two cities are known to much of the world as Sulaimaniyah and Erbil,[13] but they are known to their Kurdish-speaking inhabitants as Silêmanî and Hewlêr, the names used in this book.[14] They are located in the southern part of a region that has been called Kurdistan for centuries, but in the twentieth century that designation became particularly precarious since the region was split by the borders of modern nation-states, principally Iraq, Iran, Turkey, and Syria. Both Silêmanî and Hewlêr lie in Iraq. While the evidence described here reaches into the neighboring nation-states within Kurdistan, as well as to South Asia and Europe, it is also definitively a part of an Iraqi national historiography. "Kurdistan" was the primary geographical referent used by my interlocutors to describe where they live. But that reference was intertwined with a definitively Iraqi flavor, texture, and substance. For that reason, this book uses "Iraqi Kurdistan," often abbreviated to "Kurdistan," to describe the geopolitical context where ordinary relationships are elaborated.

The relationship between Iraqi Kurds and the Iraqi state has been tumultuous. Beginning in the 1920s, Kurds contended with an Arab nationalist vision of Iraqi unity that regarded Kurds as second-class citizens.[15] The struggle for recognition of a distinctive identity and the right to speak and write in the Kurdish language was a central preoccupation of Kurdish nationalist movements that sought varying degrees of autonomy within Iraq or independence across the twentieth century. That struggle resulted in the reaffirmation of language rights in 1970 that allowed Iraqi Kurds primary and secondary education in Kurdish, but the demand for political autonomy was met with increasing violence. During the long war that Saddam Hussein waged against Iran during 1980–1988, Kurds were conscripted along with all Iraqis for military service.[16] At the same time, however, Kurdish nationalist political parties continued guerrilla warfare against the Iraqi military. During this decade, Kurdish resistance was consolidated around two major political parties—the Kurdistan Democratic Party (KDP) and the Patriotic Union of Kurdistan (PUK)—that continued to dominate the Kurdish political landscape throughout my research.

When the war neared its end, the Iraqi military turned its attention to punishing and finally suppressing the Kurdish resistance. Saddam Hussein appointed his cousin Ali Hassan Al-Majid to oversee this final punishment, and Al-Majid's solution was a genocidal campaign against Iraqi Kurds, Yezidis, and Assyrian and Chaldean Christians who had fought against the Iraqi regime. The campaign resulted in the deaths of at least one hundred thousand people and the demolition of thousands of villages.[17] In the final years of the war, Saddam Hussein had increasingly mobilized the vocabulary of Islamic traditions to justify his war.[18] Paradigmatic of that strategy was use of the term *Anfal* to describe the genocidal campaign led by Al-Majid. Often translated as "the spoils of war," *Anfal* is the title of a chapter in the Quran that addresses Muslims at the time of a battle against unbelievers. That usage establishes an equivalence between the Iraqi state, an Arab nation, and the early Muslims who were unified in their battle against Kurds who resisted the state and were, by implication, not Muslims.[19]

Following Saddam Hussein's war against Iran, he launched a second war against Kuwait in 1990. He had maintained American and other international support throughout his war against Iran (the United States had even refused to take a strong stance against the use of chemical weapons[20]), but this second war brought fierce retribution as the United States waged war against Iraq. In the wake of Iraqi defeat in Kuwait, a mass uprising began in both the south of Iraq and the Kurdistan region in March 1991. While America did not make good on its promise to support the insurgents, it established a no-fly zone in 1991 to protect Kurdish insurgents against reprisals from the Iraqi state. Without air support to suppress Kurdish militants, the Iraqi military withdrew and a de facto autonomous region emerged. The Kurdistan Regional Government (KRG) was formed the following year.[21] While still subject to the crippling effects of United Nations sanctions that kept most Iraqis in desperate straits, the political parties constituting the KRG were able to exploit their control of the borders with Iran and Turkey to obtain cash from smuggling enterprises. In the same period, though, these parties were engaged in a protracted civil war in which each party shifted stances toward one another, toward smaller parties including the Islamist movement in Kurdistan, and toward the Iraqi and neighboring states.

In 2003, the civil war had quieted, and both major Kurdish parties offered full support for the US-led toppling of Saddam Hussein. Even though the KRG conducted extensive antiterror campaigns and detained many on suspicion of insurgency, comparatively little of the violence reported in Anglophone media took place in the Kurdistan region. On the contrary, the KRG's reintegration into the federal budget, its open embrace of foreign investment, and its relative security allowed it to lay claim to the status of "The Other Iraq." The KRG sought to distance itself from the rest of Iraq as a bastion of security and neoliberal economic development that was also uniquely pluralistic in religious terms. The KRG consistently emphasized the cooperation between Muslim Kurds and others—including Assyrian and Chaldean Christians, Yezidis, Ahl-i Haqq, and Jews.[22] During the years when I conducted the bulk of my fieldwork, 2008–2009, there was a growing sense of potential economic growth in the KRG but also an increasingly popular discontent with the KRG's inability to provide economic opportunities to anyone other than those loyal to the two major political parties.

These large-scale shifts and broad trends have contributed to a common view of Iraqi Kurdistan shared by many locals and observers that the dynamics of Kurdish identity politics are more important than the dynamics of Islamic traditions for understanding social life in Iraqi Kurdistan. Thus, a wide range of scholarship on Iraqi Kurdistan (in anthropology, history, and political science) has revolved around the questions of Kurdish identity and nationalist aspirations. The study of religion has been quarantined to the study of religious minorities such as Yezidis or Alevis. Martin van Bruinessen succinctly summarized this imbalance in scholarship on Kurdistan: "There appears to have been a distinct anti-Islamic bias in scholarship on the Kurds, or at least an implicit assumption that Islam is somehow less Kurdish than Yezidism or Alevism. This neglect of Sunni Islam in Kurdish Studies has occurred in spite of the well-known facts that the vast majority of the Kurds are Sunni Muslims who take their religion seriously."[23]

This book thus fills a crucial gap by taking Islamic traditions as the starting point and center of inquiry. My goal is not to sideline studies of nationalist politics in Kurdistan but rather to broaden the scope of politics beyond this domain and deepen attention to Islamic traditions as a productive site of study in Iraqi Kurdistan. I begin with the premise that even if scholars have not written enough about Kurdish nationalism, scholarship on Kurdistan must address more than just nationalism. Indeed, when research on Kurdistan focuses exclusively on nationalism, research itself exaggerates the risk that nationalism becomes the only recognized form of political life and, in turn, the only legitimate or inhabitable form of life. To insist that there are other dimensions of ethical and political life is not to claim that they escape or transcend the influence of nationalism, only to claim that these other dimensions are not reducible to nationalism. These other dimensions deserve scholarly attention as well. Thus, by turning to (Sunni) Islamic traditions in Kurdistan and the differences between those who seek piety and those who turn away from it, this book offers a fresh perspective on a common—but commonly overlooked—aspect of social life.

A KURDISH EXCEPTION?

During my research and writing, I encountered many voices insisting that there is nothing surprising about the fact that many *Kurdish* Muslims might turn away from piety. When the emphasis falls on the modifier *Kurdish*, it implies that Kurds are exceptional, uniquely unlike other Muslims. Two very different lines of reasoning could be at work in this idea.

The first appears most obviously in the writings of Orientalist observers—travelers, missionaries, and military personnel. But I also heard similar versions in and beyond Kurdistan, including from Kurdish nationalist intellectuals. This line of reasoning relies on ideas of racial or ethnic difference and broadly associates Islam with Arabs. According to this logic, the historical origin of Islam among Arab tribes has meant that fidelity to Kurdish identity is incompatible with fidelity to Islamic traditions. Thus, some question whether Kurds' acceptance of Islam was ever actually sincere or complete. Others suppose that even if Kurds did convert in large numbers, they nonetheless retained fidelity to some pre-Islamic traditions. This idea is often attached to the notion of ethnically or racially distinct "culture," in which it is minorities, tribes, and ancient peoples that have culture. By implication, contemporary urban Arabs, Turks, or Persians are less influenced by culture and have more direct access to religion. This line of reasoning is often at work in the English phrase "Kurdish Islam," which suggests that Islam is a broad, universal noun modified by a local, particular, ethnic adjective.

In most versions, this idea relies on the notion that a human being's capacity for commitment to Islamic traditions is determined or qualified by the person's racial or ethnic identity. It therefore often harbors subtle—or not so subtle—forms of racism. Furthermore, this idea implies that those who consider themselves fully

Kurdish and fully Muslim live in some sort of illusion or self-deception. But as the following discussion begins to show, there is no question that Kurdish Muslims have been deeply engaged with Islamic traditions for centuries. And the forms of their engagement are not unique or isolated but interwoven with the ways that Arab, Turkish, and Persian Muslims have engaged Islam.

To avoid that line of reasoning, instead of the phrase "Kurdish Islam," I speak of "Islamic traditions in Kurdistan" to describe a wide range of debates about what counts as Islamic. These debates have happened in, around, and about the region called Kurdistan (itself historically shifting) and have happened in, in conversation with, and about Kurdish language. Within this framework, it is no less puzzling when an Iraqi Kurdish Muslim turns away from piety than it is when other Muslims do.

A second line of reasoning that attributes an exceptional status to Kurdish Muslims is much more thoughtful and relies on observations of general political trends that connect Kurds to the wider region. According to this view, the marginalization of Kurds following the establishment of the four major nation-states (Iran, Iraq, Syria, and Turkey) in the twentieth century has created fertile ground for leftist political movements.[24] Because leftist political thought often values scepticism toward religion, it is unsurprising that many leftist Kurds have turned away from piety. This view has recently been magnified by the global interest in the female guerrillas in Iraq and Syria who fought the "Islamic State" and other Islamist militias beginning in 2012.[25] By depicting leftist, feminist revolutionaries as an antidote to Islamist militants, global media have often also regarded Kurdish leftists as an antidote to Islamic traditions more generally. Leftist thought is widely perceived to have had a negative impact on piety in Iraqi Kurdistan. But two points are important to bear in mind.

First, Iraqi Kurdistan has a political history distinct from that of other regions of Kurdistan. Thus, the female guerrillas have predominantly come from Syria and Turkey, where leftist movements have evolved dynamically throughout much of the twentieth century.[26] But during my fieldwork up to 2013, the vast majority of Iraqi Kurds were much more concerned with the political possibilities (and impossibilities) of the local parties (PUK and KDP) in charge of the KRG than with leftist revolutionaries in Syria and Turkey. Even though leftist ideas have moved across the borders of nation-states with Kurdish movements, political dynamics of Iraqi Kurdistan should not be confused with (or equated with) the political dynamics of Kurdish movements in Turkey, Syria, or Iran.

Second, the goal of this book is not to establish a singular cause for a diverse and varied orientation to Islam but to explore the affiliations and associations of that orientation in the contentious present. My research has not shown a one-to-one correspondence between leftist politics and the turn away from piety. Many Kurdish communists retained a commitment to the pursuit of Islamic piety, and many who turn away from piety do not evince sympathy for communist-inspired critiques of Islam. But more important, my research shows that those who turn away from piety have been disappointed or exasperated in some way with Islamist political movements in Iraqi Kurdistan. Thus, if Islamist movements have turned many toward piety, they have also had a significant impact in the lives of Kurdish Muslims who turn away from piety. So rather than ask whether leftist movements prompted a turn away from piety, this book asks about the contemporary relations between Islamist movements and those who turn away from piety.

ISLAMIC TRADITIONS

For Muslims in Iraqi Kurdistan, everyday life is saturated with Islamic traditions. That is, it is saturated with contention about what is Islamic and what is good or proper. That contest takes the form of debate about truth or rightness, but it also takes shape in subtle gestures in everyday life that show one's attitude toward others and toward Islam. Nonetheless, there are several dimensions of an intellectual tradition where debate and contest have occurred in intellectual discourse—that is, as the verbal articulation of ideas, doctrines, and the evaluations of practice. These deserve a brief introduction.

For centuries, that discourse appeared in an institution that provided a material space, a context for relationships, and access to a broad network of similar spaces. This institution is known in many Muslim societies by the Arabic word *madrasa*, commonly known in Sorani Kurdish as the *hucre*. Originally Arabic (*hujrah*), the word simply means "room," but it refers to the room, commonly in the mosque, that is often reserved for the study of texts integral to Islamic traditions: principally the Quran and its interpretation (*tefsîr*), alongside the hadith and the science of their reliability. Also indispensable to study in the *hucre* were texts on Arabic grammar and morphology (*nehu w serf*), Islamic law (*fiqh*), logic (*mentîq*), and rhetoric (*bulaxe*). A range of other texts on topics such as astronomy, medicine, and mathematics might be taken up by scholars according to their own taste. But in nineteenth-century Southern Kurdistan, the *hucre* was also an institution from which sprang a great wave of poetry.

Poetry was central to the *hucre* in three ways. First, it was a topic of formal study: elaborate treatises on Arabic grammar and Islamic doctrine were written in poetry; students learned Persian by reading epic poetry such as Sa'adi's *Gulistan*, and they studied the rhyme and meter schemes that make up the basis of classical verse in both Arabic and Persian. Second, the *hucre* was a space where Sufi ritual practice took place, which frequently included poetry. Finally, the *hucre* provided an informal environment for the meeting of poet-scholars. In addition to verse that addressed these specialized disciplines, on the evenings when serious study was set aside, scholars would pass their time by reciting, reading, and writing poetry of other kinds.[27] These included poems as historical records, poems as letters to friends in distant places, and the poetry of lampoon or satire through which serious and not-so-serious rivalries were played out in the bawdy language of insult.

The centrality of the *hucre* to the history of poetry inspired me to take up a course of study in the *hucre* while conducting research. In 2009 I spent several hours each week studying an introductory text in Arabic morphology under the tutelage of a scholar who had passed through the *hucre* himself. We usually met in a mosque for one-on-one instruction, but I also accompanied him while visiting other, older scholars who had more experience with that institution. A consistent theme in the conversations about the *hucre* was the profound sense of struggle, a sense that the *hucre* had been engaged in a fight to sustain itself for centuries.

Indeed, the material scarcity that afflicted the *hucre* in the nineteenth century is documented in the poetry that emerged from it. In one famous poem, a scholar looks back nostalgically at the *hucre* where he studied, longing to return to its paradigmatic discomforts: holes in the ceiling, bugs crawling about, and a scholar striving to find time away from other routine obligations to give attention to his books.[28] In another poem, a scholar whose verse is otherwise largely devoted to the upper echelons of mystical experience descends to the level of slang and insult to reproach the Ottoman official who cut off funding for the *hucre* where he taught and studied.[29] The material struggle to maintain a steady diet for the body and mind in the *hucre* was often intense.

Despite these struggles, Kurdish scholars who worked in the *hucre* were prolific and prominent in the production and transmission of texts they deemed central to Islamic traditions. In the seventeenth century, they even earned a distinctive reputation, alongside their Persian colleagues, for the study of rhetoric and for a unique method of study that foregrounded close engagements with written texts.[30] Kurdish scholars traveled, and non-Kurdish students and scholars also visited the *hucre* in Kurdistan. By all accounts, the *hucre* was a multilingual space. Instruction was given in a dialect of Kurdish when all parties knew that dialect, but also in Arabic or Persian if there was a great difference between dialects or a student who did not know Kurdish. Although the *hucre* has a unique name in Kurdistan and thus has a unique history inflected by the geography, it was not a space of separation for Kurds. It was above all an institution that connected Kurdish Muslims to other Muslims.

This is an important point because it helps refute the claim that Kurds' conversion to Islam was in some way superficial or incomplete. It is not simply the case that Kurdish scholars were as competent in these sources and invested in their realization in life as scholars in Mecca, Baghdad, or Istanbul, or at al-Azhar in Cairo. Scholars in all those places learned with and from Kurdish scholars.[31] Thus, the traditions of learning alive in Ottoman provinces more generally were those that thrived in Kurdistan. Kurdistan is *unique* in many ways, but it is not *separate* from the rest of the Muslim world. Kurdistan is as integrated with that world as Baghdad has been, and Baghdad is as integral to the Kurdish world as Sine (Sanandaj) has been.

For much of the nineteenth century, the Ottoman Empire was engaged in a project of fashioning itself into a modern state. It sought to centralize its administrative apparatus, grant equality to citizens regardless of religion, and regulate matters of marriage in new ways.[32] Centralization meant the abolition of the Kurdish emirates that had offered obeisance to the Ottoman sultan. It also brought the new enlistment of tribal authorities to extend the Ottoman state's authority along the borders with its neighbor empire, Qajar Iran, to homogenize the population under the sign of equal citizenship and suppress what the Ottomans perceived as threats. Thus, relations between Kurdish Muslims and Christians in the northern Kurdish emirates that had often been cordial and convivial changed course in the mid-nineteenth century. Beginning in the 1840s, Kurdish tribes were involved in large-scale violence, including massacres of Assyrian Christians, Armenian Christians, and the later Armenian genocide.[33] All of this transpired even as Muslim Kurds themselves were targeted for the same homogenizing effect to be made into Muslim Turks.[34] In further efforts to isolate and homogenize a population, Ottoman authorities increasingly policed marriage to Qajar subjects in the same period.[35]

In the midst of this tumult, the *hucre* in the Southern Kurdish emirates managed to persist (as it did in the northern emirates as well[36]). In some ways the *hucre* actually flourished since it was recruited for the Ottoman effort to forge a distinctly Islamic legitimacy. Thus, Mehwî (d. 1906), the same poet who complained about waning Ottoman patronage, supervised education in religious sciences at a *hucre* in Silêmanî that had been sponsored by Ottoman Sultan Abdulhamid II.

However, the demise of the Ottoman Empire and the advent of British rule brought new challenges to the institution of the *hucre*. And that institution posed significant challenges to the British efforts to make a liberal and secular polity out of "Iraq." Soon after the establishment of the British Mandate, the British encountered another anti-imperial and nonliberal force that would play a crucial role in Iraqi politics: communism. Communist opposition to the liberal projects of secularization in the colonized Middle East has received too little attention from scholars interested in secularism and liberalism. But communist thought forms a crucial third position in a political contest between the institution of the *hucre* and the secular liberal nationalists (which from an ideological perspective should include Iraqi nationalists and Kurdish nationalists). Recent work on Iraqi history has highlighted the ways that communist networks facilitated political cooperation among Muslim Arabs, Jewish Arabs, Christian Arabs, and Muslim Kurds in Baghdad, Kirkuk, and elsewhere.[37] For a different reason, the emergence of communism was to play a crucial role in the trajectory of religious life in Kurdistan as well.

Communism was both a revolutionary archetype and the ideological archenemy of the Islamist movement in Kurdistan. The Islamist movement began in the 1940s through relations with the Muslim Brotherhood in Egypt, but it gained momentum in the 1980s in part through cooperation with Afghan resistance to Soviet rule. It has been commonly noted that elite professions such as engineering predominated in the emergence of Islamist movements in the Middle East. But in Kurdistan the movement to Islamicize society as the precondition for reestablishing an Islamic government (either in the form of a state or more radically in the form of a caliphate) gained energy in and around the *hucre*. The *hucre* was not simply opposed to the secularism of the liberalizing nation-state; it was also often opposed to the secularism of communism. At the same time, just as many Islamist movements of the Middle East mimicked secular liberal modes of action even as they contested them, the Islamist movement in Kurdistan took communism as a model as well as a target.

Of course, the *hucre* was not only an incubator for Islamism. It was also a place where more secular Kurdish nationalism had come to thrive across the twentieth century. It provides an insightful point of entry for a discussion of Islamic traditions in Kurdistan because in that institution one can see how Sufi thought and Kurdish poetry first came to prosper in an Ottoman milieu, then how projects of liberal and illiberal secularism came to be articulated and contested, and finally how Islamism came to thrive there.

These layers of history are not lost but found on the lips of most Iraqi Kurdish Muslims. As Lila Abu-Lughod described the life of poetry in a very different context in the region, "What is said in poetry and what is said in ordinary language always exist side by side: their interplay is essential to their meaning."[38] This is true in Kurdistan as well, where poetry is commonly recited throughout the course of everyday life and where poetry intersects with or departs from other forms of speech, including Islamist discourse. Like the language of preachers and politicians, poetry in Kurdistan is not only a language of art and beauty but also of power and knowledge; it can be a philosophical expression of an entire cosmos that carries with it the moral and political struggle that characterized life in the *hucre*, as well as beyond the *hucre*.

For this book, also, poetry is neither a decorative mode of expression nor merely a subject of inquiry. Poetry offers an analytical frame through which to approach the study of religious difference. As Chapter 2 demonstrates at great length, one important dimension of the poetic tradition in Iraqi Kurdistan is its capacity to envelop paradox: poetry has the capacity to bring together two differing, even contradictory, tendencies within the same expression. Rather than resolve that paradox into a propositional claim of the kind usually sought by theology, for example, poetry is the expressive mode that allows for paradox to thrive. In this sense, the poetic tradition is where Iraqi Kurdish Muslims have historically wrestled with the paradoxes of Muslims who turn away from piety. This book suggests that the capacity to envelop paradox that is most obvious in poetry is also visible in a range of dimensions of contemporary everyday life. This paradox appears as a mood, an attitude, or a sensibility that is palpable in the way Iraqi Kurdish Muslims relate to themselves, to one another, and to Islamic traditions more generally in the beginning of the twenty-first century.

TWO CONDITIONS OF FIELDWORK

During fieldwork, I answered questions about my own religion on a daily basis, both in Silêmanî where I lived and in Hewlêr, which I visited on a monthly basis. Whether I was riding in a taxi, meeting with friends and interlocutors, visiting a home, conducting an interview, or searching out an archive, many people asked whether I had converted to Islam. In some ways this was a natural question for many Kurdish Muslims who had encountered very few Westerners who had either a serious interest in Islam or the ability to speak comfortably in Kurdish. They sometimes assumed that I was not Muslim but that my interest in Islam portended conversion or that one of my parents was Kurdish and I had grown up abroad. It took time for me to learn how to answer their questions.

I was initially uncomfortable claiming a Christian identity. Belief was a crucial part of the Protestant Christianity that I learned, and I did not believe many of the doctrinal claims learned in my youth. As far as practice goes, I never entered a church in Kurdistan (although there are many), nor did I practice other things that I had learned were essential to Christian faith (prayer, for example). Although my parents were Christians, I did not consider myself very Christian at all.

However, the terms of my interactions with Kurdish Muslims were not only my terms. I quickly realized that while there were many who could make sense of my claim to be not very Christian at all, there were many more people who could not make sense of it or else immediately made the wrong sense of it. On the occasions that I did not identify as Christian, I found myself listening to passionate arguments about the existence of God or about why religion is important for life. I came to see that I was offered these things because it was only conceivable to my interlocutors that I not believe in God if in fact no one had explained to me why there must be a God. I was also answered by expressions of deep pity that my parents had not taught me any religion. All of this was very much the wrong impression. As a teenager I had studied those arguments for God, much to my parents' delight. When I identified as a non-Christian, the response I received left me feeling terribly misunderstood, as if it was not *me* my interlocutors were speaking to.

So I became a Christian, as it were, during fieldwork, not because of any private, interior transformation or any burdensome compulsion but because it allowed my interlocutors and me to make sense of one another. As a Christian, I regularly received invitations to convert to Islam. But the style, tenor, and substance of these invitations—in contrast to the invitations prompted by my claim not to have religion—made sense to me. I realized that if I were to convert to Islam, that conversion would take the shape of a Christian converting to Islam, not an atheist converting to Islam.

There are two crucial consequences of this condition of my fieldwork. First, it offers one of the simplest illustrations of a point underlined throughout the book that belief and practice are only part of what goes into allowing relationships with others to develop or unfold. Religious orientations are much broader than identities, practices, or beliefs, and they are often not well described in (or as) statements. They *are* well described as relationships, for only in relationships can histories, expectations, and surprises accrue over time.

Second, my orientations to Islam and to Christianity conditioned the kinds of conversations that I was able to have with Kurdish Muslims. As often as I encountered pious Muslims who would invite me to convert by recounting the glory of Islam, I encountered non-pious Muslims who assumed they shared something in common with me because we were not pious people. Sometimes that assumption allowed interlocutors to try to educate me by describing their sense of ambivalence, fatigue, exhaustion, frustration, disappointment, or anger toward Islam. There was sometimes a tenor of virulence in their anger that does not appear in this book. (I met many atheists in the course of research, but they do not appear in this book.) In retrospect, I realize I could not write about that anger because it rarely turned into a conversation. It was usually a lecture for which I was an audience. In contrast, the sense of a dynamic conversation appeared most frequently when the affective tones of ambivalence or disappointment were primary. That I was not a Muslim and had decisive experiences of fatigue and disappointment with Christianity were frequently topics of conversation. This opened up a field of conversation that would not have been possible if I were either a more pious Christian or a pious Muslim.

If at first it was uncomfortable, being known as a Christian came to be as natural to my self-identification as my Kurdish name. I was given a name early in my fieldwork and came to accept it as my own. It was on the morning of a day trip for a picnic (a famed social activity) that my host's grandmother asked my name. I repeated it a few times, modulating my pronunciation to fit the sound of Kurdish—Andru, Endru, Endre—hoping she could accommodate its novelty. She was quickly satisfied when she heard something she recognized and said, "Oh, your name is *Hendrên*, like that mountain of ours" (a mountain a few hours north of Silêmanî by car). The name was a good solution, not only because it had a phonetic resemblance but also because it did not imply that I was Muslim. While my closer friends called me Andrew, many others called me Hendrên. Perhaps becoming Hendrên was rather like becoming Christian for me. My friend's grandmother was like many other people I met in Kurdistan who welcomed me with ease and pleasure. Their hospitality was warm.

Hospitality is the second condition of my fieldwork that requires elaboration, not least because of the global politics that shaped it. It may surprise some readers to learn that Iraqi Muslims welcomed an American Christian at a time when American political and military apparatuses were destroying much of Iraq. Others may recall Anglophone media's characterization of Iraqi Kurds as friends of Americans and supporters of the US-led invasion of Iraq. That characterization owes as much to the success of the propaganda of the largest Kurdish political parties as it does to popular sentiment. My encounters in public spaces as well as in homes all across Iraqi Kurdistan afforded many occasions when Kurds were surprised by the intensity of my opposition to America's occupation. But they also afforded me encounters with some who had trenchant and elaborate critiques. All of this makes for a complicated condition of hospitality. The question, though, is how we inhabited those conditions.

We did so in part through humor. A pair of jokes appeared in one form or another almost every day during my preliminary visits in 2004–2006, and they were still present during the time of my intensive fieldwork in 2008 and 2009. The first was that I was a spy for the US government. It sometimes appeared as an admonition toward older men who were reputed to prefer the company of younger men, possibly to exploit them: "Not this one," my friends would say, "he's a spy!"[39] It appeared in the very serious inquiries made about me before or after people met me or participated in my research. And it showed up in the way of a promise: people would insist that I would eventually be appointed as the first American ambassador to the independent state of Kurdistan. I protested all these accusations with a sincerity that never mattered. (After all, being a spy is the profession that requires one to disown it in order to be any good at it.)[40]

I was often compared with Major Soane, a British traveler who passed through Kurdistan disguised as a Persian merchant, managing to achieve fluency in Kurdish before being discovered and eventually returning to serve the British government during the Mandate period.[41] One of Major Soane's successors in that work was C. J. Edmonds.[42] I once took the place of Edmonds in the dream of a bookseller whose shop I visited more than once a week during my time in Kurdistan. The bookseller's dream was set in a distant past when he was just a boy. His grandfather pointed to an Englishman sitting by a tree and writing in a notebook. His grandfather said to him with admiration and a hint of mystique, "That's an Englishman who is writing your history." The bookseller, as a boy in his dream, looked and saw that it was my face on the Englishman.

That dream is just one way that I was interpolated as a researcher. I protested the identification with Edmonds just as passionately as I protested my ascribed profession as a spy—and just as fruitlessly. The bookseller meant to praise me with this story of his dream, to impress on me the importance of my task. He also reminded me that, from a certain perspective, the histories written in English tend to matter in a special way, not because they contain better research but because those histories are relayed to the imperial centers of the world before those very centers send out the planes whose bombs leave other written histories in ashes. The research for this book was conducted alongside those ashes, in the shadows of the planes, and in conversation with the poets, scholars, and ordinary Iraqi Kurds who inhabit their own history.

The second joke that appeared on a daily basis was that one of my acquaintances would eventually give in to temptation and sell me to kidnappers, who would then ransom me to the US government. With a handsome sum of cash, they would join the "terrorists" and become famous—or else, in a parody of the terrorists' hypocrisy, they would spend the money binge drinking on the outskirts of town. Some friends would evoke elaborate plotlines with a single, momentary gesture in which they assumed the posture of the hostage takers who had appeared in videos and photographs throughout Iraq during those years. The gesture allowed them to enter the plot at any point to embellish some terrible detail. I took these jokes in good humor, but not as devoid of wisdom. Even as they joked about it, the same friends went out of their way to look after me. They called me regularly, asked about the people I was spending time with, and made their own inquiries about those people. They checked up on me for my own interests, to be sure I was safe, as well as for their own. They knew the joke could lose its humor in an instant. Perhaps the joke itself was one way of reminding me of this. My friends and interlocutors absorbed the prospect of my being a spy or my being kidnapped and often transformed it by humorous exercises of (suspicious) care.

It was a main condition of my fieldwork that these prospects of betrayal were inseparable from the hospitality I received. Alongside these threats and promises, though, we enjoyed one another's company. And this book is about precisely that: how the big story becomes more complicated when we think about the everyday relationships that are conditioned by it and how relationships accommodate tendencies to friendship and estrangement. The example of these two jokes gives substance and texture to the sense in which I use the phrase "absorb and transform." The phrase does not mean escape or transcend. It just means that the relational terms given by broad structures condition, without determining, what ordinary relationships look like in everyday life. Those relationships have to be recounted in their own terms, and when that happens, the questions of structure and power come to share focus with the texture of ordinary relationships.

These were two conditions for the emergence of the evidence that appears in the following pages. It is important to keep them in mind because the evidence that I have collected did not simply "appear." It appeared *to me*, to this male, this Christian, this American who may be a spy or may be a victim of kidnapping. To name these conditions as central to my fieldwork does not imply that people were always staging themselves to me. It means that these conditions allowed for some conversations to thrive and left other conversations stilted.

Similarly, the evidence I present will appeal to a particular kind of reader. Different readers will know or discover the conditions in which they approach the book in their own way. I hope that readers will discover something about those conditions both in the book and in discussing the book with others. My own fantasy of a reader is that they read the book in conversation with another reader and that in this conversation readers may surprise each other by the difference of their reactions. As the conversation proceeds, the conversation partners realize that they are attending as much to their tone and posture toward others as to the content of ideas or opinions. Partners realize that rather than talking about disembodied ideas, they are having a conversation that moves around relationships: "I have a friend whose family is somehow similar," or "Things in my family are not quite like this." Then readers will have to launch into a long description of things. For such a description, theological accounts of faith, belief, or practice will be useful but not reliable. The conversation might not arrive at a set of claims, but claims may be a productive place to start. If this Introduction has made a case for writing from relationships, the Epilogue elaborates on the prospect of reading from relationships.

Anthropologist Marilyn Strathern described the "central problematic for the anthropologist" as follows: "what has to be done (understood, analysed, theorised) in order to gain adequacy of description?"[43] This Introduction has begun with three central claims, provided a set of key terms, and offered an acquaintance with the author. This has been the necessary first step to clear the ground for the more delicate, more laborious task of description. For that task, the chapters ahead look closely and patiently at the relationships where texts are translated into the texture of ordinary relationships. They examine the ways Kurdish Muslims themselves describe, reveal, or conceal orientations to Islamic traditions. Their task is to achieve an adequate description of how different religious orientations appear in ordinary relationships between Muslims in Iraqi Kurdistan.

Chapter 1

QURAN AND ZOROASTER

Attraction and Authority in Muslim Ethics

ANTHROPOLOGIST TALAL ASAD'S SUGGESTION TO APPROACH THE anthropological study of Islam as the study of a discursive tradition has been widely influential for the ethnographic study of Muslim ethics.[1] The concept of a discursive tradition sought to unravel a seeming contradiction between two tendencies in the anthropological study of Islam. Some anthropologists claimed that so much variety and contradiction had been observed in the lives of Muslims who claim to practice Islam that it was impossible to speak of a single thing called Islam. Those scholars suggested that there were in fact many Islams and anthropologists would be remiss to take a single approach to study the social life of Muslims because Islam could not provide any reliable similarity across different societies. Other scholars claimed that Islam provided a "blueprint" for social relations and was in fact a form of authority that prescribed predictable patterns among Muslims.

Asad highlighted the problem of both tendencies. The first overlooked the fact that there were commonalities between Muslims. These include their identity as Muslims and their insistence that they have something in common, but also that they draw on the same founding texts when they make those claims. The second, though, was inadequate for understanding how very different, even contradictory, social practices could all be called "Islamic."

The concept of a discursive tradition identified a common starting point for how Muslims organized their lives and social relations, and it allowed for very different conclusions about what was good or right. As Asad put it, the discursive tradition "includes and relates itself to the founding texts of the Quran and the Hadith."[2] That is, it draws authority from these two founding texts: the speech events attributed to the Prophet Muhammad and the Quran that Muhammad conveyed as divine speech. Yet when Muslims draw authority from these texts, they do so in an environment of contest, debate, and competition about what the texts have said, what they have meant for others, and what they mean for them. Therefore, all the variety that anthropologists have observed in Muslim societies need not be evaluated according to whether it is truly or correctly Islamic. It should instead be described and analyzed as a consequence of how Muslims have argued for what is correctly Islamic.

The notion of a discursive tradition relies on an idea of "tradition" that is not a space of uniformity and obedience but one of disagreement, argument, and contest. Asad wrote that a tradition consists of "discourses that seek to instruct practitioners regarding the correct form and purpose of a given practice that, precisely because it is established, has a history."[3] Asad here drew attention to instruction as a pedagogical approach that orients Muslims to correct practice and does so in part through reference to the founding texts. Asad has inspired anthropologists to study these pedagogies, including accounts of how Muslims learn to establish regular prayers, attend mosque, learn to recite the Quran, or listen to recitations of the Quran or sermons by Muslim preachers.[4]

Within the context of their own social and political histories, pedagogies relate to the founding texts, connect individuals to the debate about proper practice, and seek to produce a sense of commitment or a binding to what is good or proper. For example, a Muslim father teaching his daughter to fast is a pedagogy that relates to the divine command in the Quran, "O, you who believe! Fasting is prescribed for you as it was prescribed for those before you, that haply you may be reverent."[5] He may seek to show her that the "you who believe" includes *her*, implicitly arguing against anyone who might say that fasting was required only in the past. And he may seek to solicit a sense of commitment, a binding, a compulsion in her to join other Muslims to fast during the month of Ramadan. Such pedagogy is quite common in Iraqi Kurdistan.

In fact, the English word "binding" is similar to the Arabic term *iltîzam* in Sorani Kurdish. *Iltîzam* encompasses a sense of commitment, an obligation, a recognition of importance or necessity; and one who demonstrates that binding is called *multezîm*. One ordinary use of the term is to indicate commitment, such as one's commitment to a diet or a daily schedule. But another ordinary use describes someone who is committed to Islam and seeks to be a good Muslim. Someone who has *iltîzam* usually identifies the Quran and the hadith as the primary source of human virtue, and in Kurdistan today, the chief signs of being *multezîm* are a commitment to performing daily prayers and keeping the fast during Ramadan. In this sense, someone who has *iltîzam* may be described in English as someone who is "pious."

However, another common phrase in Kurdistan is *iltîzamî niye*, which means quite literally that someone lacks that binding or commitment. Even though Iraqi Kurdish Muslims commonly receive instruction through the pedagogies designed to produce a binding, some may emerge without that binding. Many Kurdish Muslims offer two other common descriptions of themselves and others: *gwê nadat*, which is similar to the English phrases "he doesn't pay attention" or "she doesn't bother"; and the phrase *lêm nayêt*, which says of religion in general or some particular practice that "it doesn't suit me" or "it doesn't become me." These expressions describe an orientation to Islam that is quite common among Kurdish Muslims in Iraqi Kurdistan, which is at the heart of this book.

This chapter aims to describe the life of one person who lacks *iltîzam*, whom I call Pexshan. She received instruction and encouragement to pray and fast in many different venues. She received instruction in the virtues that many Kurdish Muslims prize, and she was exposed to a much longer history of debate about those virtues and practices in Islamic history. And in all this instruction she engaged with the founding texts of the Quran and hadith. Despite this instruction, she expressed her aversion to Muslim piety and her attraction to non-Islamic traditions, even while she continued to engage with more pious Muslims in a variety of contexts.

Will the concept of a discursive tradition remain a useful starting point to describe the life of a Muslim who turns away from piety? What can a description of this life reveal about how Muslims relate to the founding texts? While this chapter answers "yes" to the first question and "quite a lot" to the second, it does so only after *testing* the concept against the evidence of Pexshan's life.

This chapter tests the limits of the flexibility of the concept of discursive tradition and asks whether the concept can be reanimated by a methodological sensibility that looks beyond piety. Most efforts to extend, elaborate, and critique the concept of a discursive tradition have relied on integrating it with much of Asad's later work on secularism. In returning to the starting point of the Quran and the hadith and to the arguments and pedagogies about correct practice, I seek to redirect inquiry toward the ordinary scenes of everyday life where Muslims engage these texts. Approaching the concept of discursive tradition in this way, I seek to move away from the simplistic dichotomy of offering a critique or defense of the concept, opting rather for creative redirection.

This chapter proceeds through several descriptions of when, how, in what terms, and in whose company Pexshan related to the Quran and hadith. Following her own speech, it concludes by suggesting that the language of poetry offers a useful way of describing her orientation to Islamic traditions and her manner of relating to other Muslims in the course of everyday life.

PEXSHAN

I first met Pexshan in 2004. During fieldwork in 2008 and 2009, about every other week I visited her home, where we usually read poetry of her choosing. She described that period in her life by saying, "I'm all alone, just me." By 2008, she was in her late fifties and had withdrawn from the busy life of engagements with a constantly morphing group of artists and poets in Silêmanî, where for all of her adult life she had been a poet and worked in the field of literature and the arts. The solitude to which she referred also encompassed the absence of her father, her mother, and her husband, who had long since passed away. "I've grown old," she often said with a sigh. The phrase explained why she did not know some younger poets, preferred to stay at home rather than go out for the evening, or had found it necessary to change her diet. Yet what she called solitude included the continuing presence of her teenage daughter, grandchildren from other children, and a host of other relatives in her home.

She had a stable middle-class lifestyle and a comfortable home in a middle-class neighborhood in Silêmanî. Thus, while she could not afford a lavish trip abroad, she could easily afford luxuries such as vacations in Kurdistan and dinner in fancy restaurants. Her neighborhood had a middle-class character in part because the homes had driveways for cars and the streets were not overcrowded with children playing and neighbors looking for gossip.

Visiting her home often over the years, I had developed the habit of sharing with her reflections on my fieldwork, and I often reported to her the speech of others that I found puzzling. Through descriptions of language, poetry, folklore, or politics, she would explain and contextualize phrases that interested me. I prized our relationship in part because of the way that the genre of the "interview" was transformed: I always asked questions but rarely prepared them in advance, and she frequently turned my questions back to me. I often scribbled notes as she spoke and shared with her notes I had scribbled while others spoke. The formal procedures of the interview had evolved into a four-year-long conversation. She knew that she could launch into long reflections or ruminations about the past and I would probably listen and scribble.

LEARNING HADITH WITH HER FATHER

One afternoon we spent about two hours reading poetry together when I scribbled quite a lot in my notebook. When we had finished our reading for the day, conversation wandered toward the topic of Islam. Pexshan described a sense of frustration and disappointment with the Islam that surrounded her by saying she was *bêtaqet*—tired or fed up with it. When asked whether she considered her attitude *new* in relation to that of previous generations in Kurdistan, she answered that it was. She noted that most of the critiques (*rexne*) of Islam read in her generation had been written by Arabs,[6] so she implied that previous generations of Kurds had not spent their time writing critiques. (Of course, this does not imply that there were no critiques.) Then, in an illustrative mode, she recounted how that difference of generations appeared in her own family: "When I was young, my father was always praying and worshipping [*berdewam nwêj u îbadetî ekird*], but I didn't like those things."

I asked, "Did your father tell you to pray?" In her reply, she referred to *perşêw*, which is the predawn meal taken before fasting begins in Ramadan: "Well, of course he always told us, but he never did anything. I remember when they would wake up for *perşêw* and call to me, but I would not get up to eat. But [later on] I once overheard my mother when she said, 'She doesn't fast.' I didn't like any of those things. But my faith is greater now than it was then."

I was curious about what "greater faith" meant, so I asked, "Where did that come from?" She answered,

> From experience, you know. And thinking about things. . . . Every night, my father used to gather us together and read the hadith to us. I remember one night he spoke about a hadith like this: There were two men. One of them was

faithful [*îmandar*]; he was always praying and worshipping [*nwêj u îbadet*]. The other one would never pray. When they died and they were taken before God, God asked them, "For what sake should I pardon you? For the sake of your deeds or for the sake of my own mercy?" God first asked the faithful man, and the faithful man told God he wanted to be judged according to his deeds because he had always been praying and worshipping. God sent him to hell. Then God went to the other man and asked the same question. Of course, the man had done nothing in his life, no praying or worshipping or anything, and so the man said, "Well, I can only say, on your own mercy," and God said, "Go on!" and sent him to heaven.

"So what does it mean for you?" I asked. She replied, "It means, why should you bother with all of this prayer and worship in your life if that is what will happen?" This account suggests that Pexshan took for granted that the hadith offered a reliable picture of judgment: something like this *would* happen on Judgment Day. Islamic intellectual traditions include a highly elaborate science by which to determine the authenticity and reliability of the Prophet's hadith—to separate the authentic hadith from those that were corrupted over generations of transmission.[7] In the early Muslim community, women were highly regarded as transmitters of the Prophet's hadith.[8] But Pexshan was not concerned with a scientific or scholarly evaluation of this particular hadith's authenticity or with relaying it precisely. Her narration was instead focused on the idea of getting the gist of things.

Furthermore, when her father read the hadith to her, it was not to help her become a scholar. His goal was much more mundane: to instill in her gratitude for divine mercy and fear of divine wrath on the Judgment Day. Equipped with such gratitude and fear, prayer and worship would be the only way to express it, and Pexshan would be on the path to becoming a more pious Muslim. In this sense, the spirit of the hadith in her father's recitation resembled the gist of a saying by a prominent figure in the Sufi tradition, Rabi'a al-'Adawiyya. An eighth-century Muslim in Basra, she had penned the following lines of devotion: "O Lord, if I worship you out of fear of hell, burn me in hell. If I worship you in the hope of paradise, forbid it to me. And if I worship you for your own sake, do not deprive me of your eternal beauty."[9] Yet for Pexshan, the hadith showed that God is not so concerned with ritual worship. The growth of her faith was paradoxically linked to a dismissal of ritual worship: there was no need to bother with prayer and worship if Judgment Day would look like *that*.

This scene recalls Talal Asad's notion of a discursive tradition because a hadith became one axis of Pexshan's relation to Islamic traditions. Her father sought to offer instruction on what it meant to be a Muslim and grounded it in the authoritative source of the Prophet's hadith. For her father, the hadith offers not only a reliable account of future judgment but also reliable instructions from God for how humans ought to live. Yet Pexshan makes no effort to follow divine instructions. And she does not claim that her neglect of prayers realizes a truer Islam. Rather, she describes the expansion of faith beyond the bounds of what is exemplary or prescribed. In other words, she evokes the hadith as a kind of opening to move outside the tradition. The hadith does not inspire her to become a devout Muslim but illustrates her sense that ritual worship is irrelevant to faith.

The logic in Pexshan's recitation and explanation of this hadith may be clearer in comparison to another scene described by anthropologist John Bowen in his work with Muslims in Indonesia in the 1980s, where there was considerable debate about the question of how the Islamic tradition related to practices of spirit possession and healing. Many insisted that such practices were not at all congruent with Islam since they challenged the unity of God by implying that some force other than God was capable of bringing health or sickness. Bowen described a man who responded to the illness of a relative by allowing himself to be possessed and thereby discovering a cure for the relative's illness. The man adds, though, that possession is a form of medication and recites the hadith of the Prophet that "for every illness there is a medicine." Bowen paraphrases the man's explanation: "To heal is to follow the Prophet's example."[10] In the case of Bowen's interlocutor, the citation of a hadith was an attempt to bring *into* the fold a practice that may be regarded as outside Islam. It is a recitation that makes a questionable practice into an Islamic practice and directs it toward the values and virtues already recognized as Islamic. Pexshan's recitation of the hadith appears to invert the logic of Bowen's interlocutor. Pexshan's explanation begins with the recognized Islamic practices of prayer and fasting, and the hadith opens the door to what may be called the *outside* of an Islamic tradition: a faith that spurns prayer and fasting.

Contemplating the hadith had not brought Pexshan further into the pedagogies that would bind her to Islamic traditions but instead loosened that binding. The text that for her father offered authoritative instruction in the correct attitude and correct practice for Muslims was not authoritative for Pexshan in the same way. Whatever authority it held was contestable, to say the least. Yet her engagement with the founding texts was not only a question of authority but also a question of attraction. For Pexshan had said twice that prayer and fasting were practices she did not *like* or *enjoy* (*hezm lêy nebu*). In other words, while instruction was supposed to cultivate an attraction to these practices, Pexshan was not attracted to prayer, fasting, or worship.

Although attraction surely has a dimension of interiority, it should not be reduced to a state of individualized, private interiority, because Pexshan's lack of attraction toward prayer and fasting was acknowledged and addressed by others. Her father's attitude was one of invitation, encouragement, and instruction when he had instructed her to pray and invited her fast. Her mother's attitude stood in subtle contrast. In hindsight I wish I had asked her to say more about her mother's attitude, but even this brief appearance in her description is revealing.

Rather than double down on her father's instruction, her mother simply acknowledged and accommodated Pexshan's habit. Pexshan had said, "I once overheard my mother when she said, 'She doesn't fast.'" Here is a very subtle moment of description that avoids overarching statements of good or bad, right or wrong, and makes a space in everyday life for those who do not turn to piety. Her mother's words show that Pexshan's lack of attraction to pious practice was not a matter of private conviction or an isolated conscience. It was an attitude visible to her parents when she was young and part of her relations with them. As the following sections show even more clearly, moments of description and implicit subtle evaluation are never isolated but always appear in particular social relationships.[11]

ENGAGING THE QURAN'S BEAUTY WITH A STRANGER

Exactly one month before the beginning of Ramadan in 2008, I accompanied Pexshan and her teenage daughter to a new restaurant for lunch. We arrived late in the afternoon, after the lunch crowd but long before the dinner crowd. On the second floor, in keeping with common practice in Kurdistan, was a family section reserved for parties that included female patrons. The restaurant staff were busy cleaning the floors, and the room was filled with the resounding echo of a television broadcast. The volume was so loud (and the television's speakers so poor) that it was difficult to discern what we were hearing. There were phrases of Quranic Arabic, but I did not know whether these were part of an Iraqi song (*meqam*) that was employing phrases from the Quran or the Quran itself. I asked Pexshan, who had to listen carefully for a moment before deciding that it was the Quran. Soon one of the servers passed by, and she told him brusquely, "For God's sake, change that Quran." It was a cold and curt request. The server was clearly taken aback and was not quick to comply. In the next few moments, Pexshan said plaintively, in a voice barely audible given the echoing Quran, "This is a restaurant, and we came to eat. Why this Quran?"

Why Pexshan was so displeased was unclear to me. She said nothing about the volume but asked the server to *change* the broadcast. Was it the audition of the Quran itself that displeased her? Or did she have the impression that the Quran was being *imposed* on her? With this uncertainty before me, I recounted what I had heard a few days before in the form of a hadith that when one listens to the Quran, one should give it one's full attention and not be distracted by anything else. "Isn't there a hadith like that?" I asked, to which she replied uninterestedly, "I don't know."[12] But a moment later when the Quran was still echoing over the table, she said in a tone of annoyance, "What is this? A funeral?" She then commented that the Quran creates a sorrowful (*xembar*) atmosphere.

Eventually the television station was changed and conversation wandered to the approaching month of Ramadan. Both Pexshan and her daughter let out exasperated sighs, and I remember her daughter anticipating that most of her friends—who did not usually wear headscarves—would don them during the month of Ramadan, as is common in Kurdistan. She explained how people behave, using the word *xelk*, which is just as broad and anonymous in Kurdish as "people" is in English. *People* expect her to cover her head; *people* will ask her why she does not cover her head. At the same time, though, people become lazy and sleep all day, people spend twice as much money on food when they are supposed to be eating less, and other people go on vacation then because they cannot bear it when "people" nag them about not fasting.

This scene gives a glimpse into how public space in Kurdistan is shaped by assumptions that are commonly tied to Islamic traditions. The organization of seating in restaurants as public commercial spaces enables a partial division of the sexes, but it was also surprising for such commercial space to be saturated by a recitation of the Quran. Pexshan's daughter referred to the expectation that women will cover their heads during Ramadan in any public space even if they do not do so during the rest of the year and even if they are not fasting. Yet some people were so unhappy with that expectation that they would travel during Ramadan just to avoid it. These background factors give a good sense of how different norms described in the Introduction compete with one another in Kurdistan: if those working in the restaurant seemed confident that this type of Quranic audition fell within established norms, Pexshan considered it self-evident that it did not.

This mundane event of responding to the Quran and anticipating Ramadan has complex moral, affective, and aesthetic elements. Pexshan showed a strong aversion to Quranic audition on this occasion and described that aversion in the affective and aesthetic terms of "sorrow" (*xembar*). In doing so, she touched on a key feature of much Quranic recitation as it has been described in medieval sources. In her paradigmatic study of the practice that connected medieval sources to contemporary practices, Kristina Nelson identified *huzn* (Ar.) as a cherished feature of a successful recitation. While *huzn* encompasses "sorrow," Nelson emphasizes that it is also an aesthetic feature of an overwhelming beauty that is necessarily tied to a "softening of the heart" and a fear of God.[13] Feeling sorrow and beauty at the same time is evidence of a pious attitude toward God, a correct relation of awe at divine beauty and fear of divine wrath. In this model beauty and truth are entirely contiguous: the moral goal of developing a pious attitude is inseparable from the aesthetic impact of Quranic verses. However, Pexshan's response showed that she isolated sorrow from the virtues. She did not connect sorrow to a fear of impending judgment but to the more mundane sadness of attending a funeral. Pexshan felt that because it resembled the atmosphere of a funeral, it was not appropriate to a restaurant.

Furthermore, Pexshan was not moved by my explanation of a hadith, which had offered a way to say that *this way* of listening to the Quran was not the properly authorized one—one should instead listen with attention. Pexshan had dismissed this explanation without interest. Contrary to what occurred in the first scene, here her engagement with the founding texts shows no hospitality toward the hadith.

Yet it would not suffice to say that a Quranic recitation was being broadcast in the restaurant. The passive tense is misleading. It is better to say that someone was broadcasting the Quran in the restaurant. Perhaps it was the server whom she asked to change it. Perhaps it was another server. Perhaps it was the manager. But someone made the decision and thus made the restaurant into a space of moral education. In this sense, Pexshan's response was not only to the Quran but also to those who practice Quranic audition in public. That public practice effectively extends an invitation to anyone within earshot to join in and exercise a form of moral pedagogy. Pexshan had declined the invitation that someone had extended to her.

Pexshan and her daughter had here offered a critique of what "people" do in Ramadan. Their critique registers disappointment and fatigue or exhaustion.

Obviously, pious Muslims might also feel disappointed at the bad conduct of others during Ramadan and criticize them in an attempt to bring them back to the true meaning of Ramadan. But Pexshan and her daughter were not trying to recover a more correct practice. They were simply annoyed.

Their relationships to the widely accepted requirement that Muslims fast during Ramadan, and to the common practice of veiling even if one does not fast, is not only a matter of accepting or denying the authoritative claim of the founding texts on their moral lives. It is also a question of how Pexshan and her daughter gauge their attraction to the practices and how much they can endure the pedagogies that call on the founding texts. In lieu of attraction, there is aversion. In response to invitations to piety from strangers, they show fatigue and exhaustion.

As she turns away from piety and declines the invitations to piety offered by strangers and her father, what does Pexshan turn toward? In the space of fatigue and exhaustion, what animates and refreshes moral aspiration? These questions set the stage for a third scene from my conversations with Pexshan.

FASTING IN RAMADAN WITH NEIGHBORS

One afternoon during the first days of Ramadan, Pexshan and I read a poem by 'Ebdullah Goran, who is one of the most prominent Kurdish nationalist poets of the 1950s–1970s. Goran is known for the musicality of his free-verse poetry as well as his attraction to the poetry of the European Romantics. Pexshan praised him by saying that in addition to his political poetry expressing communist commitments, he had a Romantic capacity to appreciate the beauty of nature.[14] That afternoon we read a poem that described his trip to the Hewraman region. Much of the poem is devoted to his rapture at the natural beauty of the region and the native genius and good manners of its inhabitants. Hewraman is sometimes associated with Kurdistan's pre-Islamic past, and some speculate that Hewraman is the original home of Zoroaster, founder of the Zoroastrian religion. In the midst of his rapture at the pristine beauty of Hewraman, Goran encounters a mela (mullah)—a scholar of religion—and describes him as follows:

> A mela was snuggled up beneath his turban
> his beard sprawling down and across his chest;
> A slumping posture, like an old book,
> a sweet tongue and a slight pout;
> His soul is full of poetry and letters,

> like the old-fashioned Arabs and Fars.
> What an honor for tonight's guests;
> our gathering is full of melas!
> You and your mela, some poetry, Islamic philosophy,
> the simple obedience of the masses;
> It comes to resemble this, no more and no less:
> a written letter read aloud by the blind![15]

I believe that this poem, which celebrates the natural beauty of a Kurdish landscape and offers a critique of religious figures who seek to shore up their own authority, set the mood for the conversation that transpired in the ten minutes before I left her house that day. In my own reading of this poem, it offers a critique of a figure of religious authority. Even if such a critique had been quite common in the Kurdish poetic tradition, it was more often a critique that demonstrated faith in true religious authority. For the many poets who preceded Goran and offered critique in this vein, the caricature of an ignorant scholar worked as a provocative call to pursue true knowledge. Yet for Goran, this critique of an ignorant scholar seems to stand for all religious scholars. Rather than criticize a mela for not having accurate knowledge of Islam, this poem hints that even if the mela's knowledge were accurate, it would be meaningless. The mela in the poem pretends to be literate and knowledgeable but knows that his knowledge is in fact weak, so he seeks to prevent others from developing literacy and studying on their own. Finally, the sarcasm evident in the poem's celebration of a gathering "full of melas" suggests that the entire class of scholars could be grouped together as ignorant.

Similar critiques of the figure of the mela were common among communists of Goran's generation. While many communists retained their internal "binding" to Islamic traditions, many also directed criticism at the scholars of religion in the form of caricature such as this one. In the apt metaphor of another interlocutor who drew on this caricature, the melas treat religion as their own "private property" that they want to keep away from the masses. Drawing on figures like Karl Marx, Vladimir Lenin, and Joseph Stalin, this version of communism was not a critique internal to Islamic traditions but a critique of Islam from outside Islam.

This passage and the longer poem of which it is a part thus bring together the two themes that Pexshan had emphasized in Goran's intellectual personality: a capacity to appreciate natural beauty and deep political commitments to a non-Islamic tradition. These two themes also form part of the background for the conversation that transpired in the few minutes before I left her house that day.

I had told Pexshan that I wanted to get home in time to dine with my host family as they broke their fast in the first week of Ramadan. Pexshan asked if everyone there fasted, and I answered (with a wink) that almost everyone fasts, but everyone eats together. Then she said, "It's been three or four days now that I fasted." Surprised and incredulous, I asked, "Really?"

> Yeah, it's nice. I stay up all night watching TV, then get up late in the morning, and I don't want to eat anything. Next thing I know, the day is over and I haven't eaten anything. The problem is that we [i.e., Kurds in Kurdistan] eat so much: rice, bread, fruits, tea. But it's nice; when you don't eat for a whole day, you feel comfortable [*îsrahat ekeyt*].

In this last sentence she made a gesture with her hands to indicate that she meant a corporeal comfort, so I asked if her fasting was for religious or health reasons. She said, "No, it wasn't religious reasons. We can say it was approximately health reasons."

"That means, you fasted, but you didn't pray," I said, earnestly wondering whether some dramatic transfiguration had taken place.

She responded as if by wondering whether she had prayed, I had conceived the inconceivable: "Nooooo!" Then after a pause she went on: "You know, you look around and everyone is praying and fasting, and so you are somehow compelled to fast, for whatever reason."

The conversation became even more interesting, but her comments thus far already show three paradoxical dimensions of her relationship to fasting. First, she denied that it had been intentional. She reports it as an accident, something that happened as a result of staying up late and waking up late. Quite significantly, during my fieldwork in Kurdistan I never heard anyone claim that an accidental fast would "count" as a proper fast. Indeed, scholarly traditions suggest that intention—*niyet* is the term used in Kurdish—is essential to the act of fasting. According to one survey of classical works in Islamic law, *niyet* "turns the undifferentiated flow of human gestures and movements into *particular named actions*, especially the actions required by God and regulated by *fiqh* [law]."[6] Thus, according to one commentator, fasting without intention to do so is merely "lack of nourishment."[7] So among my interlocutors and in classical sources, there is a broad consensus that fasting without intention is simply "not eating." Thus, while Pexshan called it a "fast," neither she nor many of her neighbors would call it a "proper Islamic fast."

Second, in claiming that fasting has health benefits, she echoed the comments of many pious Muslims in Kurdistan. I frequently heard people recount those health benefits in scientific terms as proof that divine wisdom in requiring Muslims to fast far preceded the discovery of modern science that it does have benefits. The difference, however, is that the health benefits seem to have been enough for Pexshan. She did not describe it as divine wisdom and did not mention anticipating any heavenly reward for her good deed.

Third, even if she does not claim an intention to fast in the legal sense, she does claim a desire to fast—an attraction to the practice of fasting. And that attraction lies on the nexus of her relations to others. She describes those others ambiguously as "everyone" (*hemuy*), the people whom you see when you "look around." Perhaps "neighbors" is the best term available in English for that relation that allows for fluctuating proximity and distance. Her words "for whatever reason" suggest that she is not quite clear about the reason for her fasting. But it does seem to exclude the explanation that it was the invitation, verbal encouragement, or explicit advice of her neighbors that had compelled her to fast.

Readers of this book will all have their own ways of sensing or not sensing what it is that their neighbors are doing. Perhaps they see people coming or going in patterns, overhear people, or smell food. Or perhaps readers feel firmly separated from their neighbors and cannot sense what their neighbors are doing. Each of these is a mode of relating that reveals or conceals knowledge in different ways. In Pexshan's neighborhood, one could sense what neighbors were doing. The mode of sensing was primarily aural and visual: If neighbors are eating, one may hear the clang of dishes during the preparation of a meal or the cleanup after a meal. One may notice the arrival or departure of guests around meal time. One may hear the instructions of a parent to a child to go pick up fresh vegetables from a shop on the corner. Or one may note a sudden silence from the neighbor's patio when everyone there sits down to eat behind closed doors. All of these factors likely contributed to Pexshan's sense that all of her neighbors were fasting. And they also contribute to the sense that she kept company with her neighbors during her accidental fast.

Thus, Pexshan's turn away from the Quran and her exhaustion with the pedagogies of moral advice offered by strangers also include a turn toward distinctively

Islamic practices she engaged with her neighbors. As the conversation continued, the terms of her engagement became even more complicated.

After her enthusiastic denial that she had prayed, and the attribution of her fasting to the feeling of everyone around her fasting, she continued speaking in a tone of imaginative muse. My notes do not record any mention of Zoroastrianism in our conversation until this point. Yet they do record her mentioning it here as if we had discussed it earlier in our meeting. It is for that reason that I described Goran's poem as having set the mood for our conversation, as it contained allusions to the region that is sometimes associated with Zoroastrianism and nearly always associated with nature. Moving from the theme of the health benefits of fasting and her relation to her neighbors, Pexshan said,

> But there was no fasting in Zoroastrianism. He had some beautiful sayings. He said, "Think well, speak well, do well." That's brilliant. Because thinking well without speaking well is nothing. And speaking well without doing well is also nothing. You need all three. Zoroaster himself was a doctor. He looked at those he treated. He saw that some of them were healed, but others died. He was very sad for those who died, and he wanted to know why it was that some died and some recovered. So he went to the mountains to ask, What are the forces that save or kill? He said that there is darkness and there is light. That darkness is what brings the bad, but the light is what brings the good. It's beautiful [his idea]. I think the same thing, really. I don't think that the one who creates is the one who destroys also. Just like what Khayyam says about that glass: Would God create humans only in order to destroy them?[18] Here they say that they worshipped fire. But it wasn't like that. They thought fire was sacred. They lived in a place where it was cold, and rainy, and snowy, and so fire was sacred. He had a beautiful saying. He said that there are three things that should not be polluted: earth, water, and wind. So don't throw your trash out into the open, and don't dirty the springs. He said that if you want to become a good person, go be a farmer, because then you will understand that humans are just like the earth. They depend on the light of the sun for life. The sun does not make any distinction between humans and animals and plants. It shines on all of us. It's a beautiful religion.

This short description of Zoroastrianism is provocative. In Kurdistan at the time there was a small movement of Kurds around Silêmanî who professed adherence to Zoroastrianism. Historian of religion Edith Szanto has described a burgeoning of conversions to Zoroastrianism in Iraqi Kurdistan after the rise of the Islamic State of Iraq and al-Sham (ISIS) in 2014.[19] Yet as Szanto shows, that movement drew from long-standing efforts to connect Zoroastrianism to Kurdish nationalism.[20] By claiming that Zoroastrianism is the "original" religion of the Kurds, many seek to distance themselves from Islam. When such arguments racialize Islam as the religion of Arabs and Turks, they appear to ironically reverse the claims made against Kurds that Kurds were never truly Muslim to begin with. Pexshan was familiar with all these claims, yet she sidestepped the more dramatic claims that as a Kurd she was originally Zoroastrian or that she would herself convert to Zoroastrianism. She instead declared an attraction to Zoroastrianism.

Pexshan's explanation bore all the features of a stereotypical university professor's account of religion: It began with a famous slogan, then moved through biography to a cosmology that included a vaguely materialist explanation of religion, with a little poetry added along the way for flavor. However abbreviated, this is precisely the kind of description of religion that one may find in a contemporary text in the study of religion. And in fact, most of the works about Zoroastrianism available in Kurdish at the bazaar were translations of twentieth-century Arab and Western academics.[21] Thus, in some ways this was an abstract, intellectualized account of a religion that was not *alive* to her. But in other ways, perhaps Pexshan's description was an attempt to bring Zoroastrianism to life.

Pexshan described Zoroaster's views of the body and the environment as if she were offering an explanation for the wisdom of fasting. There was no logical link to suggest that she was following a Zoroastrian version of fasting. Instead, she sought to align two different logics and imply that they had something in common. In contrast to those who would suggest that the Islamic prescription of fasting anticipated the truth later discovered by twentieth-century biological sciences, Pexshan suggested that the prescription was perhaps drawing on an older, pre-Islamic wisdom. However, it is not truth, belief, or practice that forms the nexus of her relation to Zoroastrianism. It is attraction: Zoroaster has "beautiful sayings," and the religion is "beautiful" (*cwan*). Pexshan aligned her fasting with the attractive power of Zoroastrianism, diverting attention away from the authority of Islamic texts and prescriptions.

Pexshan then contrasted the attractive forces of Zoroastrianism with her aversion to the Islam that surrounds her. Immediately after her summary remark that Zoroastrianism was a "beautiful religion," she cringed and said, "But this Islam . . . *this* Islam . . ." She emphasized the demonstrative pronoun in Kurdish—*em Islame*—an indexical that refers to the Islam that is the "here and now" for her. Then she briefly described documentaries she had seen on television about the rule of the Abbasid caliphs in ninth-century Baghdad and all the violence associated with them:

> There is a series on now for Ramadan that talks about Abu Ja'afar Al-Mansour. It describes all that he did to become caliph. Oh, how many people he killed! [Here again she makes a disgusted face.] All these people he killed!

I asked, "In Ramadan they talk about these things in a critical way?" She replied,

> No, it just talks about how he became caliph and what he did. But these caliphs in Islam, some of them had children imprisoned who were heirs of relatives of theirs. One jailed a few children who were six or seven years old, and after a few days, he sent someone there. He took them out of the jail. And he killed them. Because he didn't want them to claim the caliphate when they grew up. What a repulsive culture [*yek kulturî pes bêtewe*]. Islam, from the very beginning, was about killing people. Whatever got into its path, it killed them. Like that boy Hussein, the son of Ali, they killed him, too, but he was so smart. He spent all day and all night praying, praying and reading. But they killed him . . . stealing money and killing people.

In the last few sentences, Pexshan evokes a well-known episode from Islamic history. After the death of the Prophet Muhammad, his closest companions successively assumed leadership of the Muslim community. The last of these was Ali ibn Talib, commonly known as Imam Ali. His rule was contested, and his death inaugurated an even greater controversy and struggle for power that is often narrated as the beginning of a split between Sunni and Shi'i Muslims. Ali's son Hussein was killed in this struggle during the battle of Karbala. Sunni Muslims in Kurdistan and elsewhere acknowledge the injustice of his death and the heroism of his fight against injustice.[22] In the nineteenth century, Hussein's status as a hero and martyr was a recurring theme in the poetry of (Sunni) Kurdish poets.[23]

Yet in the late twentieth century, the commemoration of his death was increasingly associated with the sectarian dynamics of politics in Iraq and Iran, in part because the Iranian state compared those who died fighting against Iraq in the long war of 1980–1988 with those who died alongside Hussein. Commemorations of Hussein's death have often involved self-flagellation and sometimes insults against early Muslim figures whom Sunni Muslims hold in great esteem. In contemporary Iraqi Kurdistan, some Sunni Kurdish Muslims become apprehensive when Muslims speak passionately of Hussein's martyrdom because they associate that passion with heretical Shi'i tendencies.

In this context, Pexshan's evocation of Hussein presented several ambiguities in her critique. It lent ambiguity to the wholeness of Islam that she criticizes because it suggests that this Islam is the distinctively *Sunni* Islam that surrounds her and left open the imagination of *another* Islam. It also made clear that Muslims are the first and primary victims of the violence that she described. And finally, it introduced an element of irony: Pexshan evoked the image of Hussein as the paradigm of a pious Muslim who suffered injustice at the hands of other Muslims. Despite these ambiguities, the predominant sentiment in her account of Islam's past is disappointment and exhaustion in the face of violence.

Pexshan's description of this distant past was very much present to her, in part because it was linked to contemporary debates that followed Kurdistan's civil war. Throughout the 1990s, different political parties fought for control of the Kurdistan region after the United States and its allies imposed a no-fly zone on the Iraqi military following the Iraqi government's suppression of uprisings at the end of the Gulf War in 1991. The main political parties were the PDK and the KDP, both secular parties. Those two engaged with other secular parties as well as several factions of an Islamist movement in a struggle for power that cut across the Islamist/secular divide. Yet in 1999, factions of Islamists consolidated power in the region of Hewraman. A broad opposition between Islamist and secular approaches informed much public debate throughout the early 2000s, in which the violence of the secular parties was sometimes attributed to their supposed separation from Islam, and the violence of the Islamist parties was sometimes attributed to Islam itself. In public debate, some voices insisted that the violence of Islamist rule in Hewraman was a natural product of Islam, while others insisted that the violence was a betrayal of Islam. Those debates about whether Islam is violent or not are the context for Pexshan's next remark: "Now they say that Islam is this or that. I don't even know. But it is a violent religion. What do you say?"

In her question, the sense of exhaustion reappeared. Yet this time she turned to me—a foreigner who was then unambiguously *not* Muslim—as if she held on to the hope that I might be outside the debate. If I was asking her for descriptions of her ordinary, everyday experiences of Islamic traditions, I believe that she was asking me for a view of Islam from somewhere else, some perspective far from those experiences. While a predominant image of anthropologists is that they ask questions and interlocutors answer them, those roles are commonly reversed. In my case, as an American anthropologist in Iraq at a time when the US military occupied much of the country, I often answered questions about America. Yet on this occasion, Pexshan had not asked me to speak about America per se. She had asked me for my anthropological perspective, for my view of Islam based on my studies.

I tried to think of the truest and shortest thing I could say, something that would deflect the conversation away from the familiar terms of Islam, secularism, and violence. I responded by telling her that I had been impressed by the words of a journalist friend who, coincidentally, was from the region of Hewraman. My friend had recently told me,

> I accept all the prophets, and I even accept Prophet Muhammad as the last prophet, but he himself said that he was the last prophet. And if we look at history, what are the things that have brought benefit to humans after that? All the great contributions are in literature and philosophy. So how I can refuse those accomplishments?

I had cited a Kurdish friend to her, and Pexshan responded by citing an American to me. "There's a novelist—what's his name? He's American... Colin... Colin... Colin Powell?" I told her he had been the secretary of defense, and we shared a good laugh before she finally found the name she was looking for:

> Colin Wilson! Colin Wilson said somewhere that when humans learned to write novels, they had no more need for heaven, because both are imagination [*xeyal*]. But this religion... this religion... it plays with your mind [*mêşkt egat*]; it doesn't let you believe, and it doesn't let you not believe. But like Khayyam says, there is no need for doubt [*guman*] and no need for certainty [*yaqîn*].

I later learned that Colin Wilson was a British novelist, and a friend reminded me that Colin Powell had actually been secretary of state. But these facts were hardly relevant to the conversation. Here again Pexshan had used the indexical *this religion* (*em dîne*) and then in the same breath connected what was present to her, "here and now," with the religion of the twelfth-century Persian poet Omar Khayyam (d. 1126). While many contemporary scholars doubt that Khayyam was himself a practicing Sufi,[24] the widespread assumption in Iraqi Kurdistan has been that only a practicing Sufi could give voice to the ideas that Khayyam put into his quatrains. In the early twentieth century, several prominent Kurdish poets translated Khayyam into Kurdish with such eloquence that the translations have taken on a life of their own. Pexshan was most fond of translation by a poet named Sheikh Selam, and here is my English rendering of Sheikh Selam's translation of the poem to which Pexshan referred:

> Some are obsessed with sect and religion
> Others are plagued by doubt and certainty
> "O, fools!" The voice of the town crier shall come
> "You are all blind and do not see the way!"[25]

Nestled in the prose of her speech was a poetic turn of phrase that offered some respite from the debate. The town crier in Khayyam's poem is a truth-telling figure who suggests that Muslims' preoccupation with debate and contestation is debilitating. Arguing about sectarian difference and matters of creed is fruitless. Similarly, those Muslims who struggle with Islamic traditions in a search for intellectual certainty are missing the point. Pexshan acknowledged the impulse to frame her relation to Islam in terms of doubt or uncertainty, but she took poetry as a reminder that this opposition will go only so far. And true to Khayyam's style, even as his town crier demolishes the only two commonsense ways of relating to Islam, he offers nothing to take their place.

Right before I left, the conversation turned to the topic of the hajj—the pilgrimage to Mecca that is recounted as a requirement for Muslims. She said that the hajj was something that was "outdated" or had "expired" (*be ser çu*). She continued:

> It existed before Islam. It was a yearly journey to Mecca for trade. And the Prophet didn't dare to interrupt that, and so he told the Muslims to make that journey, too, so that Mecca would not fall. They needed that trade. But look at it now; look at all these millions of dollars that the Saudis have collected from the people making the hajj. I told this to my brother, and he said, "Oh, you are a *kafir*!!" and I said, "Well, look, don't make the hajj; take that money and give it to the home of someone who is poor." But going on the hajj, what kind of virtue is that?

In this report of her interaction with her brother, several possible orientations to Islam appear. It is possible to tease out those possibilities while recognizing that neither party's intentions are transparent in this account. Among many Muslims, it is common knowledge that there was a practice of pilgrimage in place on the Arabian Peninsula before the Prophet Muhammad made it an obligation for all Muslims.[26] It is similarly common knowledge that trade and broader economic life were organized around the pilgrimage. There is nothing inherently heretical or scandalous about those claims. Yet that historical knowledge is by no means universal, and it sometimes appeared when someone wanted to challenge a Muslim's understanding of his or her own religion—as if to say, "what you think is unique about Islam is not so unique after all." It is not quite clear if this was the tone of their interaction at this point, but the possibility is certainly there. In any case, that historical knowledge is not necessary, in contrast to what *is* regarded as universal among Kurdish Muslims: the knowledge that Islam requires Muslims to conduct the hajj if they are able.

"If they are able" is a significant qualification that has been a subject of debate in Kurdistan and throughout Islamic history. Jocelyn Hendrickson, a historian of Islamic law, has examined a provocative position in that debate that appeared in different forms from eleventh-century Andalusia to nineteenth-century West Africa. In both settings, Muslim jurists took the position that it was virtually impossible for Muslims of that time and place to be able to conduct the hajj. Given conditions of ongoing warfare and the dangers of the journey, the prominent eleventh-century jurist Ibn Rushd claimed that it was much more important to defend the Muslim community. He even went as far as to state that "the obligation to perform the pilgrimage has lapsed in our times" and considered it reprehensible to conduct the hajj.[27] Hendrickson also reports that a nineteenth-century West African author had approvingly recounted an anecdote about a wandering Sufi who settled in Baghdad in the ninth century. When he encountered a Muslim who claimed that his motivation for conducting the hajj was purely to please God, the Sufi "advised him to give his travel money in charity to poor men, debtors, or those caring for orphans or large families. Removing hardship from others and bringing them joy is better than a hundred pilgrimages, he said."[28]

During fieldwork in Kurdistan, I heard different explanations of the conditions of ability. One of the most interesting was that before one ventures out for the hajj, one should be sure that no one in one's family had any debts and that none of one's neighbors was hungry. In recurring conditions of widespread poverty in Kurdistan, that condition would be hard to meet. Thus, many pious Muslims would suggest that the proper course of action under these circumstances is not to conduct the hajj but rather to support one's poor neighbors. Part of Pexshan's commentary draws on that possibility and resonates with the provocative spirit of the ninth-century Baghdadi Sufi. Is this the interpretation described earlier as the reformist's approach, where the true spirit of the hajj is reclaimed against a merely technical or legalistic interpretation of its requirement? Or is it a rejection of the requirement altogether? Pexshan's suggestion that it had "expired" perhaps leans toward the latter interpretation. At least, that is how her brother seemed to interpret it, because he responded as if Pexshan had crossed a line.

This dispute had taken place as a conversation among close relatives, probably within the household. To have made public declarations on television or in writing about either the contemporary viability of the hajj requirement or about Pexshan's status as a *kafir* would have changed circumstances dramatically and raised the stakes to a level of conflict that was present in their interaction only as a distant possibility. This conversation was instead one in which Pexshan explored the limits of skepticism in her relationship with her brother. Nonetheless, the suggestion that Pexshan was a *kafir*—or gave voice to a *kafir*'s words or had a *kafir* tendency within her—was her brother's answer. His words took the shape of an accusation, declaring that Pexshan had reached the limit of experimenting with skepticism in conversation with him.

AUTHORITY, ATTRACTION, AND AVERSION

What then do these scenes demonstrate about Asad's concept of the discursive tradition? Pexshan was continuously engaged with the founding texts of the Quran and the hadith. Throughout her life, she encountered pedagogies from a range of relationships with others: her father and mother, strangers at a restaurant, and her neighbors during Ramadan. They all offered an opening into Islamic traditions through a range of pedagogies that sought to establish the authority of the founding texts, to instruct Pexshan in "correct" practice, and to instill an attraction toward Islamic traditions. Yet two problems appeared.

First, the pedagogies did not work. Rather than pious obedience and attraction to pious practice, they inspire a sense of fatigue, exhaustion, and disinterest. Whatever attraction Pexshan experienced toward her neighbors when they fast, it did not overcome her aversions to prayer, to the recited Quran, or to the reproof and instruction that strangers would offer to her and her daughter during Ramadan.

Second, and consequently, her relation to the founding texts is not well described in terms of their authority to prescribe conduct for her. If the goal is to describe her relation to the texts and the traditions that bring the texts to life, then we cannot ask only whether she offers assent and obeys or hesitates. There are other forces at work in her relation to the texts and other dimensions of her relation to Islamic traditions. Shahab Ahmed also argues that Asad's insights on questions of authority should be supplemented by insights on other questions. Taking up Asad's description of how the discursive tradition usually works in an effort to prescribe a particular version of correct practice for Muslims, Ahmed suggests:

> To understand the discursive tradition of Islam, we must conceive not only of prescriptive authority, but of what I should like to call *explorative authority*—the *authority to explore*. Whereas the proponent of prescriptive authority views his authority as a license to prescribe to another, the bearer of explorative authority views his authority as a license to *explore* (by) himself.[29]

Exploration is certainly a useful way to describe the form of experimentation that Pexshan practiced on several occasions. And much of her exploration was done, in a sense, "by herself." That is, in pushing back against the prescriptive modes in which her father and brother engaged her, and in turning away from the paths that those around her took to piety, she seemed to be looking toward her own path. Furthermore, hers were explorations *of* herself, insofar as she was often taking stock or recalibrating what dimensions of Islamic traditions were attractive and what dimensions prompted aversion.

This quality of her exploration offers a crucial explanation for the method here of focusing on Pexshan's life as an individual. While it is true that many of my interlocutors shared this experience of departing from a well-worn path and turning toward uncharted paths, to frame Pexshan's experiment as merely one within a pattern of interviews would deflect attention from the experiential quality of her striking out on her own. Instead of a simplistic opposition between individual experience and broad social patterns, this close account of a few scenes from Pexshan's life allows one to appreciate the difficulty of describing one's own experience to begin with. Focusing on a single life shows that the singular experience of experimenting with Islamic traditions occurs in ongoing relationships with others. In those relationships and the conversations that happen as part of everyday life, simply pointing to a broad social pattern cannot solve the question of whether a given practice is "proper" or "Islamic." Rather than escape the ambiguity of these ethical questions by achieving an outside perspective, I seek to follow these questions as they appear in everyday life, which is always shared with others.

Thus, if part of Pexshan's experiments were conducted by herself, they were not exactly conducted *alone*—quite the opposite. Her experiments were conducted in the give and take of everyday life in encounters with others: strangers, relatives, and an anthropologist. For this reason, it would be a mistake to equate her exploration with isolation, aberration, or alienation from others. It would be equally mistaken to overemphasize qualities of autonomy or defiance. For at one key moment, an unusual form of fasting during Ramadan did become attractive and inhabitable to Pexshan, and she attributes that to the vague influence of what "people" are doing all around her. Thus, as Chapter 5 explores in greater detail, those who turn away from piety still find pleasure and companionship with pious Muslims who practice the prescribed disciplines of prayer and fasting.

The explanation Pexshan offered for her attraction to fasting took the virtues of fasting and associated them with a non-Islamic discourse. Pexshan never said that she wanted to transform her identity and become a non-Muslim, and she never outright rejected Islam. Pexshan was striving to find a different way of relating to Islamic traditions or, say, a different way of living in relation to Islamic traditions. The journey involved listening to the critique of communists, asking a Christian foreigner's opinions about Islam, and making a kind of imaginary passage through Zoroastrianism as a non-Islamic religion.

For these reasons, I argue that Asad's concept of a discursive tradition remains a useful starting point for the description of the ethical lives of Iraqi Kurdish Muslims who turn away from piety. At the same time, my conversations with Pexshan show that starting with the discursive tradition allows for a longer, more paradoxical journey than the one that strives for piety. In Iraqi Kurdistan, Islamic traditions are much more capacious than that, and they are no less Islamic for being so capacious.

In Pexshan's life, questions about the authority of the founding texts share space with questions of attraction and aversion to the texts themselves as well as to the practices that those texts authorize. To focus on the themes of attraction and aversion allows one to imagine some of the more paradoxical relations that Muslims have with Islamic traditions, as well as the relations they may have beyond such traditions. Pexshan's struggle to find a different way of living in relation to Islamic traditions involved turning outward, in part toward the non-Islamic tradition of Zoroastrianism. One might say that journey involved a turning or stretching toward a non-Islamic tradition. Yet even if she turned to look beyond Islam, she did not depart from Islam.

Pexshan remained embedded in a shifting set of ordinary relationships where her attractions and aversions were expressed. While she and her daughter seemed to share a similar disposition, Pexshan lived with the memory of her parents' commitment to piety, and she encountered her brother's inclination to pursue piety on different occasions. Furthermore, the two of them together encountered other pious Muslims in public spaces—both at the restaurant where they were indirectly invited to engage in Quranic audition and in other spaces where, for example, her daughter was asked to explain her choice not to veil. These ordinary relations encompass subtle perceived aggressions as well as modes of accommodation and acceptance. Those relations show as much about Islamic traditions as Pexshan's speech does, if not more: Kurdish Muslims' relations to others and their relations to Islamic traditions encompass a wide range of attractions and aversions.

A LANGUAGE FOR DESCRIPTION

How can one turn toward a non-Islamic tradition without departing from Islam? It is difficult to answer this question with a statement. But following Pexshan's own evocations of Khayyam's poetic sensibility, perhaps a poem will suffice. And perhaps this poem, which summarizes the argument in this chapter, will offer a response to the initial question about the language available to describe the lives of Muslims like Pexshan. Pexshan herself never referred to this poem, and I have not seen it in Kurdish translation. Its attribution to Khayyam is subject to all the skepticism for which the poet is himself so well known, and my translation is subject to all the contestation that any translation of poetry provokes. But the verse clarifies something that is otherwise muddled in prose. The poem refers to the magus, or Zoroastrian priest, who is marked by the *zunnar* (P.). In his study of similar themes in Persian literature, Franklin Lewis describes the *zunnar* as "a cord-like girdle with knotted or tassled ends" that was a part of an Orthodox priest's clothing and also became "a marker of the Christian's non-Muslim status in the medieval Islamic world." He adds, "The zunnar's association in Persian extends beyond Christians to Zoroastrians, who for sumptuary reasons wore a similar belt."[30] It was a common symbol in classical Persian and Arabic poetry.

> How long shall I flaunt this ignorance of mine?
> How distraught by its confusion is this heart of mine!
> I'll tie the *zunnar* of the magus around her waist,
> Why else? Since she's Muslim, that self of mine![31]

The poem begins by announcing dissatisfaction with malaise, apathy, or confusion that constrains or binds the heart. The motion of binding then takes the material form of the Zoroastrian priest's *zunnar*. In this case, though, paradoxically, it does not bind a Zoroastrian but a Muslim self. The poet's self is a Muslim, yet the poet binds that self with the signs of being a non-Muslim. The poem thus shows how a Muslim can belong within an Islamic tradition without being fully pious and how a Muslim may pass through a non-Islamic tradition without becoming a non-Muslim.

Chapter 2

CHRISTIANS, *KAFIR*S, AND NATIONALISTS IN KURDISH POETRY

KHAYYAM'S POEM DISCUSSED AT THE END OF CHAPTER 1 OFFERS A memorable image of a Muslim passage through non-Islamic traditions. Through many different permutations, that image was common in much Sufi poetry, and the poetry written in Sorani Kurdish in the early nineteenth century is no exception. Figures of Zoroastrians, Christians, and *kafir*s more broadly were quite common on the terrain of the poetic imagination. These figures were sometimes cast as the beloved—as the subject of the poet/lover's longing. They were also sometimes a version of the poet's self, as in Khayyam's poem or other poems in which the Muslim poet contemplated being or becoming someone else. In both cases, they frame the poet/lover as a Muslim who is attracted to, and passes through, a non-Islamic tradition. These scenes of passage offer abundant ways to imagine how Muslims relate to non-Islamic traditions, an imagination that can have different relations to historical conditions. Themes of attraction, desire, and beauty stand in the foreground of those relationships.

Some readers of Kurdish poetry insist that the poets' imagination of a passage through non-Islamic tradition is evidence of the poets' desire to reject the derivation of legal norms from the texts of the Quran and the hadith. These readers consider an attraction to Zoroastrianism as a rejection of Islam, or an attraction to a Zoroastrian as a mode of casting doubt on Islam. This view relies on an opposition between Sufi tendencies and Islam more generally when it suggests that Sufism stands on the side of religious pluralism and antinomianism, while Islam stands for legalism and religious exclusivity.

This view of a relation between Sufism and Islam appears clearly and succinctly in 'Eta Qeredaxî's history of Sufism in the city of Silêmanî. In the opening pages, he brings two claims together that consolidate a widely held view of Sufism. On the one hand, he writes that Sufism (*tesewuf*) is "negatively opposed to the structure and authority of Islam,"[1] which suggests that Sufism has more in common with other religions, such as Zoroastrianism, than it does it with Islam.[2] Yet at the same time, he writes that Sufism "is still established on the foundations of Islam."[3] Bringing these two claims together shows a vision of Islam in which a foundation evolves in two different directions: it moves toward law, structure, and authority that rejects other religions; and it moves toward Sufism, which rejects the laws, structures, and authorities of Islam and embraces other religious traditions.[4] This view resonates with broad stereotypes of Sufism among Anglophone observers.[5] More important, it thrives in the cafés and teahouses that I frequented in Silêmanî and elsewhere in Iraqi Kurdistan.

However, this chapter dissents from that view. It argues that the early nineteenth-century Kurdish poets did not consider Sufism as a negation of Islamic traditions. Consequently, their descriptions of a passage through non-Islamic traditions are entirely consummate with a hierarchy of religions that enshrined Islam as superior and assumed the ascendance of Islam. For the early poets, a passage through non-Islamic traditions was a productive paradox that enabled the achievement of true Muslim piety. Furthermore, in the context of the early Ottoman Empire this assumption was tied to an explicitly depoliticized literary imagination—that is, the relation between Muslims and non-Muslims described in poetry was not assumed to bear any resemblance to the reality of sociopolitical relations between Muslims and non-Muslims in everyday life. Non-Muslim figures of thought were figments of an imagination that was only contingently related to the concrete, embodied others (Christians and Jews) that Muslims encountered in everyday life.

Alongside this argument the chapter tells a story. For by the mid-twentieth century, the question of religious difference had come to relate to a very different set of political conditions. Following more extensive contact with European colonizers and missionaries, the figures of Christians, Zoroastrians, and *kafir*s in Kurdish poetry became historical, political figures in a new way. As Kurdish nationalism grew during this period, these figures increasingly appeared in Kurdish poetry as opponents and external threats to the Kurdish nation. Thus, if these three figures were once an imaginary other internal to the poet's self and allowed the poet to pass through a non-Islamic tradition en route to Muslim piety, by the mid-twentieth century they become real, external threats to the political unity of the Kurdish nation. Telling the story of how Christian, Zoroastrian, and *kafir* figures were transformed between approximately the 1820s and 1950s also tells the story of how Kurdish Muslim poets imagined ordinary relations with non-Muslims and how their orientations to Islamic traditions changed in this period.

Within the wider scope of the book's effort to describe the lives of those who turn away from piety but stay within Islam, this chapter plays a crucial role. For Kurdish Muslims who turn away from piety in the twenty-first century do so as historical beings who stand to inherit and contest the terms of religious discourse that have shaped Islamic traditions in Kurdistan. Rather than ask how state-driven initiatives have restructured those traditions, this chapter looks to the history of poetry to ask how Kurdish Muslim poets have found a voice within those traditions. It does not offer a history of poetry in any comprehensive or representative sense. It instead offers a glimpse into some significant ways that Kurdish Muslim poets imagined religious difference in a more distant past and allows for a better appreciation of how religious difference is described in a more recent past. It is the capacity to express oneself in terms of unresolved paradoxes that provides the link across these two times. I suggest that the older poets' capacity to imagine the *kafir* within the self is the nearest model for the paradoxical sensibility of contemporary Muslims who turn away from piety without departing from Islam.

A LIVING ARCHIVE OF POETRY

This chapter is based on a study of seventeen *dîwans*—or "collected works" of poetry.[6] It is the fruit of a reading project conducted after I completed my fieldwork. It was carried out largely in the quiet solitude of a university office, but I drew from long periods of tutelage in poetry I received during fieldwork. Pexshan was one of almost a dozen different teachers with whom I sat for hours reading poetry line by line. I sat in bookstores, parks, cafés, and homes, taking notes in an effort to find my way through a library of images and metaphors. Even with that training, I found many of these texts difficult, and thus throughout my reading project, I returned to Kurdistan to consult my most perspicacious teachers.

The *dîwan*s I studied were available in the bazaar throughout Kurdistan during my fieldwork, although some were more difficult to obtain than others. In the nineteenth century, Kurdish poets kept handwritten collections of poetry, and their work circulated both through aural recitation and performance and in written manuscripts. The *dîwan*s available in the marketplace are the result of later editors' labor in collecting and comparing those manuscripts. A few were published in the early twentieth century, but most available for sale in bookstores during my fieldwork were the result of efforts that culminated in the 1970s and 1980s. The editor of a *dîwan* would seek out the remaining manuscripts of poetry, compare them in an effort to weed out copyists' mistakes, and gain access to the poet's complete oeuvre. For the older poets who wrote in a slightly different script, the editors revised the script to reflect the newer standards of Kurdish orthography. For newer poets who published in journals and magazines in the twentieth century, editors had to scour many copies of the Kurdish journals to collect a poet's works.[7] Editors usually took on this momentous task on their own time, at their own expense, while employed as religious scholars or less commonly in public universities. The Ministry of Culture or a wealthy patron often subsidized publication.[8]

The result of the editors' work is a series of *dîwan*s that range from a sixty-page booklet to eight hundred pages of text spread across two volumes. The difference in length is partly due to the presence or length of running commentary (*şerh*) that editors compose and place below the text in footnotes. The commentary has three primary goals: to note relevant differences between different manuscripts; to provide translations or descriptions of words in Arabic, Persian, Turkish, or Kurdish that are not a part of the everyday vocabulary of contemporary Sorani Kurdish speakers; and to elucidate meaning (*me'na*) through an exposition of images, historical contexts of composition, and the technical devices of rhetoric, as well as references to the Quran and hadith.[9] Intense engagement with the Quran and hadith show how this era of Kurdish poetry is deeply entwined with the Islamic discursive tradition described in Chapter 1. These tomes of poetry are commonly found in the homes of Kurdish Muslims throughout Iraqi Kurdistan. Even homes that do not contain collections of books will often have a copy of the Quran and at least a few *dîwan*s of Kurdish poetry.

The *dîwan*s of poetry that circulate on the market are edited and curated windows into the past—"curated" since dozens of poets have been left out of this selective process. Thousands of manuscripts have been destroyed over the centuries, and many others have not been gathered in libraries where researchers could have access to them. Precisely for that reason, though, the prism of collection, commentary, publication, and circulation that frames the archive of *dîwan*s available in the bazaar provides important insight into the range of orientations to Islamic traditions that contemporary Kurdish Muslims inhabit and transform. The history of Kurdish poetry reveals a landscape of poetic imagination that not only stretches deep into Kurdistan's past but also belongs to its present.

The *dîwan*s of poetry constitute a living archive that says as much about the interests and aspirations of those who construct, control access to, and contest the archive as it does about the past they purport to represent through it. Contest over the archive occurs at several levels. At the level of published commentaries, an editor with great knowledge of the Persian poetic tradition, for example, may compose a commentary that highlights the ways a Kurdish poet built on the precedent of fourteenth-century Persian poet Hafiz. Yet before the commentary reaches publication, another editor may consider that precedent less relevant and significantly abbreviate the work of the first editor. Contest also occurs at the level of reading. One reader may seek to explain a verse's vague reference to the Quran. Another reader may object that the effort to tie everything to the Quran will miss the true spirit of the poetry. Finally, recitation can become a scene of contest because poetry circulates in fragmented form as a single couplet, a half line. Even a phrase from an old poem used in a new context can lend new meaning to the poem. I witnessed these and other forms of contest over the archive of Kurdish poetry while conducting fieldwork. Debates often revolved around these questions: What did the poet really say? What did it mean to the poet? How did the poet relate to Islam? What does it mean for us?

Learning about that contest required participating in it, which was one of the greatest intellectual challenges of my fieldwork and one of the most pleasing as well. I memorized couplets I did not understand in order to recite them to others and ask for explanations. I found groups of men in teahouses who habitually recited puzzling lines of poetry and challenged one another to explain their meaning. Naturally, one cannot simply be an observer to such a contest. I was drawn in. I, too, was called on to offer my own accounts of poetry. And this chapter itself is one such account. Rather than argue with scholarly consensus about Kurdish poetry,[10] the chapter argues with elements of the contest that I encountered in Silêmanî and were captured in 'Eta Qeredaxî's position described earlier. Thus, the chapter does not simply treat the tradition of interpreting Kurdish poetry as a "local" one that could be put in dialogue with "anthropological" or other modes of interpreting poetry. It engages a tradition of debate and argumentation by participating in the debate, arguing against some modes of interpretation available on the Kurdish intellectual landscape rather than arguing with Anglophone scholarship per se.

Through the prism of the *kafir*, I emphasize how my vision of the Kurdish poetic tradition also relies on more widely available Islamic themes that touch on early Islamic history (e.g., the relation of Muslims to non-Muslims and the figure of Imam Ali), Persian poetic traditions (e.g., the interpretive lens of Sufi poetry given by Mahmud Shabistari and the tales told by Farid al-Din 'Attar), as well as references to the Quran and hadith. All of these locate the poetic production of the nineteenth century squarely within Islam as a discursive tradition.

Perhaps readers will be tempted to join the contest of interpretation as well. Indeed, I hope that they will. Readers may approach these texts with a familiarity with Islamic traditions. Or they may find the interpretive tools they have from engaging other traditions are useful for engaging these texts as well. Engagement in this contest does not require passion for poetry per se because the poets' efforts to describe a journey to piety also entail the production of an ostensibly comprehensive categorization of religious identities. In this sense poetry might be approached as a kind of political philosophy that describes kinds of religious difference in verse. According to these poets, the categories "Muslim," "Christian," "Jewish," "Zoroastrian," or "*kafir*" encompass virtually all the categories of their prospective readers. Readers of this book, too, may find themselves interpolated by one of those categories, however incompletely or awkwardly.

CLASSICAL POETRY IN SORANI KURDISH

There is a long tradition of popular poetry and music in Sorani Kurdish and a poetic tradition in the Kurmanji dialect that reaches back to the sixteenth century. Yet the tradition of Sorani Kurdish poetry that is now called "classical" rose to prominence only in the early nineteenth century. This followed the work of Mawlana Khalid Naqshbandi (1779–1827), a prominent Sufi figure who inspired a revival in the religious sciences as well as in Sufi practice at the turn of the that century.[11] Today Mawlana Khalid is known in Kurdistan in part for having composed a few verses of poetry in Sorani Kurdish and a short creed in prose meant to allow ordinary Kurdish Muslims precise knowledge of Islamic doctrine in their own tongue.[12] Therefore, the poetic production in Sorani Kurdish that followed Mawlana Khalid is not *only* or *simply* an expression of linguistic or nationalist identity (though it may also be that). It is also an expression of an orientation to Islamic traditions. It insists that Kurdish can stand alongside Arabic and Persian as a language for Muslims' pious striving.

The poetic production in Kurdish that followed Mawlana Khalid was a disciplined and creative form of imitation. Kurdish poets of the nineteenth century were already able to compose poetry in the rhyme and meter schemes of Arabic and Persian poetry—and often in Turkish as well. In acts of creative imitation, they brought the music of established schemes of rhyme and meter in Persian poetry into harmony with Sorani Kurdish.[13] This creativity included poetic forms of macaronic language (Ar. *mulammaʿ*) that would borrow the second half of a Persian couplet from Hafız, for example, while crafting the first half in Kurdish (without simply translating Hafız) or crafting three prefatory lines in Kurdish before copying the original couplet in Persian. This form of creative imitation was quickly taken up within Kurdish poetry as well when poets would add three of their own lines of Kurdish to two lines of a Kurdish poem. In addition, the themes, metaphors, and techniques of reference in Kurdish poetry were quite similar to those in Persian.

Their work was supported in part by the political power of the Baban emirs. The Babans founded the city of Silêmanî in 1784, and the Ottomans deposed them in 1847. While always formally subject to the Ottoman pasha in Baghdad, the Babans had also been reliant on steady relations with the Qajar authorities since they were precariously located at the borders of the two empires. This formal subjection and precarious reliance were costs that the Baban emirate paid for practical autonomy in matters of governance. But their governance was modeled on Ottoman political structures and, far from a mere coalition of tribes, the Baban court was a highly organized administrative body that patronized the arts.[14] The relations of kinship and patronage that linked the Babans to the great poets of the age earned three of those poets the nickname *sê koçkey Baban*, which I translate as the "Baban Pillar Poets" and refer to more simply as the Pillar Poets. The term "Pillar Poets" itself is instructive because it suggests that the entire Sorani Kurdish poetic tradition since then has relied on these poets as pillars for support.

Among the three Pillar Poets, 'Ebdulrehman Muhemmed Begî Sahibqiran (1800–1866) left the most poems for the living archive that I encountered. He is known today by the pen name Salim. He was educated in the *hucre*, although his passion for poetry distracted him from completing his studies.[15] While born in

Silêmanî, he traveled often to Sine (Sanandaj) and Tehran, sometimes because of the political instability of Silêmanî under pressure from the Ottomans.[16] The second Pillar Poet is Salim's younger cousin, Mustafa Begî Sahibqiran (1812–1851?), known as Kurdî. Both Salim and Kurdî were members of the Baban ruling family. Kurdî also spent time in Sine and had good relations with the Ardalan emirs there. But also because of political instability, he fled Silêmanî frequently, and at the end of his life he even changed his pen name to Hijri, "the exile."[17] Nonetheless, the living archive retains his name as Kurdî. The third and perhaps most famous is Mela Xidr Ehmed Şaweysî Mikayelî (1797–1877?), known as Nalî.[18] Nalî is one of the most commonly cited poets of the living archive, and contemporary scholars have devoted much energy to the study of his poetry.[19] Even so, it has been difficult to pinpoint the date of his death in part because he also lived in exile and died in Istanbul.[20]

These poets led peripatetic lives in which they traveled frequently from Silêmanî to Sine, Tehran, Baghdad, Kirkuk, Koye (Koy Sanjak), Istanbul, Damascus, and other locales, including the Arabian Peninsula, where they conducted the hajj. Their travel was a product of established networks of scholarship in the *hucre* system but also the result of instability during the final years of the Baban emirate.[21] The living archive considers Silêmanî a center of Sorani Kurdish poetic production, partly because these poets held Silêmanî in high esteem as the city of their birth, and partly because Silêmanî was the seat of the Baban emirate, the last bastion of Kurdish self-rule before the reassertion of Ottoman authority.

This legacy is very much alive in contemporary Silêmanî, even for those who do not enjoy poetry. Many residents regard Silêmanî as more progressive than other cities in Iraqi Kurdistan and often point to Silêmanî's productivity across the twentieth century in terms of literary, theatrical, and plastic arts and, later, cinema. Contemporary historians who write about the Baban emirate have emphasized its status as an urban environment where tribal forms of social organization had to contend with other forms of power that cut across tribal lines, including class, rising religious groups, and hierarchies of knowledge and education. Thus, historian Mamosta Ce'fer, for example, was keen to emphasize that even in the nineteenth century when Silêmanî was barely one hundred years old, the city had a ratio of commercial shops, public baths, and mosques similar to that of other cities of comparable size that were much older.[22] These were signs of urbanity that contribute to a widely shared sense in contemporary Silêmanî that it has long been the center of a small universe. Rather than cast Silêmanî as a marginal space, as many observers of the region frequently do, this discussion thinks alongside the local intellectual tradition that has regarded Silêmanî as a center in its own right.

NON-MUSLIM FIGURES IN THE POETIC IMAGINATION

How did the nineteenth-century Pillar Poets imagine the relations between Muslims and non-Muslims? And what kind of orientation to Islam does that imagination show? The common vocabulary of the poetry itself suggests that the largest category to include any variety of non-Muslim is *kafir*. This includes Muslims who reject Islam to become full-fledged apostates, as well as Jews, Christians, and Zoroastrians.

But there are fine distinctions between these various groups. Some of those distinctions draw directly on the Quran. In a succinct survey of the Quran's view of Christianity and Judaism, Joseph Lumbard highlights three key points. First, the Quran acknowledges Christians and Jews as "People of the Book" who received a revelation from God and correctly believe in God and in the coming day of judgment.[23] The Quran recognizes Jesus, Moses, Abraham, Adam, and other familiar biblical figures as prophets who preceded the final Prophet Muhammad. Second, while the Quran supersedes those revelations and is the final revelation, it does not abrogate the previous revelations. That is, while the Quran is the final revelation and the Prophet Muhammad is the final prophet, Muhammad "was not sent to destroy previous religions, but to reaffirm their essential content."[24] Third, according to the Quran, the "essential content" of Christianity does not include considering Jesus as a "Son of God" or as "God incarnate."[25] Thus, while the Quran enjoins Muslims to respect Christians and Jews who follow previous revelations, it also warns them against the mistake of some points of doctrine. In the history of Islamic thought Zoroastrians were often regarded as among the "People of the Book," but this was not universal.[26]

In seventh-century Arabia when the Quran appeared, some Christians, Jews, and Zoroastrians considered the revelation brought by the Prophet Muhammad as superior and embraced Islam. Many others did not, and for this reason they have come to be called *kafir*s. *Kafr* (Ar.) is a person who commits an act of *kufr*, and the semantic range of *kufr* is broad with many degrees of variation and nuance. It implies the heart and mind's refusal to acknowledge the veracity of God's signs (including the Quran), as if those signs were covered over. It also implies an affective state of arrogance, of refusing to show gratitude to God for all of God's favors.[27] As one scholar pointed out, the Quran opposes the act of *kufr* both to acts of *iman* (Ar.), having faith or believing, and to acts of *shukr* (Ar.), showing gratitude.

Later, *kufr* could be used to refer to Christians' denial of the final revelation. In this sense, even though Christians correctly believed in God and the last day, they were still called *kafr*s. *Kufr* could also refer to a range of actions that Muslims themselves carry out that show a lack of gratitude for divine bounty or instruction. Acts of *kufr* thus commonly include failure to honor the obligations established in the Quran, so a Muslim who knowingly and intentionally neglects the performance of required prayer may be said to commit an act of *kufr*. Finally, and most comprehensively, any act that bears the trace of a multiplicity of gods (Ar. *shirk*, or "polytheism") is regarded as *kufr* since it is a rejection of divine unity. (Divine unity is the doctrine that denies God any partners [in existence, omnipotence, or omniscience], any multiplicity, or any corporeal body.)

The following discussion of four groups of couplets illustrates how the Pillar Poets, and the subsequent generations of poets who wrote in their style, imagined their relation to Islam through the figure of a *kafir*.

Beholding the Face of the Beloved

Given the theological imperative to deny that God has a body, one of the paradoxes of Sufi poetry is that it often refers to divine unity through the corporeal features of *the face*. The metaphor is meaningful within the framework of a love that can have only one beloved. For the lover in that scheme, the face of the beloved is absolutely singular, irreplaceable, the direction of all striving. It is also bright and full of light. In contrast, hair that sometimes crowds around the face is both dark and multiple. It clouds one's vision, tangles one up, keeps one away from the face.

According to Mahmud Shabistari, one of the most famous expositors of Sufi poetry who wrote in Persian in the fourteenth century, the bright face of the beloved evokes the singular unity of God, and the dark curls or tresses hide that unity with the illusion of multiplicity or repetition: "The wavy curls have overwhelmed straight truth, / thus the way of the seeker has become confused." In further explanation, Shabistari writes of the beloved (the translator uses the feminine English pronoun for the beloved): "Were she to shake those fragrant tresses from her face, / not one impious soul would be left in the world. / Were she to hold them still so as to hide her face, / not one true believer would be left to existence."[28] These verses suggest that the brightness and beauty of the beloved's face exert a force of attraction that supersedes any other means of finding faith. Those subject to the attractive force find faith, but nothing can guarantee the faith of those who do not feel attraction. Thus, in the poetic imagination, the brightness and singularity of the face reflect divine unity, while the darkness and multiplicity of locks of hair suggest the *kufir* of polytheism. For the same reason, the face of beloved is often a metaphor for God.

I begin by considering the following couplets, excerpts from three different poems by the Pillar Poet Salim. Several refer to the face of the beloved.

> As your lovely locks bend around your face;
> Christians come bend their knees in the Church.[29]

> Around the friend's face are curling locks and layers of down;
> like Zoroastrians they form rings around the fire.[30]

> This is Salim's piety: from the pleasure of beholding your face
> every morning I exalt the fire, like the dark, curly Hindu.[31]

> Though you cannot save me from judgment, you are my hope;
> I am as pleased by you as the monk is with his cross.[32]

These four couplets all present Christians and Zoroastrians as religiously devout figures. The Christians pray in the church, and the hearts of Christian monks are pleased by the sign of the cross. The Zoroastrians are presented as those who worship fire, and my teachers in Silêmanî told me that the term "Hindu" was often used interchangeably with "Zoroastrian." From the perspective of the Muslim poet, this image of worshipping fire conveys a laudable awareness that everyone must bow in worship. If the Muslim poet would insist that the only one worthy of worship is a God who transcends and denies any form of material manifestation, the poet can still admire Zoroastrians' recognition that humans must bow in prostration.

The devotion of these non-Muslims to their own religion is compared to the poet's devotion to the beloved. In keeping with the neighboring Persian tradition in preceding centuries, the beloved is androgynous—both in grammar and physiognomy. The curling locks and the soft down on the beloved's cheeks are features of beauty shared by both women and young men.[33] Whatever the gender, the key features of the beloved's face are its brightness and singularity. According to Shabistari, the darkness and multiplicity of the locks that curl around the face ultimately point to the threat of polytheism.[34]

In sum, the relationship of Muslims to *kafir*s in these couplets revolves around a basic similarity that both share: both are subject to the law of attraction that compels them to worship. The poems establish an analogy between the way that the poet is attracted to the beloved and the way that people of various faiths are attracted to divinity.

Yet the very last couplet evokes a second theme. The first line describes the beloved as one who cannot save the poet on the day of resurrection. That is, the beloved is not God, the Prophet Muhammed, or anyone who might intercede on the part of a Muslim. The poet's devotion to the beloved thus appears as a transgressive tendency to misplace the poet's faith, here called "hope."

Converting to Christianity

A number of poems from the Pillar Poets and following generations draw on precisely this possibility that Muslim poets misplace their faith and become either Christian, Zoroastrian, or simply apostates, *kafir*s. Two couplets from poets of the second generation bring out this theme clearly:

> I took the cross of your locks to my neck and turned Christian
> have mercy, dear friend, my faith and devotion are now lost.[35]

> Your eyes and your curls have become my guide on the path of love:
> I pray toward the arc of that magus's temple, kneeling on the prayer
>   mat of their garments.[36]

In both couplets, the beloved is human, a non-Muslim, and androgynous. The Muslim poets' maddening love for the beloved drives them to forsake their devotion to Islam and take on the religion of the beloved. The first couplet describes a Christian beloved, and the second one provocatively mixes metaphors, drawing on imagery of a Zoroastrian priest—called magus—and also on the sartorial marker of non-Muslims that was very common in Sufi poetry. What is translated as "garments" is actually the *zunnar*, the belt or girdle that was the famously prescribed (if not often adopted) dress of non-Muslims who lived under the protection of the caliphate.[37]

The figure of a Muslim poet who is so enraptured by a non-Muslim that they give up their devotion to Islam and take on the beloved's religion is common to Sufi poetry. A widely renowned story of Sheikh San'an is central to the tropes analyzed here. Those who regard Kurdish Sufi poetry as a rejection of Islam commonly evoke his story as the paradigm for the Sufi who leaves Islam. Several details of the story merit discussion.

The most famous version of the story of Sheikh San'an appears in Farid al-Din 'Attar's *Conference of the Birds*, in which a learned sheikh has a dream that prompts him to travel with a retinue of disciples to Byzantine Rome. On the path, he falls in love with a girl whose Christianity is marked by her wearing the *zunnar*. The girl requires him to forsake Islam in several dramatic acts: drinking wine, renouncing faith, burning the Quran, and bowing to an image. He carries out the first two and declares his willingness to do the others. Referring to her hair as locks and making himself obedient to her, he says, "Your slave submits—lead me with ringlets twined / As chains about my neck; I am resigned!"[38] The girl then requires him to act as her swineherd, and he consents. His disciples promptly abandon him, but the Christian girl accepts him.

Sheikh San'an is a familiar figure in Kurdish poetry, not least because poets are consistently suggesting that his path must be their own path, or as a way of bragging, they suggest that their love is deeper than his and that their beloved is even more seductive than his was:

> The mullah's straight fingers and the beloved's curling locks have nowhere to meet
> unless, like the sheikh, I take up the Christian path. What can I do?[39]
>
> My progress on the path of love is a step beyond San'an:
> his Christian was the disciple, my irreligious friend the master.[40]

It may be easy to suppose that this story is about love that transcends religion. In the contests of interpretation in which I engaged in Silêmanî, some readers of couplets like these insisted on just that: they described a love that "left religion" (*le dîn hate derewe*).

But one key to the story of Sheikh San'an is that he eventually repents of his infidelity. He abandons his Christian wife and sets out to rejoin his Muslim friends. On the way, his Christian wife catches up with him, herself repents, and becomes a Muslim just before she dies.[41] Although the figure of Sheikh San'an holds out the prospect of the Muslim poet giving up Islam, it does so only as the prelude to the climactic return to Islam. On closer inspection, the story does not show that love transcends religion. I argue that it suggests love *cannot* flourish between two persons of different religions.[42] Love between a Muslim sheikh and a Christian girl can be realized only if one forsakes one's religion and joins the other. Thus, the story does not imagine a love that affirms and inhabits religious difference. The lovers are united only on the condition of sharing a religious identity. Finally, the end of the story is a "happy ending" insofar as both of them turn toward Islam, the sheikh realizing a degree of piety that had been unavailable to him before his attraction to the Christian. This affirms both the ascendance of Islam and the status of attraction to a non-Islamic tradition as a stage through which a Sufi passes on the way to a higher piety.

In these Kurdish verses, the passage through a non-Islamic tradition has two important features. First, the passage is never final but is a stage that becomes necessary for the discovery of a more pious orientation to Islam. The living archive of Kurdish poetry from the nineteenth century does not offer any work by a Muslim poet who finally renounced Islam and embraced another religion. Yet poets commonly contemplate that act as a trope that is always subordinate to the inevitable return to Islam. Second, the Muslim poet's passage through non-Islamic traditions is not a horizontal movement among equals. If the poet recognizes the force of attraction in (or *of*) non-Islamic traditions, the poet also recognizes that this attraction is not compatible with a commitment to Islam and regards the attraction as a falling, a slipping, or a movement downward in a hierarchy. The incompatibility of attraction to different traditions is not the incompatibility of equals. It is the incompatibility of Islam with the traditions that Islam supersedes. In other words, Islam is assumed to be ascendant.

Reclaiming the Beloved for Islam

The fact that the poets assume the ascendance of Islam is clear in a third group of couplets from Pillar Poet Salim. Here, alongside these descriptions of how the Muslim poet might become a *kafir* are descriptions that explicitly reclaim the beloved *from* any other religion and *for* Islam. The first sets the tone of an oral dispute or debate in which Christians and Muslims are described as at odds with one another. In the space of two lines, this couplet manages to both exalt the virtue of humility that Christ exemplified and to criticize Christians for debating with Islam rather than accepting it. These lines do not suggest that the beloved *is* a Christian but that the beloved is *like* a Christian in some way:

> In the beginning they were humble, like Christ
> but in the end they talk back, like the Christians.[43]

Another pair of couplets by Salim takes the theme of oral disputation a step further. They begin by repeating the theme of the non-Muslim hair curling around the brightly lit face of unity (in this case the face is the text of the Quran):

> Muslims and Christians debate the status of a single strand of hair:
> one says it curls in the shape of a cross, one says it conceals the true face.
> The priest has set that strand as a trap for Muslims,
> grab him by the beard, set him straight in this debate![44]

Here Salim presents Christian priests and Muslim scholars as participating in debate, in which the face of the beloved is the object of contest. Looking into the face of the beloved, the Christians see their theology affirmed by the cross formed by the strands of hair intersecting on the beloved's face. The Muslim scholars regard that cross as a distraction from the face itself, which is bright, as the pages of the Quran are often described. Salim insists that the true beloved is the divine and that the final revelation was not Christ, as the priests believe, but the text of the Quran. He does not hesitate to assert his position through the violent image of grabbing the priests by the beard.[45] Thus, these couplets not only underline the fact that Salim assumed Islam's superiority over Christianity, but they introduce the theme of a potentially violent confrontation emerging around that difference.

Executing Kafirs

Violence appears in other ways in this poetry as well. For even if the Muslim poet's act of *kufir* is entertained as a productive paradox, it appears within a frame that assumes that death is the eventual result for those who turn away from Islam. In discussions of death the juridical categories and punishments outlined by Muslim scholars of the law mix with the embodied passions of a lover whose experience touches death. Quite commonly, the poet dies as a result of an encounter with the beloved. There are several causes or explanations of such a death that appeared in the contests of interpretation in Silêmanî. One is to invoke the French sense of *la petite mort*, in which death is an idiom for the peak of ecstasy: when the lover experiences union with the beloved, the sensation of ecstasy resembles death.

Another way to explain the death of the poet valorizes death not as the extinction of the poet's entire being but as the execution of the worst tendencies within his being. That explanation resonates with a saying that is quite famous among Sufis, and often attributed to the Prophet, in which Muslims are instructed to "die before you die."[46] In that phrase, the second death is the usual extinction that occurs at the end of life, but the first death refers to the dying of a small self, a wicked self that lives within one's being and provokes one to evil deeds. The instruction, thus, is to kill off the smaller wicked self within before one reaches the end of one's life. According to this explanation, when the poet speaks of dying in an encounter with the beloved, it is a death of the *kafir* within. In these terms, the terrain of the poet's self is again imagined as plural: it offers a space of contradiction or paradox that the poet must confront in order to overcome. By overcoming that paradox, the poet gains a higher piety.

The execution of *kafir*s is assumed to be their deserved fate, and the image of Imam Ali ibn Talib is frequently evoked as the executor of that justice. Imam Ali was the fourth "Commander of the Faithful" after the Prophet Muhammad. His son Hussein suffered a cruel death in battle at the hands of fellow Muslims (a death to which Pexshan alluded). Imam Ali himself, though, was renowned for his military prowess on the battlefield as he fought for Islam. His execution of *kafir*s appears alongside other images of executing *kafir*s, as in the following verses by Salim and Kurdî:

> They shot an arrow from their brow across my face
> like Ali's sword across the necks of the *kafir*s.[47]
>
> Though it appear unjust that I be killed like that,
> the sentence for a *kafir* is just when it is just that.[48]

Thus, as much as poets may indulge the imagination of themselves becoming *kafir*s, they do so within a context that assumes the ultimate fate of the *kafir* is the tragedy of execution and, by extension, a divine judgment that would cut them off from eternal happiness. Contrary to the persistent claim of some readers that Sufism and Islamic law (*şerʿ*) were opposed to one another in Kurdish poetry, these lines show how the legal judgments that lean on the Quran were assumed to be just, even if they were not practically applied.

In this framework, attraction to any nominally non-Muslim tendency is a threat, in part because it holds out the possibility of undermining the poet's relation to the divine. If such attractions cast doubt on the finality of the Quran as revelation or on the unity of the divine, then they are subject to the violent reassertion of authority. At the same time, "flirtation" with other religions is the means by which the Muslim poet sets up a response to the threat and a recovery of piety. In this sense, true piety for the Pillar Poets allowed for the paradox of attraction to non-Islamic religion. And it was precisely in this passage that, through the non-Islamic, the identity of the Muslim poet, and the authority of God and the Prophet, could be reasserted.

GENDER AMBIGUITY OF LOVER AND BELOVED

Given the centrality of attraction to the poetic imagination, one may wonder: What is the role of gender and sexuality in this imagination of the beloved, and what is its role in the poet's relation to Islamic and non-Islamic traditions? A preliminary response to the questions will allow for a more thorough reply later in the chapter. The gender ambiguity of the beloved has been a source of great interest for many scholars and commentators. Several scholars have demonstrated that neighboring traditions in Turkish, Persian, and Arabic thrived on the ambiguity of the beloved. The essential features of the beloved—the face, hair, gait, lips, mole, "down" that covered the lips or chin—could belong to either females or males.

This also holds true for the Pillar Poets and the first generation following them. Of course, sometimes beloveds were given clearly gendered names. Kurdî's beloved was Qadir, an explicitly masculine name; Nalî's beloved had the feminine name Hebîbe. But this simply underscores the fact that when the beloved was *not* named, they were not necessarily male or female. For all of the unnamed beloveds, grammar allows for this ambiguity since pronouns in Kurdish are not gendered. (For that reason I have used the English word "they" to indicate a singular figure with ambiguous gender.)

Scholars have been less preoccupied with identifying the ways that the poetic self has been gendered. In the romantic *ghazal* in Kurdish (a poetic form including seven to fourteen rhyming couplets), it is noteworthy that the poetic voice is not explicitly gendered and may be assumed by either male or female poets.[49] This is proven by the case of Masture Erdelan. Although her remaining poems in Sorani Kurdish are few, they do suggest that a female poet was able to assume the poetic "I" in ways comparable to how a male poet would assume it. As important as the presence of these poems is the fact that existing poems in the romantic genre by ostensibly male authors bear no features that would necessarily identify them as male. In this regard, the availability of the Kurdish poetic imagination to female poets whose voice is not necessarily "feminine" resembles the availability of Persian poetry to female poets in the same period.[50]

To summarize, the poetic imagination of the Pillar Poets and the generation immediately following them, about until the turn of the twentieth century, was one in which a Muslim identity and pious striving were taken for granted. Figures of Christians, Zoroastrians, and *kafir*s introduce a productive paradox, allowing the poet/lover to pass through a non-Islamic tradition on the way to higher Muslim piety. These figures remain squarely subject to the superiority of Islam, and they ultimately assume that the Muslim poet is oriented toward Muslim piety as the top of a moral hierarchy.

In this imaginary landscape, the non-Muslim *kafir* is most essentially a tendency within the pious Muslim self. Acknowledging the tendency is both a way of cultivating humility—reminding the poet that small acts of infidelity proliferate in their lives—and the first step toward killing the *kafir* tendency within. Acting on one's attraction to the *kafir* and even becoming a *kafir* are tropes that emphasize a plurality internal to the pious Muslim self.

The poetic imagination affords a picture of an orientation to religious traditions that is primarily one of productive paradox. The paradox of attraction to Islam and attraction to non-Islamic traditions is quite similar to the paradoxes of attraction and aversion that Pexshan inhabited in her life. True, Pexshan turns *from* piety, and the productivity of the paradox is visible in her sustaining relations with more pious Muslims; and the Pillar Poets insisted that the outcome of paradox is a *return* to piety. But both orient themselves to Islamic tradition by means of productive paradoxes. This is the sense in which the Introduction identified poetry as not merely a subject of study but an analytical frame: poetic expression makes audible and sensible a relation between a Muslim and an Islamic tradition that is first and foremost a relation of paradox. However, those productive paradoxes were soon subjected to historical pressures that worked against them.

NON-MUSLIMS BEYOND THE POETIC IMAGINATION

If the poetic imagination of the nineteenth-century Kurdish poets offers a creative transfiguration of the *kafir* and the Christian in the Quran, how does that imagination relate to the political conditions of non-Muslims during this historical era? Was the figure of the non-Muslim beloved in Kurdish reflective of the historical condition of non-Muslims? From what is available in the English and Kurdish archives thus far explored by historians, it is difficult to make more than a few general observations. Nonetheless, piecing together a general trend with the statistics collected by European travelers, oral history in contemporary Silêmanî, and a few crucial events allows for a useful sketch of how religious differences in other regions of Kurdistan influenced social life for the Babans and their successors in Silêmanî.

Numerous Jewish and Christian populations were spread throughout the Kurdish emirates in the nineteenth century. Historians have devoted increasing attention to the Armenian, East Syriac, and Assyrian Christians (the latter two were called "Nestorians" by Western observers) in the northern emirate of Bohtan, around Hakkari and Urmia, in what is currently the border areas connecting Turkey and Iran;[51] and several works have focused attention on Jewish populations north of the Baban emirates.[52] Yet considerably less attention has been given to Silêmanî's Jews or Chaldean Christians (affiliates of the Catholic Holy See).[53] And as comparative work by Metin Atmaca on the politics of the Bohtan and Baban emirates has shown, one cannot assume that the conclusions reached through study of the northern Kurdish emirates may be imported to the southern region around Silêmanî.[54]

In his 1820 visit to Silêmanî, Claudius James Rich, the representative of the British East India Company based in Baghdad, reported that the population included 2,000 Muslim families, 130 Jewish families, and 14 Christian families. Of these Christian families, 9 were Chaldean and 5 were Armenian.[55] Despite numerical minority, especially as compared to northern provinces of Kurdistan, these non-Muslim populations were a recognized part of urban life in Silêmanî. Three facts collected through oral history demonstrate the participation of non-Muslims in the social fabric of life in Silêmanî.

First, a study of oral history conducted among Kurdish Jews who had migrated to Israel included a report that the founder of Silêmanî had said that "a town with no Jews is not considered a proper town" and had for that reason asked Jews in nearby areas to move to Silêmanî in the first efforts to populate the town.[56] Thus, Kurdish Jews were an essential part of Silêmanî's social landscape even before its founding.

Second, during my research in Silêmanî in 2004–2013, I heard from several sources a story about a famous Muslim-Christian marriage. Kak Ehmedî Sheikh (1794–1888) was a prominent scholar of religion and a sheikh of the Qadrî Sufi path. Kak Ehmed's grandfather had encouraged the Baban authorities to suppress another Sufi path, the Naqshbandi, that had begun to spread through Mawlana Khalid, by expelling him from Silêmanî in 1820. So Kak Ehmed himself was no stranger to the power struggles that may accompany religious differences internal to Islamic traditions. Yet in regard to relations with Silêmanî's Christian population, he was eager to prove friendship—so eager, in fact, that he arranged for a marriage between one of his sons and a local Christian woman.[57]

The third story involves a descendant of Kak Ehmed's named Sheikh Mehmud Berzencî (1878–1956), who was a major political figure in Silêmanî in the 1910s–1930s. Following the collapse of the Ottoman Empire and the inauguration of British rule, Sheikh Mehmud was initially favored by the British to rule Silêmanî in their stead. Late in 1918 he was appointed governor of Silêmanî. He quickly fell out of British favor, though, and despite several organized uprisings he was finally subdued in 1927.[58] Sheikh Mehmud's declaration of jihad seemed to confirm British officials' stereotypes about Muslim hostility to non-Muslims.[59] Yet the jihad was not a campaign against non-Muslims sui generis. First, and most obviously, the fight was directed against the violence of the British occupation and Assyrian cooperation with that occupation; it was not against the local Christians *as* Christians. But second, the same British officials neglected to take account of what the residents of Silêmanî have remembered for a full century:[60] in the initial government authorized by the British in 1918, Sheikh Mehmud had appointed a Chaldean Christian named Kerîmî 'Eleke (1845–1948) as a minister and adviser in his cabinet.[61] This suggests that it was not a matter of simple opposition either to the British or to Christians. It was rather a question of how political power would be distributed and which local populations the British were willing to empower.

The precise reach of the transformations in sociopolitical relations that occurred in the first decades of the twentieth century becomes clear in one final event. According to the observations of the British colonial officials, the proportional population distribution along lines of religious difference in Silêmanî had not substantially changed since 1820. In 1925, C. J. Edmonds reported "10,000 [individuals] of whom 9,000 were Muslim Kurds, 750 Jews, and 120 Chaldean Christians."[62] He did not count any Assyrian Christians as residents of Silêmanî.

Yet Assyrian Christians were increasingly present in the regions around Silêmanî. Many Assyrians and Armenians had fled the violence in regions farther north that had its beginnings in the 1890s but was especially pronounced in 1915.[63] By 1918, a refugee camp sixty kilometers north of Baghdad (and around three hundred kilometers south of Silêmanî) held more than twenty-four thousand

Assyrians and almost fifteen thousand Armenians.[64] Other displaced Assyrians had been recruited as levies for the occupying British forces, and one of their strongholds was in the city of Kirkuk, itself about one hundred kilometers from Silêmanî. A string of events in May 1924, recounted in detail by historian Arbella Bet-Shlimon, illustrates how the politics of religious identity were affected by colonial violence. When violence broke out in the bazaar in Kirkuk, insults directed at religious identity were traded between Muslims in Kirkuk and the Assyrian Christian levies. The Assyrian levies soon commandeered the house of a local Chaldean, against his objections, and used it to fire on people of Kirkuk. This fueled a rumor that Chaldeans had sided with Assyrians, and, consequently, the few days' violence fell along lines of Muslim-Christian difference.

In Bet-Shlimon's analysis, this type of violence appears surprising for the local context in Kirkuk. (As indeed it would have been for Silêmanî.) Acknowledging that the Assyrians had brought with them the trauma of their experiences farther north, where the language of jihad had been used against Christians more generally, Bet-Shlimon concludes that these events "revealed the potential for tensions and violent actions amongst Kirkuk's communities that would persistently be linked with the British presence in Iraq."[65] In other words, latent tensions between Muslims and Christians at the local level developed into this kind of conflict when combined with the traumatic memories of violence elsewhere and the violence of colonial occupation.[66]

In sum, if the social relations of the northern and southern Kurdish regions were quite different through most of the 1800s, then by the first decades of the 1900s the two regions had become deeply entangled as a result of migration and colonial occupation. More important, if the politics of religious identity in nineteenth-century Southern Kurdistan had emphasized accommodation and engagement, a sharp turn was apparent in the 1920s. This sharp turn in fact built on decades of increasing interventions from European and American forces—not only in government and trade but also in the realm of missionary activity. Indeed, missionary activity had been a growing concern for the Ottoman authorities throughout the nineteenth century.

From the perspective of the Ottoman state, the consolidation of religious and ethnic identities as viable grounds for political claims *beyond* the Ottoman state became a problem, and it sought to enact a series of reforms that would keep Ottoman subjects loyal. Chief among them was the effort to establish universal citizenship that would place all Christians and Muslims, Armenians, Kurds, Arabs, and Turks on even footing for claims on the Ottoman state. Ironically, the state's effort to reduce tensions between the communities often translated into a firm stance against religious conversion, supposing that firm boundaries would allow for peace between the communities.[67] Policies aimed at producing homogeneous citizenship dovetailed with a project of centralizing the state. The campaign to guarantee religious pluralism through strong state power further coincided with the campaign to mitigate regional autonomy that resulted in the end of the Baban emirate in 1847. Thus, one of the broadest conditions in which Sorani Kurdish poetry emerged in the nineteenth century is an extended crisis around issues of religious and ethnic identity in the Ottoman Empire.

In this context, what is most remarkable about the poetic production of Southern Kurdistan is that it was *not* deeply marked by the anxieties about religious difference that had begun to inform Ottoman policy in the nineteenth century. In the poetic imagination, Kurdish Muslim poets' attraction to non-Muslim others was largely unhindered by the question of how embodied, historical Muslims and non-Muslims related to one another in politics. Within the poetic imagination, paradox thrived that allowed for both abiding attractions to non-Muslims and the assumption of an established hierarchy that kept Islam supreme. In a sense, religious difference in the poetic imagination was depoliticized insofar as a Muslim poet could speak of attraction to a *kafir* and attraction to non-Islamic traditions without fear that such speech could undermine the predominant sociopolitical order. Poetry was depoliticized not because embodied Christian beloveds in Kurdistan had no relation to Muslim poets but because that relation was made irrelevant to the way Muslim poets imagined Christian beloveds in verse.

Several decades into the twentieth century, this changed. The passage through non-Islamic traditions was politicized in a radically new way as a betrayal of Kurdish national identity. At the same time, the sense of plurality that had been internal to the pious Muslim self was dislocated and appeared on a political landscape where plurality was a political and historical problem to be solved. The demand to win a zero-sum game of politics that admitted no contradictions replaced the productive paradox of attraction to *kafir*s.

The remainder of the chapter examines a dramatic shift in poetic imagination whereby the nationalist project comes to politicize religious identity in new ways. Christians were increasingly associated with foreign powers. Piety and moral virtue more generally were increasingly associated with allegiance to the national cause. Even if poets themselves were not pious, they cast infidelity to the nationalist cause as the real infidelity—true *kufir*. This turning point is crucial context for the larger ethnographic project of the book because it highlights the emergence of an opposition between those who seek piety and those who turn from it. That opposition had been found within the poetic self in the nineteenth century. But in the twentieth century, it became a social opposition between self and other. That opposition, shaped specifically by the history of poetry, is a key point of reference in the everyday lives of people in twenty-first century Iraqi Kurdistan, including Pexshan and others who appear later.

"ENOUGH TALK OF THESE EYES AND TRESSES!"

Two distinctive tendencies in Kurdish poetry elucidate the transformation in poetic imagination that appeared early in the twentieth century. The first is a trenchant critique of the Sufi paradigm of images. Several poets launched a full critique of the Sufi vocabulary and considered it a distraction from the real struggle of the age, which was one of national awakening and liberation. One of these was Ehmed Muxtar Caf (1898?–1935), who was a poet, writer, and politician. He served as mayor of the town of Halabja in 1922 and then as a member of Parliament in Baghdad under the British Mandate in 1924.[68] His novella *The Matter of Conscience* (*Meseley Wîjdan*) is hailed as one of the first works of prose fiction in Sorani Kurdish. His oeuvre is unique because while he began composing poetry in the old style of the Pillar Poets, he soon made a dramatic shift and denounced that style. Here is a poem that performs that denunciation dramatically:

> Kurdish poets, enough talk of these eyes and tresses!
> Lay off the locks and curls a little
> Move on from all this talk of flowers and figures
> Take up the state of this heartbroken nation
> Quickly now, try it if you can, before you lose the chance to work.
>
> You go on about wine and cups, flowers and blossoms
> On and on about figures and gaits
> Would you rather be drunk than free? Then why this way?
> How far will you go on this path of nonsense?
> Quickly now, try it if you can, before you lose the chance to work.[69]

The poem continues for three more stanzas that end in the refrain of the closing line. Throughout the poem, the poet emphasizes the need for modern education and industry and decries the ruinous state of Kurdistan as a colonized land. While the Pillar Poets and their first generation of heirs had famously lamented the loss of Baban authority and decried the reestablishment of Turkish rule, those poets had not considered the denunciation of imperialism as incompatible with speech about the beloved. Neither was their speech about the homeland within the modern framework of demanding a nation-state. Now, though, poets faced a choice: *either* speak about the beloved (in the language of eyes, tresses, flowers, and drunkenness) *or* take up the cause of the modern national freedom.

Alongside this shift appear several new features of the Kurdish nation. Ehmed Muxtar Caf here invites Kurds to prove their intelligence and virtue by winning independence and making progress in modern education and industry. In doing so, he implicitly invites comparison with other nations who are making that progress and assumes the cleavage that would inform much Kurdish nationalism in the twentieth century: Kurdish difference from Arabs, Turks, and Persians was the main factor affecting those relations—a difference that would trump other forms of similarity, including Islam. Finally, when Caf speaks of the urgency of accomplishing "work" (*îş*), he does not speak within the older temporality that takes divine judgment as its horizon but rather within the national time in which Kurds realize national self-consciousness.

In another stinging indictment of poets' attraction to the features of the beloved, Mufti Pêncwênî (1881–1952) writes:[70]

> What a shame for a poet of this age to befriend tresses and combs
> or heavenly faces and figures in a garden.
> Whoever feigns to be a poet
> shames himself with such myth and illusion.
> "Poet" put simply means thoughtful and aware;
> who could be truly thoughtful and yet so scared?
> When a poet is hung up on moles, wrinkles, and locks,
> we are better off without him, may God silence him.[71]

Much like Ehmed Muxtar Caf, Mufti frames his polemic against the beloved as a choice: poets can either seek national liberation and progress or choose to continue regurgitating the same tired images and metaphors.

Yet Mufti Pêncwênî is famous in contemporary Kurdistan in part for the means he prescribed for the realization of liberation and progress: the *mekteb*, or the publicly funded state school. Mufti himself had been trained in the *hucre*, where a prominent religious scholar of the Naqshbandi line gave him the pen name Mufti in recognition of his legal scholarship, and he spent most of his life in the bazaar tending to a store that sold tobacco.[72] Yet his poetry was often a polemical argument for expanding access to public education. Drawing on an opposition common to many other poets, Mufti often contrasts the forms of knowledge and virtue that were proper to the old poetic tradition in the *hucre* and the forms of knowledge and virtue that are proper to modern education. In the *hucre*, knowledge was old and outdated, and acquiring knowledge required unthinking submission to scholars and sheikhs. It was also off-limits to females. In the *mekteb*, however, education was universal and secular and emphasized modern sciences that would allow technological progress in Kurdistan and Iraq more broadly.[73] Mufti Pêncwênî was later praised as having a "rebellious and revolutionary stance" by advocating for women's rights, including the right to education.[74] In short, Mufti characterized the *hucre* as a space of hierarchy and oppression and the *mekteb* as a space of equality and liberation.

In the following poem, Mufti opposes an old-fashioned, *hucre*-trained poet's obsession with the features of the beloved to pursuing education in the *mekteb* and becoming industrious. At the same time, he introduces a gendered poetic voice that is quite different from the one in which the Pillar Poets composed:

> The poets of this age, from this day on,
> should cease speaking of lips and eyes, wrinkles and moles.
> What a shame for a noble man
> to speak of a necklace, bracelets, an anklet.
> If you Kurds do not turn to education and industry,
> no one will employ you, not as a janitor or porter.
> Without knowledge and ethics, you'll never become human;
> it is knowledge that makes iron fly without feathers.[75]

In the final line, Mufti makes a provocative equation between the achievement of full humanity and the construction of a modern aircraft. Both achievements are the result of knowledge (*'îlm*), a term that Mufti often pairs with industry (*sen'et*) and ethics (*edeb*).[76] For Mufti, becoming fully human entails modern education and good conduct (*edeb*). The ethics in question, though, is far from the journey to piety that had inspired the Pillar Poets. Ethics is here paired with avoiding what is "shameful" (*'eyb*), which Mufti associates with speech about the features of the beloved's face. Instead of the hard road full of suffering that Sufis had traveled in search of their beloved, ethics for Mufti is achieved through maintaining honor and gaining scientific knowledge.

The gender dynamics here are complex and deserve careful analysis. If the beloved had been of necessarily ambiguous gender for the Pillar Poets, Mufti makes the beloved into a female, in part by equating the features of the beloved to the accessories of feminine jewelry. Furthermore, he sets up an opposition between speech about the female beloved and the nobility proper to manhood expressed in public speech in the bazaar. According to Mufti, poets who are truly men would not stoop to speaking of feminine jewelry. With these words, Mufti effectively emasculates those who would hold to the tradition inaugurated by the Pillar Poets. And when enjoining poets to cease describing the features of the beloved, he assumes that the beloved is female, thus rejecting the gender ambiguity of the beloved that had characterized earlier poetry.

Yet this matter should not be confused with confining poetic speech to a masculine voice. Mufti himself composes several poems in the feminine voice. Even in those poems, he does not stoop to speaking of jewelry. He instead directs his feminine speech to the Iraqi state in a demand that the state provide *mekteb* education for females in the town of Pêncwên, where he lived.[77] Thus, Mufti's poetry does not restrict the poetic voice to men. However, by requiring a masculine voice of men and a feminine voice of women *within poetry* (whatever the author's own gender), Mufti's poetry rejects the *ambiguity* of the poetic voice.

Ehmed Muxtar Caf and Mufti Pêncwênî directed their polemic against the tendency to describe a journey to Muslim piety through the features of the beloved's face. They were not alone in doing so but drew on a much wider sense of disappointment with imitation as well as growing aspirations to articulate a modern nationalist Kurdish identity. Yet the figure of the beloved was not entirely abandoned. Rather, it had shifted, and the Kurdish nation was to become the new object of the poet's unflinching love and dedication.

Within this new tendency, the goal of poetry was to inspire nationalist self-realization and modernist "progress." But by disavowing talk of the beloved and the beloved's face, these poets also endangered the productive paradoxes expressed through that image. Attraction to the beloved's face had been the means through which the Pillar Poets allowed the pursuit of piety to encompass the paradox of attraction to Islam *and* attraction to non-Islamic elements. Yet the poetic self that emerges in the nationalist era was anxious about that attraction and anxious about plurality internal to the self or to Islamic traditions. The new tendency inaugurates an opposition, an unbridgeable gap, between a pious Muslim and a non-Muslim or *kafir*. In doing so, this opposition irons out the paradoxes of Muslim identity in Iraqi Kurdistan. And ultimately, it contributes to the broader discursive environment that prompted Muslims like Pexshan to turn away from the vision of Muslim piety that eschews paradox. The next section examines what happened to the role of the Christians and *kafirs* as the new nationalist tendency grew in Kurdish poetry.

KURDISTAN BECOMES A CHURCH?

The notion of a tendency is a useful way to describe change in the Kurdish poetic tradition in part because it does not imply that one tendency will entirely replace the other. In fact, dimensions of the older tendency have continued to thrive in some ways to the present.[78] At the turn of the twentieth century, several poets, such as Ehmed Muxtar Caf and Mela Kake Hemey Bêlu, known as Narî (1874–1944), gave expression both to the old tendency to describe the features of the beloved and the new tendency to inspire national self-consciousness through poetry. Unlike the former's elite background, Narî began as a farmer and later completed his studies in the *hucre* and spent his life as a religious scholar. He was also committed to the Naqshbandi Sufi path and wrote many poems in praise of the sheikhs who traced their lineage to Mawlana Khalid Naqshbandi. While many of Narî's poems address the beloved in the older style, others address the homeland. When they do so, they invariably assume that the audience is Kurdish Muslims. These poems are interesting in part for the sharp contrast they offer to the older style. The poet does not address his own attraction to another religion, or his own inclination to *kufir*, but those attractions and inclinations in the national body. And rather than allow those attractions to reshape the self, he seeks to purge the collective self of the threat of internal difference. In a sense, these poems trade an obsession with personal salvation for a concern with collective religious identity and collective piety.

One poem addressed to the homeland (*xakî weten*) begins with the complaint that people in the Kurdish nation have not been faithful Muslims because they have neglected the contemplation of God (*yadî xuda*) and divine commands (*ehkamî îlahî*). It gives a list of complaints that include preoccupation with desire and worldly matters and neglect of true knowledge. Narî evokes the figure of the beloved, but rather than describe the beloved through physiological features, he names it simply as *teqwe*—which can be translated as the "virtue of fearing God" or more broadly as "piety." Addressing the Kurdish nation, Narî asks, "Why are you so bothered and annoyed with the beloved of piety?" Here, the figure of the beloved, in contrast with the old poetic tendency to identify the beloved by a set of recognizable features characteristic of the human body, is reduced to the rather abstract concept of piety. But most provocatively, Narî concludes one section of the poem with the following couplet:

> The Christians now seek to drink from your fountains,
> I fear that in the end you will become a church.[79]

Here the figure of the Christian is a long way from its place in the story of Sheikh San'an. Christians are no longer local, thus part of the religious hierarchy, but definitively foreign. And rather than being busy with their own piety or tempting the poet's attraction to their piety, Christians are seeking a resource in Kurdistan. And tellingly, the conversion at stake is not the poet's own but a collective and apparently irreversible conversion that happens as a result of pressure and imposition rather than attraction. In short, Christians appear as a group that intrudes on the homeland, and thus they are an explicitly political opposition.

Indeed, the beginning of the twentieth century was a time when foreign, Christian nations such as Britain were keen to exploit Kurdistan's riches. While the *dîwan* offers no information on the date of this poem, it shows anxiety about the extraction of resources that was a key feature of British imperial interests in Kurdistan and Iraq more broadly. One of the key interests was oil, which had been discovered in Kirkuk in 1927.[80] As Samira Haj notes, it was not until the 1950s that the Iraqi government was able to negotiate a treaty whereby oil profits could be recovered and invested in development projects across Iraq.[81] Until that time, British companies led a coalition of Europeans that extracted oil from Iraq and invested very little in the local economy.[82] Narî's poem links the extraction of resources to a missionary effort, expressing fear that foreign Christian powers will not only subdue Kurds but also eventually convert them.

The foreignness of Christians stands at the heart of another Narî poem. The editor of the *dîwan* offers a prefatory note: "This poem was composed in 1935 about an Armenian girl who became Muslim for a boy."[83] The poem begins by describing the girl as a "foreign heroine" (*zumrey xarîce*), but this phrase is difficult to interpret. Why does Narî call this Armenian girl "foreign"? Most obviously, it could be that the girl was not born in Southern Kurdistan, but perhaps she or her parents had fled Northern Kurdistan in the wake of the massacres and genocide of Armenians. The girl would thus be foreign in a geopolitical sense. However, she could have descended from the Armenian families that C. J. Rich had counted in 1820. In that case, calling her "foreign" would refer to her status as non-Kurdish, non-Muslim within a Kurdish Muslim polity. The fact that it is so difficult to know is not merely evidence of what researchers do not know. It is also evidence of how deeply entangled the politics of religious and national difference had become in Southern Kurdistan twenty years after the Armenian genocide.

In this poem, Narî describes the girl's conversion to Islam as part of Islam's defense against foreign incursion. The girl is even compared to Ali—mentioned previously as a paradigmatic warrior—and Ali's predecessor, Omar, in having fought off those foreign enemies.

> O, foreign heroine, I would give all for you:
> for the sake of your courage, your determination, your faithfulness.
> You turn the haughty speech of foreigners to dull spittle:
> one glance from you does the work of a hundred sharp spears.
> Whether English troops or French brigades,
> with a single stone you scatter that gaggle of geese.
> Imam Ali is your comrade facing the foreigners;
> Omar is captain and commander of your cavalry.[84]

This poem suggests that conversion to Christianity was a result of a foreign incursion, and it evokes Christian conversion to Islam as a militant defense against that incursion. In contrast to the ambiguous identity of the Christian in the older tradition, where that identity was signaled by a mode of dress or worship, this poem refers to an actual Christian woman whose conversion is not a literary trope but a social reality.

Toward the end of the poem, the addressee shifts, and instead of praising the girl, the poet addresses the Muslim Kurdish nation:

> When this girl clings to the path of Muhammad
> How could you lose your grip on the path of God?[85]

Here the literary trope of conversion has been completely transformed. For the first generations of Sorani Kurdish poets, it was the prospect of the Muslim poets' conversion to Christianity that provided the productive paradox through which poets might recover their "grip on the path of God." Yet for Narî, a Christian's conversion to Islam serves as inspiration to an entire nation of Muslims to hold that grip. In a sense, nothing could be further from the depoliticized figure of the Christian who had appeared in the early nineteenth century. The plurality internal to the self that allowed for attraction to a non-Muslim in the Pillar Poets has been replaced by an anxiety about the plurality of political identities on the landscape of nationalist politics.

A NEW POLITICS OF THE *KAFIR*

The new politics of the *kafir* in Sorani Kurdish poetry in the twentieth century is a consequence of the changes discussed previously. Once the locus of knowledge and ethics shifted away from the *hucre* and the goal of poetry has become national self-realization, fidelity to Islam and fidelity to Kurdish nationalism became deeply intertwined. Qani' (1898–1965) was a poet whose intellectual biography matched that trajectory. While trained in the *hucre*, he developed strong commitments to socialism in the 1940s. His contemporary reputation rests on the way he described his own poverty in a rapidly developing capitalist economy as well as his willingness to criticize the sheikhs and religious scholars who were unconcerned with nationalism or the struggles of the poor and downtrodden. Qani' expresses this succinctly in the following two couplets of the poem "The Pillar of the Nation" (*payey nîştîman*):

> You must be pure of heart with your fellow countrymen, O Kurds!
> Love of country is a pillar among the duties of worship.
> Qani'! If you are not serving mother country,
> Go straight to the mosque and begin your prayers [*munacat*]![86]

The word choice here reflects an equation of nationalism with faith. While the title uses the Kurdish term *paye* for "pillar," the first line uses the Arabic term *rukin*, which places the concept squarely in the province of religious discourse. Second, when he describes love of country as a duty of worship, Qani' uses the term *'ibadet*, which has a similar effect. The second couplet describes the failure to serve the nation as a religious offense.

It should come as no surprise, then, that the figure of the *kafir* in the new political landscape defined by Kurdish nationalism is one who has betrayed the nation. The poet Bêkes (1905–1948), whose pen name means "alone" or "lonely," had not studied in the *hucre* but in state-administered schools where he later became a teacher.[87] He describes this new *kafir* in the following lines from a poem composed in 1939. Bêkes uses the term *dîn* in a way that captures its polyvalence, as it could mean both "Islam" as a religion and a broader sense of moral grounding.

> Today there are many who for the sake of food
> sell their country for a single coin
> throw faith and *dîn* underfoot.[88]

These lines also bear testament to the problem of widespread poverty that had not been solved by industrial development. Poor Kurds who would betray their nation for a single coin would abandon their faith by doing so.

One final poem, again by Qani', demonstrates the extent to which the terms of faith and *kufir* were appropriated by the nationalist discourse. The editor notes that the poem was composed before the end of the Second World War, and Qani' calls on Kurds to revolt against the imperial yoke imposed by Britain under Winston Churchill at the time. Reflective of his own communist leanings Qani' sets up Stalin as the ideological figure who offered an alternative to British imperialism:

> There is no use in worshipping idols or serving Churchill,
> so quickly turn back to Stalin.
> That crook has stolen from our hands for years;
> cut his hand at the wrist—that faithless *kafir*![89]

If the theme of the *kafir*'s looming punishment should be familiar to readers of older Kurdish poetry, this *kafir* is no longer a tendency internal to the poet but an outsider seeking to exploit Kurdistan.

The Pillar Poets and the generation following them inhabited a poetic imagination in which the aspiration for Muslim piety was taken for granted and the tendency to *kufir* was a means by which to retune and recover that aspiration. Non-Muslim figures represented nodes of attraction—they staged productive paradoxes insofar as they both posed a threat to faith and allowed for its deepening. The passage through a non-Islamic tradition was possible for a poet who acknowledged plurality of tendencies within the self. The non-Muslim figures were depoliticized in that context insofar as their status could not speak to or challenge the assumed hierarchy in which Islam was ascendant.

While those tropes and figures continue to thrive in twentieth-century poetry, a new tendency appeared that offered a different perspective on questions of faith and infidelity in which the presence of Christians was a clear and present danger to the newly configured addressee of poetry in Sorani Kurdish: the Kurdish nation. Christians are no longer literary tropes but now historical figures who bear political claims. They were either paradigmatic *kafir*s such as Winston Churchill, against whom Kurds must struggle, or an individual Christian woman whose conversion to Islam supports that very struggle against the imperialism of Christian nations.

This shift, in turn, suggests a broader, deeper transformation in the relation of poetic discourse to political context across these two centuries. The earlier tradition was depoliticized in the sense that its political vision transcended immediate political circumstances and was not compelled to directly answer developments in the politics of religious difference. The Pillar Poets spoke from and to the broader political context of their day, but in the matter of Muslim–non-Muslim relations, their poetry cannot be considered a mirror of social relations. By the mid-twentieth century, the gap between literary tropes of the previous generations and the social reality of the present was a problem that demanded resolution. To abandon the established vocabulary of the features of the beloved and take up national self-realization was a revolutionary maneuver that brought the political context of relations between (Kurdish) Muslims and (non-Kurdish) non-Muslims to the heart of poetry.

However, as the next chapter shows, these transformations in the context in which poets produced Kurdish poetry do not in themselves determine the life of Kurdish poetry in contemporary Kurdistan. Attending to the reception of poetry in everyday life, nestled within a unique set of ordinary relationships, one sees that Iraqi Kurds not only draw on diverging aspects of Kurdish poetry's past but also improvise in addressing that poetry to their present.

Chapter 3

MYSTICAL DESIRE, ORDINARY DESIRE
Love, Friendship, and Kinship

SITTING WITH NEWZAD IN A BAR ONE EVENING AFTER A LONG DIS-
cussion of Kurdish poets that intertwined with other topics, he said something that captured my attention and became the kernel for this chapter. Speaking about the poet Mehwî, Newzad said, "This world... that's how Mehwî comes about: God becomes a lover; a lover becomes God.... You get mixed up."

Here Newzad touched on the famous theme of the divine beloved. The idea that God is the poet's true beloved is discussed in Chapter 2. In referring to God as a lover, Newzad evoked that discourse, and the switch of roles was part of the condition of being "mixed up." It was clear from the rest of the conversation that he spoke from a place of sympathy with that confusion. Quite provocatively, he also made it clear that the cause of confusion is something quite general that he, and I, and all the people we knew, necessarily shared: this world. So what is it about this world that is confusing? What is it about that confusion that makes God into a lover and makes the lover into God? This chapter investigates that question by examining several layers of context for Newzad's speech, both the conversation we shared that day and a series of other conversations that are all a part of the way he understood Sufi poetry, the figures of the lover, the beloved, and the divine.

To say that God becomes a lover is to set up an analogy between the divine and the ordinary, to suppose that one who experiences love acquires the elements for experiencing divinity as well. But there is no reason to assume that Newzad's analogy is the same as the analogies that the Kurdish poets relied on. And in fact I argue that Newzad's analogy means something quite different. If the previous chapter told a story about how the figure of the beloved was transformed in the poetic imagination across historical contexts, this chapter tells the different but related story of how the figure of the beloved appears in the course of everyday life in contemporary Kurdistan. In Marilyn Strathern's description of the emergence of analogous relations between persons and objects in Melanesia, she writes, "It is not the way anthropologists control the analogies, then, that seems at issue, but the way the actors do."[1] If the last chapter was about my own vision of the analogy between God and the beloved, this chapter tracks the way that Newzad controls those analogies.

Other anthropologists have tracked the way actors control similar analogies. Zuzanna Olszewska has described how the analogy of lover and beloved has been crafted through the composition and recitation of poetry in Iran and shown that the beloved can signify political events such as a revolution, or the lover can become a political activist.[2] And historian Afsaneh Najmabadi has described how the figure of the beloved came to signify a newly feminized homeland in nineteenth-century Iran.[3] Following the lead of these scholars, I take the historical work of the previous chapter as a background and examine how Newzad sets up an analogy between the divine and the ordinary in his own life. What features of Newzad's ordinary relationships made this analogy possible for him? And what imagination of a Sufi mystic made this possible for him?

Given the interpretive framework outlined in Chapter 2, it is certainly possible that linking the divine and the ordinary through the figure of the lover and beloved is part of his striving for proximity to God. One may guess that Newzad was like the pious Sufi poets whose description of desire in erotic terms was simultaneously a description of desire for religious virtue. Several facts make that explanation unlikely to succeed. First, Newzad did not belong to any of the Sufi paths in Kurdistan that celebrated the mystical dimensions of poetry. Second, and more important, when discussion turned to Islam, Newzad was quick to point out all of the "killing, filth, and lies" peddled in its name. He neither prayed nor fasted, and he often drank with his friends at a bar. Newzad sometimes joked that he went to the mosque only on the occasion of a funeral or for a public restroom. He told me that he was Muslim only on his state-issued identity card.

Yet he never claimed not to be a Muslim. Newzad displayed the tendency that is at the heart of this book: to turn away from piety yet not to leave Islam. He expressed strong aversion to Islamic traditions but never flatly disowned them. Thus, the question of how the Sufi trope of the lover and beloved became accessible and meaningful to him cannot be explained either as an unreflective reaction or as part of his striving to become a better Muslim.

Scholar of Sufi literature Michael Sells once posed a provocative question that is a useful starting point for this inquiry. Using the term "nonreligious" to refer to those who, like Newzad, are not particularly devout or pious, Sells asked, "Why are the poems most loved by the religious and the nonreligious alike those in which the identity of the object of desire (divine or human) is as ambiguous as the desire itself is infinite?"[4]

The question tethers two additional concepts to the status of Muslims who are averse to Islamic traditions: the ambiguity of the beloved and the infinity of desire. The ambiguity of the beloved, introduced earlier, refers to the paradox that the God who has no body can be described in poetry as an embodied beloved, and the embodied beloved described in poetry may eventually refer to God. The infinity of desire was only implicit in the discussion: in the long journey to piety that was characteristic of the Pillar Poets, one discovers that the farther one travels on the route to piety, the farther one has to travel. The concept of the infinity of desire rests on a feedback loop by which the more faith one finds, the more *kufir* appears to be lurking below and the more desire one finds to pursue piety. "Infinitude" then refers to the endless dimension of that process, where the poet/lover's desire to reach God seems to be always renewed, despite also always being nearly empty.

Desire has other ambiguities as well. The English term "desire" might be used to translate several terms used in Kurdish. The most obvious are *hewa*, a term of Arabic origin that describes corporeal desire for food or sex; and *arezu*, which, similar to its usage in Persian, encompasses both that corporeal desire and the more simple notion of "wanting" to do something or become someone. Both belong to the broader semantic field of *xoşewîstî*, a general term also translated as "love" (including love for friends, God, famous persons, strangers, or consumer goods). Finally, the kind of love that verges toward madness because of the way it consumes one is called *'işq*. Rather than separate these terms from one another or lament their untranslatability into English, this chapter allows the ambiguity of "desire" in English to encompass the ambiguity that appears in Kurdish as well when these terms intersect and intertwine.

One way to answer Sells's question is to suggest that even those averse to Islamic traditions seek to achieve transcendence and reach God on some level. In this reading, there is an essential human craving to reach God that cannot be denied but may be transformed, for example, by displacing the Quran and hadith and turning instead to poetry as a guide toward piety. According to this view, it is the persistence of an urge to piety, the persistence of a desire to meet divinity, that makes the analogy of God as lover or beloved possible. God can become a lover when "infinite desire" allows the Sufi to overcome or transcend all the small failings of desire.

This chapter argues that Newzad's life and speech reverse those terms: God does not become a lover (or beloved) when desire is infinite. God becomes a lover because desire is finite, because ordinary relationships in this world are characterized by limits, boundaries, failures, and disappointments that can only be endured, not transcended. In this view, the baseline experience that makes Sufi poetry relatable is not the persistence of pious striving toward divinity but the persistence of threats and failures in ordinary relationships. In other words, it is not because Newzad has Sufi tendencies that the analogy makes sense but because Newzad understands Sufis to have ordinary relationships in which people are in danger of failing or disappointing one another.

Making this argument also shows a new way that ordinary relationships absorb and transform texts. Chapter 2 examines how different kinds of religious difference were historically transformed, moving from a difference internal to the self toward a social difference in politically precarious historical conditions. This chapter examines how fractures of difference appear in ordinary intimate relations—particularly the relations of friends, love and marriage, and other kinship relations.

I aim to describe the *texture* of those intimate relations in Newzad's life. Philosopher Sandra Laugier identified texture as "an unstable reality that cannot be fixed by concepts, or by determinate particular objects, but only by the recognition of gestures, manners, and styles."[5] Following this idea of texture, I describe some of the gestures, manners, and styles that make up the ethical life that Newzad shares with others. If Laugier's definition of texture subordinates "fixed concepts" and "particular objects," it by no means dismisses them. Accordingly, I also describe several fixed concepts (e.g., Sufism, Salafism, companionate marriage) that appear in Newzad's life and how those concepts are creatively mobilized in the manner and style of relating to others in ordinary life.

The focus here on an individual allows for a proximity to lived experience that would be sacrificed if I were to attempt to survey too many different lives. As anthropologist Michael Jackson has suggested, lived experience is a personal matter. In a discussion of how the density of lived experience often complicates abstract universals, counters an intellectual impulse to perceive patterns in social life, and bends our desire for consistency in our worldviews, Jackson cites philosopher William James: "The universal conscious fact is not 'feelings and thoughts exist,' but 'I think' and 'I feel.'"[6] Jackson concludes his reflections with the following reminder:

> Much as we extol the value of consistency in our views, constancy in our relations, and logical coherence in our thinking, we sometimes need to be reminded that our survival depends on our ability to change as circumstances change, to go with the flow, and to draw on a diversity of past experiences in response to who we are with and the situations in which we find ourselves.[7]

Because I had the privilege of hearing a great deal of "I think" and "I feel" from Newzad, a close description of some events in his life allow this chapter to show how he "goes with the flow," adapting big concepts to the manners and styles that suit the people "he was with." Accordingly, I am unconcerned with the question of whether the texture of his life with others represents any larger portion of Iraqi Kurdish Muslims. I am much more concerned with the already daunting question of how a single chapter can render the texture of one individual's life, with all the complexity and density of Newzad's lived experience of religious differences. While much remains obscure to me about Newzad's life, this chapter includes the thoughts and feelings he shared with me that offer insight into the goals of this book.

SALAFI, SHI'I, SUFI, AND NEWZAD

I met Newzad in my first years of research in Kurdistan, and we were already well acquainted when I returned in 2008 for a long stint of research. He had held a series of jobs that brought him in contact with journalists, writers, and artists at bars, cafés, and newspaper offices, but he was not a public figure. His income was modest, and his family was not prominent in the city. He married for love early in life, his wife kept a steady job in the field of education, and together they raised their children in Silêmanî.

Early in 2008, I met Newzad for a walk at the main bazaar in Silêmanî. He mentioned that his brother, a devout Muslim, was involved with Islamist groups in Silêmanî. Given Newzad's relationship with Islam, I expressed my surprise at his brother's involvement with those groups. Newzad described the features of such a movement that he thought attracted his brother: it is a "system of morality" (*sîstemêkî exlaqî*), he said, and the people in that movement all love and help one another.

In the 1990s, the Islamist movement became a more prominent force in Kurdistan, eventually controlling areas around the town of Halabja in a protracted civil war. Following the US-led invasion of 2003, the already-fragmented Islamist movement split yet further. While many were killed, some were integrated in the political process as official political parties. A third group reverted to secret political operations, and a fourth group shunned politics altogether. Chapter 4 addresses one of the most prominent figures among the last group, who usually identify themselves as Salafis. I never spoke directly to Newzad's brother, and Newzad referred to him only as an "Islamist," but from the descriptions Newzad offered, I gathered that his views were not far from those of the Salafis.

Salafis in Kurdistan are part of a wider Salafi movement that Muslims all over the world have encountered to varying degrees. Key features of the movement include a strong emphasis on the unity of God (*tewhîd*), a passion to replicate the exemplary practices of the earliest Muslims (who are called the *salaf*, Ar.), and an eagerness to cease all forms of practice that either deviate from the practice of the Prophet and the earliest Muslims or imply a challenge to the unity of God.[8] In the everyday experience of Kurdish Muslims, these doctrinal points can be inferred through particular modes of conduct and orientations: Salafis largely reject political parties because the Prophet and the early Muslims did not participate in such organizations. Men keep a distinctive style of beard (a closely trimmed mustache and a long beard) that is otherwise uncommon in Kurdistan, and they often wear distinctive clothes (for example, trousers or Kurdish pants that leave the ankles visible rather than cover them, as is more common). And beyond those who hold resolutely to the entire scheme of doctrine and conduct, many exhibit sympathies or tendencies toward Salafism.

Since 2004, the Salafis who rejected political involvement in Kurdistan have been a small but influential minority in Kurdistan. In rejecting party politics, they claimed to focus on the moral reform of the Muslim community, calling Muslims to reject all forms of illicit innovation and return to the perfect model set by the Prophet Muhammad. This is what Newzad glossed as their providing a "system of morality" and a community in which they helped one another. Many in Silêmanî harbored suspicions of these nonpolitical Salafis. Principally, they criticized the Salafi disavowal of politics as a cunning political move, a weak attempt to depoliticize their movement in the short term, while it was evidence that their long-term goals were nothing short of the complete transformation of Kurdish society. Those goals were evident in a strident way of engaging other Muslims—insisting that they, too, abandon the innovations that polluted the practice of the most pious Muslims. There was also deep suspicion of these groups' ties to foreign interests—principally Saudi Arabia.[9] On this front, many in Silêmanî saw these groups as an unwitting bridge for foreign interests to reshape religious life in Kurdistan in accordance with their own geopolitical goals. Another critique I heard was rooted in a dismissal of the Salafis' claim to superior piety: some insisted that if the Salafis were really pious, then the strenuous task of perfecting prayer and fasting in their own lives would not leave time to reform *other* Muslims.

Thus, when Newzad reported that his brother often advised him to pray, it was clear that his brother belonged to the group of Islamists who seek to reform those around them and bring them on to the more pious path. Whether or not he identified as Salafi, it seemed that he had been deeply influenced by these groups. When I asked how he responded, Newzad said, "I don't say anything." I asked, "Does he think you are someone you are not?" He replied, "No, but it seems to him that I believe, that's all. [*Na, bes pêy waye bawerim heye.*] But we get along well." I then asked, "What does your father think of that [his brother's involvement with Islamists]?" Newzad mimicked his father's lack of concern by sucking his teeth to produce a sound like "tchk."

When beseeching Newzad to pray, his brother was giving moral advice (*nesîhet*), discussed in greater detail in Chapter 4. But Newzad sidesteps a declaration of what he "believes" and avoids altogether making claims about an ethical orientation. Newzad does not say but implies that he does not have belief, and paradoxically his brother does not mistake him for someone he is not by thinking that Newzad does have belief. In such a delicate situation, his brother seems to consider Newzad's relation to Islam different from his only in degree, not in kind. This allows his brother the opportunity to demonstrate care by advising him to pray, and it frees Newzad from the obligation either to reveal the condition of his belief or (what would amount to a different but also burdensome thing) to conceal it. Both brothers carry on in the subjunctive modality of "as if"—*as if*

Newzad were a believing Muslim—illuminating a central truth of the fictional dimension of human relatedness. Rather than explicit debate or disagreement about propositions of belief, tensions are sustained in a relationship where belief is pushed to the background.

The fact that their father was indifferent to one of his sons' involvement in the Islamist groups is also significant since it shows how participation in those groups is only one aspect of a person's social world. From his father's perspective, his son's commitment to an Islamist group was of secondary importance; it was a fact that was woven into the fabric of a longer relationship between them.

Since Newzad had used the English word "system" in reference to his brother's "Islamist" orientation, I used that word in my next question to him: "Well, it's clear that you're not with that system of morality that is Islamist, but I wonder what your system of morals is—or is it a system?" He answered quickly, "It does have a system. [But] it is a natural system [*sîstemêkî siruştî*]. For example, I cannot take your freedom away from you." He then began to describe Imam Ali. He said that he had read Islamic history, and "although I'm Sunni, I feel like I love Imam Ali more than anyone else in the history of Islam." He said "although" because, like most Sunni Muslims in Kurdistan, he associated the love of Ali with Shi'ism, so it was somewhat paradoxical for a Sunni to love Imam Ali above all others.

To my query of why he loved Imam Ali, Newzad answered, "Because he's smart [*zîrek*] and peace loving [*aştîxwaz*]." He then told a story: when the Prophet captured a city, he killed everyone; when Ali once subjugated a group of fighters, one of them spat in his face, and Ali did not kill him.[10]

When Newzad described his religious orientation as a "natural system," he was not pointing to an established, normative discourse that set out rules or principles of conduct. It was rather in the mode of improvisation that he spoke, spontaneously stitching together an idea of a natural ethics with the idea of a system he had just mentioned. The term "natural system" was a kind of placeholder that allowed him to deflect attention away from Islam toward something else. But the deflection did not last very long, since he immediately returned to describe a paradigm of Islamic virtue: Imam Ali, who was the cousin and son-in-law of the Prophet Muhammad and the fourth leader of the Muslim community after the Prophet's death.

When Newzad described Imam Ali as "smart" and "peace loving," he emphasized a dimension of Imam Ali's character and teachings that Tahera Qutbuddin has called "humanitarian virtues." Qutbuddin notes that among the humanitarian virtues is "perceptive sagacity"—that is, the ability to take lessons from the world and from human experience. This virtue, in turn, is intertwined with the virtue of taking wisdom from revelation and from the example of the Prophets. In Imam Ali's sermons, "Humanitarian virtues are explained on a religious plane, while religious concepts are parsed and presented in terms of humanitarian ethics."[11] For Imam Ali the two were inseparable, but Newzad was attracted to the more "humanitarian" aspect of the virtues.

For many Sunni Muslims in Kurdistan, the two remain inseparable. In fact, Sunni Muslims are enjoined to passionate attachments to Ali. In a sense there is nothing surprising about the fact that a Muslim would evoke him as a model of virtue. At the same time, though, among many pious Sunni Muslims in Iraqi Kurdistan there is considerable anxiety about an excessively zealous love of Imam Ali. The anxiety takes the shape of a worry that love for Ali could displace love for the Prophet Muhammad. That excessive love is associated with Shi'ism, and many Kurdish Muslims frame their critique of Iran or Shi'ism by saying that they take the love of Ali too far, even to the point of divinizing him. Among the Salafis, there is no more reliable example of an incorrect "innovation" than the practices of Shi'i Muslims.

Newzad's association of Imam Ali with Shi'i tendencies became clearer to me later that year. One evening we met with the explicit purpose of discussing the only book I could find in the bazaar that contained some of Imam Ali's sayings.[12] When I handed Newzad the thin volume in Arabic that included a selection of those sayings along with explanations, he looked at it for a few minutes and then expressed his disappointment. He looked at the author and the publication data: it was clearly written by a Sunni Muslim. He quipped, "The Sunnis don't know anything; you have to go to the Shi'a to learn about Imam Ali." He then mentioned the doctrine (which he attributed to some Shi'i Muslims) that prophethood was actually sent to Imam Ali through the angel Gabriel but Muhammad had stolen the office. He also described the practices of Kurdish Alevis in Iran as "worshipping" Imam Ali, less to endorse those practices than to prove how morally persuasive Imam Ali can be.[13] The idea that Imam Ali might *outdo* the Prophet in some way animated his version of the story of the Battle of Badr, in which Imam Ali refuses to kill an enemy.

Thus, what other Sunni Muslims find heretical about that tendency to love Imam Ali is precisely what Newzad found attractive. Rather than an endorsement of the Prophet's pious precedent, his invocation draws on the possibility that Imam Ali subverts that precedent. Newzad never claimed the superiority of Imam Ali to the Prophet. Yet Imam Ali was a locus of attraction that Newzad considered transgressive of the Sunni norms. By foregrounding his attraction to Imam Ali as "love," Newzad shows an orientation to Islam that acknowledges orthodoxy and heresy and moves creatively between them. Newzad's admiration for Imam Ali should be understood in this context as both an insistence on the more humanitarian of his virtues at the expense of the religious virtues and a declaration of attraction that might appear heretical to Sunni Muslims.

After he described Imam Ali, Newzad and I walked on without speaking, suffering the distractions of the bazaar. Then he started to speak again, and I soon realized he was reciting a poem.

> By the squinting of her black, intoxicated eyes, she intoxicated us
> with one kiss from her lips; she robbed us of the pleasure of any other taste.
> Her shirt opened upon a floral red when I sighed "Ah,"
> but she covered it; she denied us a glimpse into the garden of quince.
> Behind the clouds of her locks and brows, she hid her face and cheeks;
> she darkened the shining splendor of that waxing crescent moon.[14]

I insisted that he repeat it slowly for me to copy down. He repeated it for me and told me that it was a poem by Narî. I told him that it was beautiful. He then named another poet he found beautiful. Omar Khayyam (d. 1131) was remarkable, Newzad said, because he "criticizes God" (*rexne le xwa egrê*). He did not recite the poem he had in mind, but he described its theme. To paraphrase, he asked: Why would God create beauty just in order to destroy it? Sensitive humans, even when they are drunk, are not so cruel—they do not even break the glass they drink from!

Newzad here referred to the same poem mentioned by Pexshan. Here is my English rendering of a Kurdish translation by Hejar, who was Newzad's favorite translator of Khayyam:

> A drunk is never so cruel as to shatter his glass,
> he just spills a little then sets it to rest;
> these shapely beauties and supple figures,
> whose grief does God slake when he makes them rot?[15]

Newzad then connected this poem to Narî's poem. He said that when Narî describes hair, he means human beauty, and why shouldn't we enjoy the beauty of humans? Next, he pointed out that when Narî says *mest*, he does not just mean drunken intoxication (*serxoşî*) but also the imagination (*xeyal*) formed in such intoxication. After he said this, we parted ways, and I sat down to write the notes from our conversation that became the basis for this short narrative.

Several features of the poem recall themes described earlier. The poets are affected in the modes proper to the genre of the love poem at or before the turn of the twentieth century in Kurdistan: being love-struck is like intoxication; the girl's lips, like the lips of Christ, bear the promise of restoring life, but she has no intention of sparing her lovers from death or of giving them more than a glimpse of her beauty.

Newzad's description of poetry departs in small ways from the scholarly manner of reading poetry that I learned from other interlocutors. When he said the tresses of the beloved referred to "human beauty," he bypassed the stricter analogy of the tresses as the threat of polytheism (dark and plural) encroaching on the truth of divine unity (the single and bright face). Rather than fend off the threat of the tresses, Newzad described the tresses as part of a broader picture of human beauty—a necessary complement to the face. When he said that Narî's idea of experiencing "intoxication" upon seeing the beloved was a kind of imagination, he moved away from a strictly literal idea of drunkenness but resisted making it only a metaphor for the poet's passion for God. Newzad's interpretation privileges the complexity of the earthly beloved, who is conceived as a metaphor for all of God's human creations rather than a metaphor for God.

I later learned part of the context of the poem's composition, which is widely recounted by lovers of poetry in Silêmanî even if Newzad did not recount it on this occasion. As the story goes, it was jointly written by Narî and Taher Beg. The poets were sitting together in their opulent garden when they saw a beautiful Jewish girl who inspired this poem. As the description of this beloved indicates, the two poets write from that tendency of the poetic imagination that assumes non-Muslims do not, as such, pose a challenge to Muslim political authority. The Jewish beloved is depoliticized. Later I return to the theme of how the non-Muslim beloved recurred in my conversations with Newzad.

Yet the context of Newzad's recitation perhaps shows more about his religious orientation than a textual analysis of the speech he recited. After he had described his brother's orientation as a "system of morality," I asked him about his own system. His answer traversed the notion of nature, the figure of Imam Ali, and the poetry of Narî, Taher Beg, and Khayyam. What do those figures have in common, and how do they show a religious orientation?

The common virtue that ties those figures together according to Newzad is a sympathy or reception to human beauty: it was Imam Ali's recognition of the terror of killing that prompted him to spare the life of his enemy, it was the poets recognition of another human's erotic attraction that put them in a state of heightened perception called imagination or intoxication, and it was Khayyam's attraction to human beauty that emboldened him to ask how God's judgment could ever turn beauty to rottenness. This gloss of vulnerability or receptivity to human beauty as a human virtue is helpful, but Newzad did not use the language of virtues. He began with a principle, turned to several illustrations, then offered a short lesson on poetry. While it was easy to begin in declaratory language, it was apparently easier for Newzad to carry on in the language of poetry. Poetry for Newzad showed an affective state that was part of his religious orientation.

Yet what he said was all a response to my question that was explicitly comparative: Newzad was not describing his religious orientation as he might when taking a survey or introducing himself to someone new. Rather, he described it as different from that of his brother, as something that stands in tension with an Islamist perspective but does not prevent him and his brother from getting along. In this short conversation, Newzad's relations to Islam, poetry, and kinship were deeply intertwined. Poetry offered a way of describing a general religious or ethical state of being, whose primary features are not named virtues or singular principles but a sensibility, an ethos, an affective orientation to others.[16]

Religious orientation is thus embodied in a sensorium that creatively borrows from conflicting fields of discourse and connects people to one another in ordinary relationships. Responding to others within those relationships only rarely takes the form of announcing a position in a debate. Rather, a kind of argument emerges through the labor of description—describing passions, attractions, and aversions as much as principles.

COMPANIONATE MARRIAGE

Early in 2008, Newzad and I met at a park near the main bazaar. My mood that day was despondent, and he quickly noticed and asked about it. When I implied that my sorrows involved romantic love, he did not ask for any details. Though he must have been curious, to indulge curiosity by asking questions would have forced me into either revelation or concealment. Rather than require me to lie, or take up the burden of knowing too much, Newzad exercised kindness in his silence. I took it as his way of caring when he suggested a distraction by gazing at the women who walked by as we sat on a park bench. "That will not help," I said inconsolably. I thus had revealed myself despite my desire not to: it was obvious that I was sad about a woman. Quietly he sighed to acknowledge my sadness, "Ehhh." Then he said, "It's true, when you're in love [*ke tuşî 'işq buyt*], the others are all nothing. I'm the same way, you know. Don't misunderstand: it's true I like [looking at] women, but just as something beautiful in the world. I cannot betray my wife. Even if I wanted to, I cannot do it. I love Sana a lot." Though he did not specify what he meant by "betray" (*xeyanet*), we were both familiar with the type of relationship in question. That kind of relationship—involving secret meetings, cell-phone conversations, text messages, and possibly also sexual contact—was a common topic of conversation among our male acquaintances. Stories about those relations were not always true, but the referential truth of the stories was secondary to their creation of intimate relations between males who celebrate stories of extramarital liaisons with women. So when Newzad rejected such a relationship, implying that his enjoyment was limited only to gazing and invoking his love for his wife, he seemed to share with me the idea that he was bound to an idea and affect of love that allows only one beloved. That idea, though, was oriented toward me when my own sorrow shared the same affect of love.

While Newzad's descriptions of love resonated with me in my lovelorn state, they also resonated with a widely available and relatively new discourse of companionate marriage in Iraq. Across many Muslim societies in the region before the nineteenth century, marriage had been described as "a sexual contract for procreation" in which relations between husband and wife were conceived first and foremost as rights and obligations to sex and maintenance. Companionate marriage was a relatively new idea that made marriage into a "romantic contract" in which "the object of exchange was now love, companionship, and mutual attendance to each other's desires and needs."[17] While much research remains to be done on how that discourse was made available in the Kurdistan region, two proximate historical contexts are of immediate relevance.

First, since the 1910s, Arab and Kurdish reformers in Iraq have worked to consolidate an image of the family built around a reproductive couple that married for romantic love. This required increasing restrictions for polygamy, banning the marriage of children and marriage by force, making divorce more difficult, and encouraging marriage based on romantic love.[18] As Sara Pursley has shown, even those who critiqued some of those reforms frequently affirmed the romance of companionate marriage.[19] While these efforts were increasingly directed to the domain of civil law, they were never separable from poetry and in fact received some of their earliest expression in poetry.[20]

Second, Amy Motlagh has traced this connection in neighboring Iran through her study of the modernization of Iranian fiction. Because of the intensity of different forms of exchange between Iraqi Kurdistan and Iran—including intellectual exchange through the Persian language and literature and marital bonds between Kurds that reach across the borders of Iraq and Iran—Motlagh's study provides insight into a second historical context for companionate marriage in Kurdistan. In contrast to the narrative of redemption through secular law that animated much reformist discourse during this period, Motlagh draws attention to the grotesque dimensions of companionate marriage and the forms of violence that appeared alongside it in Persian fiction of the twentieth century. Placing the figure of the beloved in the context of Persian literary history, Motlagh identifies the labor that was required to draw the beloved from its transcendent, ambiguously gendered form in classical Persian poetry toward the female companionate spouse. Far from a simple liberation, this transformation of the beloved sometimes resulted in gross violence, as occurred for the beloved figure who was killed in Sadegh Hedayat's famous novel *The Blind Owl*.[21] Domesticating the beloved in the twentieth century could be fraught with agony or violence.

Thus, for men such as Newzad, if contracting a love marriage and sustaining a relationship with his spouse was a mark of urban modernity, it could also be marked by modern forms of failure, violence, or despair. So how did Newzad come to describe and inhabit his marriage, which seems self-evidently companionate?

Newzad frequently made passionate confessions about his love. He often praised his wife's beauty, her cooking, and her intelligence and spoke of his inability to live without her. Though common among newlywed men of my acquaintance in Silêmanî, I had rarely heard such unabashed praise from men such as Newzad who had been married for more than ten years, with children. It was more common for men of that age to refer to their spouses as *malewe*, a kind of objectification of the beloved as a home.[22] But Newzad always used her name, Sana, when he spoke to me. They lived in an inexpensive rental with a neglectful landlord in one of Silêmanî's older neighborhoods. There I saw his relationships with his family. He flirted with his wife by telling me, "I'm glad you're here because my wife never makes such good food just for me"; his wife asked if I thought the remodeled kitchen looked good so that she could boast about Newzad's craftsmanship; his children hung around his neck, hugging and kissing him, begging him for an exception to the rule that they not ride their bike in the alley after dinner; all of us laughed as Newzad clumsily mounted a bike that was too small for him. His wife even suggested that rather than go to the bars where everything is overpriced, where the food is dirty and tasteless, and where scenes of violence between drunks are inevitable, Newzad and I should stay in the tiny courtyard of their house for drinks.

This gesture of hospitality was remarkable given that his wife was a pious Muslim. She kept the fast and prayed regularly and wore a headscarf during Ramadan (as Pexshan's daughter reported she was expected to do). She described her husband's nonobservance with a common term described at greater length in Chapter 5: *gwê nadat* (he doesn't listen, doesn't pay attention). This was a subtle way of rendering a stark religious difference, which was perhaps part of the companionship their marriage afforded them.

NOT BECOMING A CHRISTIAN

Once Newzad and I met by chance in the bazaar and spoke for a few minutes. His first words to me were "How are you getting by in this immoral city?" (*Çonît lem şarey bêaxlaq?*) I chuckled at his dry humor; then he told me he was going toward the Palace Hotel, which was for many years the tallest building in Silêmanî. It was less than a hundred meters from where we stood and directly in front of the park where we had earlier sat and he had told me about his love for his wife. "I'm going to the Palace. I'm going to throw myself down [from the top]." I laughed again and asked him what had inspired this decision. He answered that he had just "loved a girl" (perhaps, *fallen in love*). Recalling the way he had expressed his love for his wife and the impossibility of other liaisons, I was surprised and questioned whether it was shameful (*'eyb niye*). His reply was quick and cool, with a hint of sarcasm: "What should I do, become a Christian?" In retrospect, and as I explore later, I see that this comment is both an allusion to a very famous couplet of poetry and a joke. At the time, though, I did not understand it at all. My incomprehension must have been evident, since Newzad then explained, "Muslims can have four wives; only Jesus forbade that." He then described a fleeting encounter he had at a bus stop, and when I protested that he would break his wife's heart, he said, "Love? [*'îşq*]. There's no such thing in this country."

My protest was surely misplaced; I took his joke too seriously. Readers of early drafts of this chapter have also reacted quite seriously, even regarding the scene as the revelation of Newzad's hypocrisy. Such reactions are understandable if one finds no room to joke about monogamy. But an encounter with a stranger at a bus stop hardly made the kind of affair that his wife would bother to take seriously. I had seen him make such jokes in her presence, and she usually responded by calling his bluff.

These jokes were not unique to Newzad but part of a very common practice among men in Kurdistan. Sometimes the joke was an assertion of power in the guise of humor, in which a man calls up the prospect of exercising the right (commonly granted in Islamic law) to unilaterally divorce his wife or to take up a second wife. But at other times, those jokes backfired and became the space in which a man's authority appeared vacuous, as when I once heard a wife respond to her husband joking that way by issuing a challenge: "Sure, let's see if we can find anyone who will put up with *you*!" Even one such effective challenge in the history of a relationship could mean that every subsequent evocation of the joke was reduced to the performance of homosociality among men, in which the joke actually works to forge an affective bond between men who share an interest in women. In any case the jokes show some lingering ambivalence about the ideal of companionate marriage as a domestication of infinite desire.

Newzad's joke about being allowed multiple wives also shows an important dimension of his religious orientation. While much of Newzad's conversation about his status as a Muslim sounded like submission to fate as it had been decreed on his identity card, his remark about Jesus's forbidding polygamy sounded like an ironic boast about the adventures afforded to Muslims. To evoke conversion to Christianity was to evoke something practically unthinkable for Newzad.

Newzad had also referred to a famous poem with his question, "What should I do, become a Christian?"

> The hands of a mela cannot graze the *zunnar* of the beloved's locks,
> Unless like the sheikh I chose the sect of Christians. What can I do?[23]

Newzad's words echo this phrase: *Çi bikem, bibime mesîhî?* (What should I do, become a Christian?). This couplet is from a longer poem by Mehwî (d. 1906) and is one of the most frequently memorized couplets of classical poetry in contemporary Silêmanî. Newzad recited it to me on other occasions, and it is clear that the slight grammatical rephrasing of his question in our conversation referred to it. Chapter 2 described the couplet in relation to Farid al-Din 'Attar's story of Sheikh San'an, the Sufi sage who converted to Christianity to win the favor of a Christian girl. Recall that while the tale of Sheikh San'an raises the specter of a love that transcends religious difference, it does not imagine a love that affirms and inhabits religious difference. I argued that the lovers are united only on the condition of transforming—and so sharing—a religious identity.

In Mehwî's couplet, the "I" of the poem, an educated scholar and pietistic Sufi, finds himself hopelessly in love with a Christian and asks, "If I don't become like Sheikh San'an and become a Christian for the sake of my love, what else could I do?" Newzad's allusion to the poem evokes at least two dimensions of the historical transformation of religion, love, and marriage as they affected his ordinary relationships.

First, his evocation of the prospect of becoming a non-Muslim bears little in common with the trope of conversion that had animated the poetic imagination in the early nineteenth century. This imagination is certainly not a part of any quest on Newzad's part to become a better Muslim. However, neither does this allusion bear any resemblance to the anxiety about Christians converting Muslims to Christianity or Christians dominating Muslims. Thus, this allusion illustrates exactly how far the everyday usages of poetry can travel from the historical context of their composition. The history of poetry does not illuminate what Newzad meant as much as it illuminates the creativity he demonstrates in expressing what he meant. The history of poetry is not a library of concepts and tropes inherited as ready-made tools for deployment in everyday life. It is like a library that is sometimes plundered or looted, where concepts travel so far from their homes as to be almost unrecognizable.

Second, in the more immediate context of modern efforts to forge heterosexual nuclear families, Newzad's description of his extramarital flirtations shows ambivalence about the project of companionate marriage. Newzad was already engaged in that project, since both before and after this incident he continually proclaimed his love for his wife. For that reason, to simply accuse him of hypocrisy (for turning away from Islam until Islam offered him the fantasy of polygamy, whereupon he returned) would neglect several facts. Not only had Newzad never claimed to have left Islam, but in these moments suffused with tension and frustration he did not claim to be pious. In fact, the tension and frustration led him to the hyperbole of throwing himself off the roof of a tall building. He only named the conditions of describing desire the way he did, and he clearly understood being Muslim as essential to that description.

In a sense, Newzad was here acknowledging a limit, that as much as he would like to have a marriage in which desire for a singular beloved is infinitely renewed and refurbished, when he looks at his own desire, he finds limits. While at one moment he aspires to a marriage that exemplifies transcendent love and infinite desire by conjoining the classical lover's madness with contemporary notions of companionate marriage, at another moment he finds himself confronted with the finitude of that desire. Living with the knowledge that desire is limited may sometimes seem a disappointment. But it may also be a key element that enables relationships.

ADVICE ABOUT FASTING DURING RAMADAN

Later in 2008, Newzad and I sat together at a bar one evening. He mentioned that his son had told him that he wants to fast, which became the topic of a short exchange. When I asked why, he answered that since the boy sees his uncle and everyone around him fasting, he wants to fast. Newzad continued, "And because my brother told him, 'You should fast,' and, 'God will see it,' and those things." I asked, "Does your brother tell you that you should fast?" He answered, "No, he doesn't tell me that. But he told my son in a sneaky way [*be dizîyewe*]." I asked, "Why? Do you see this as pointing to your disagreement in that aspect, or do you think of him as respecting you?" He said, "No, it is because he respects me. He loves me a lot, you know. When I [do some work on the house], he comes and does the work of a day laborer on the house. I don't even tell him, but he does it. And when he gets angry, later he'll come back and say, 'I beg your pardon, forgive me.'" I asked, "But you felt like he told your son in a sneaky way?" He said, "I mean, we can say that without my being aware of it; he told him these things."

Newzad's descriptions here are subtle and complex. He clearly thought there was something remarkable and not exactly necessary about his brother's advice to his son. His son was then at the precarious age when fasting was commendable but not yet a formal duty. So his brother's encouragement was a kind of advice (*nesîhet*) that anticipated the boy would have a long-term relationship with fasting that would evolve over time. By encouraging the boy to fast at an early age, Newzad's brother set a precedent for other kinds of guidance or advice as the boy grew up. Without a doubt, Newzad's brother knew that the boy would not receive that kind of advice from Newzad.

It is difficult to understand exactly why his brother had advised the boy without Newzad's knowledge. Had he done so in Newzad's presence, one can imagine an awkward scene in which the boy asks, "Will you fast, Dad?" Newzad would have to explain himself to his son in the presence of his brother, which could open the door to conflict. That sort of direct argumentation, though, is precisely what Newzad and his brother successfully deflected. Perhaps the ongoing effort to deflect that disagreement is what prompted Newzad's brother to advise the boy discreetly and thus also why Newzad wanted to emphasize that respect was at the core of his brother's relationship to him. Chapter 4 explores at greater length this mode of interaction within families, which was an explicit matter of public debate among Islamist intellectuals.

But Newzad was keen to emphasize that his brother also showed love and respect for Newzad in many ways. Working together on projects around the house was just one form of cooperation that proved that love. That cooperation, though, was precisely the way that Newzad had characterized the relations within Islamist groups. That his brother offered Newzad the same form of cooperation shows that forms of Islamist activism were deeply implicated in ordinary relations that extended beyond the bounds of those groups. Was his brother's cooperation a form of activism or simply brotherly love? From the perspective of their relationship, it seems unknowable—not unlike the status of Newzad's belief.

I asked what he told his son, and Newzad said, "I told him that he is still young, that he is thin, and he needs to take care of his health. [That was all I could say,] because I can't tell him not to fast." I asked why, and in Newzad's answer he referred to the two ostensibly "secular" parties that make up the Kurdistan Regional Government—the PUK and KDP. He said, "Because if I tell him not to fast, these parties will arrest me. Sure, supposedly they are secular and everything, but at the root, at the very base of them, these parties are based on Islam. There are laws about it. For example, if I told my wife, 'Don't fast,' she would immediately summon me to court and divorce me. It's like that in this country." He then concluded with a statement that combined his frustration with the two main political parties and his frustration with the Islamist movement by calling the Islamists "them" and insisting that there is not much difference between the secular and Islamist parties. "The parties are with *them*."

This interaction affords rich insight into the texture of both the threats and promises that arise in this family, given their differing religious orientations. Newzad acknowledged the possible boundaries of his wife's desire to live with him as her husband. If he were to discourage his wife from taking up a duty incumbent on all Muslims, he risked alienating her. There was a sense of joking exaggeration about his imagination that she would summon him to court and divorce him. But like Newzad's jokes about other wives, this joke worked because there was a legal framework to allow for it.[24]

Furthermore, Newzad understood his words to his wife about fasting as belonging within a wider network where they could be used against him. Even if he did not intend to terminate his marriage or prevent her from fasting, and even if she did not take his words in this way, they could be used as evidence to issue a divorce against Newzad's or his wife's will. Newzad named the prospective actors in such a hypothetical case as "them," by which he referred to the Islamist activists in or beyond the political parties. The fact that his brother had some affiliation with them would not likely offer any protection.

Thus, his marriage is a kind of gamble against the chance that desire itself might fail altogether in the face of intervention by others (with the support of the law). At the same time, his marriage is also a gamble that his wife will not reach the limits of her desire to live with him. He knew that desire was finite: it had boundaries and limits that could not be crossed without grave consequences. For Newzad, this means that loosening his tongue could be courting disaster. Holding his tongue, then, was one condition of enabling a future in view of the finitude of desire. Here again the work of desire is not conditioned by the transcendence of the beloved with whom one can never attain union. Desire is conditioned by the simple willingness to go on in the face of intractable religious difference and the promise of a future together, however unstable and uncertain. Sharing such a future does not prove a desire that will transcend religious difference as much as enact a love that strives to bear that difference.

The picture of ordinary relations here is complex: his brother, his wife, and his children are all engaged in a network of relations in which pious striving is explicitly encouraged. Also at work are broader political conditions, activist programs that already had an effect on his house when his brother came to help with household projects but could also materialize into a strange actor intervening in his marriage at any time.

ENGAGING THE QURAN'S BEAUTY

Later in the same evening, Newzad touched on another small event that was part of his ongoing relationship with his brother. It returns to the theme of "human beauty" that Newzad had evoked in describing the poetry of Narî and Khayyam. Newzad described a night of drinking he had shared with a friend and then said something that I later glossed in my notes as the following: "Then that night I went home, and I was watching TV. I like these Islamic channels. I watch them all the time, and sometimes I'll call my brother and tell him to watch something that is on. That night, this guy was reading the Quran, and he was crying. It was amazing; his voice was just amazing." I was surprised to hear this from Newzad. So surprised that I wanted to be sure I was not, once again, missing some dimension of his dry humor: "Do you really enjoy listening to those things?" He answered, "Yes, because this isn't a religious thing; it is a human thing. I started crying, too. I listened to this, and I started to cry. And so I called up my brother and told him to watch it."

Chapter 5 returns to the theme of Kurdistan's Islamic television stations. For now it will suffice to say that they frequently broadcast readings of the Quran, sometimes with accompanying visual images of the reciter but more often with the text of the Quran on the screen, allowing the listener to follow along with the text. Newzad described what he heard as "amazing" (*'ecîb*): the beauty of the Quran had inspired tears in the reciter. These were precisely the tears that Kristina Nelson described as appropriate to recitation and that Pexshan did not find accessible. If Newzad and Pexshan shared some dimensions of a religious orientation, they surely were not the same. For Newzad found the beauty and the tears of the recitation to be infectious, and he cried himself.

In his description to me, though, Newzad makes it clear that his attraction to the Quran—his vulnerability to its beauty—does not follow the terms of vulnerability that the discourse of Quranic reception has outlined for it. Rather, the attraction of the Quran was explained as a "human thing," so Newzad compared the effect of the Quran on him to the effect of beauty on the poets. When Newzad said this, the point was not to deny that the Quran is a religious text, nor was it a comment on the origins of the Quran. He was not saying that the Quran *is* poetry (though this was a common critique in Kurdistan, just as it had been a common critique at the time of the Quran's appearance).[25] He was saying that the beauty of the Quran can affect a listener whether that person is religious or not. Implicitly, then, one can also be affected by the Quran without necessarily *becoming* more religious—or in the language this book has adopted, without turning to piety.

In that moment of heightened emotion and affective sensitivity, he was reminded of his brother, and the phone call he placed to his brother extended the line of affective contact even further, to encompass his brother as well. I have often wondered how exactly his brother responded to that phone call. Might he take it as evidence that Newzad will eventually repent and take up the pious path? Would he consider Newzad's appreciation of the Quran beauty deficient and thus take the phone call as an occasion for disappointment? Or are such judgments completely unnecessary and even foreign to a relationship that is founded precisely on sustaining affective modes of connection that cross lines of doctrinal difference? My own analytical impulses—my desire to take a claim to its logical conclusion, and my supposition that Newzad's brother does the same—incline me to one of the first two answers. But all the ways that Newzad described his relationship with his brother, and with his wife, suggest the latter. In other words, to recall Michael Jackson's words, I believe this event demonstrates why the analytical impulse for "consistency in our views" and "logical coherence in our thinking" needs to be complemented. It also requires an acknowledgment that thriving in human relationships (not only "survival") requires us "to go with the flow, and to draw on a diversity of past experiences in response to who we are with and the situations in which we find ourselves."[26]

MEHWÎ: "GOD BECOMES A LOVER"

One evening I made an appointment with Newzad to discuss Khayyam. We spent some time reading Khayyam and talking about the poems. At a certain point when he picked up the book to find another poem of some interest, he closed it and said that in fact he loved Mehwî more than Khayyam. Another of Kurdistan's accomplished poets of the nineteenth century who was deeply devoted to the Naqshbandi path, Mehwî was regarded by many as the acme of beauty in Sufi poetic expression in Sorani Kurdish. Although he studied abroad, Mehwî was born, raised, and died in Silêmanî, where the *hucre* built for him by the Ottoman sultan Abdulhamid II still bears his name. When I asked why he preferred Mehwî, he replied, "Because Mehwî talks about *'işq*, and he talks about it at the level of humans, of God, and of society." With that phrase he evoked the broad tradition of commentary: not only the mainstream interpretations of classical poetry but also the twentieth-century critics who, as I did earlier, began to explain the metaphors of lover and beloved in terms of social and historical change. After a pause he said, as if to explain the social dimension of Mehwî's discussion of *'işq*, "For example, he has one poem that says 'if someone has poor conduct, I retreat from him.' I hide myself from him. That's it. That's important!" Moved by what he said, I read to him from the poem that I had studied earlier that day with another teacher, in which Mehwî laments the lack of virtue among Muslims and names himself as the greatest offender:

> My days were borne off by the wind while I did the work of a nobody;
> grant me a few more days, God, that I may die on the stoop of somebody.
> Resurrection may be tomorrow, dear friends, so today is your chance;
> get far away from me lest you be resurrected beside me.[27]

Newzad picked up the *dîwan* and read the whole poem quietly. Then he said, "When I read this, I feel that I have been lazy. I should have memorized some of this. I should have read it more carefully. I wish that I had been better, or else that I had not been at all!" That last phrase was a convoluted expression in Kurdish that I had to ask him to explain. He did so in such a way that I saw a dimension of existential angst in it: live as a noble human being or do not live at all. The idea resonated with Mehwî's complaint that the world is full of people who lack virtue, and in such a world it may be better not to exist than to go on with that immorality. At the same time, Newzad's words showed an aspiration or striving to become a good person—an aspiration so intense that he is willing to say that he would rather die than fail. In the conversation that followed, he gave a name to that aspiration and described its relation to poetry:

> In humans, there is a continual striving [*renc*]: it is a kind of interrogation [*lê pirsînewe*] that is always happening. You ask yourself every night what you did today, what was good and what was bad. Not necessarily about moral things, but about normal things, everyday things: buying and selling and talking to friends. . . . And why is Mehwî important? Because he deepens things. He sees into the depth of things, and in just two words, he gives it to you, and you can think about it; you can go into the depth of things with those words.

Poetry is connected to moral striving not because it tells you how to live but because it allows you to see some aspects of life in a new way. In a sense, Newzad here encapsulates the concluding suggestion of Chapter 1. Poetry gives a language of description that allows one to see new things in a new way. He then described teaching himself art and spoke admiringly of our mutual friend Ahmed, who practiced that self-interrogation in his artwork. Mention of this friend became a bridge to talk about friendship more generally. Then, more soberly, he said, "But you should also know this. In this country, there is a kind of friend you will find everywhere who will simply tell you that you are doing good work.... He tells you this just because he wants to spend an evening with you and pass the time."

My notes from our conversation indicate that there is much I did not write down. I wrote simply, "We mused on the bitterness together for a minute and on bad friendships." I thought about my own lost friendships, and I did not conceal my disappointment. Nor did he conceal his. We ran through a long list of shortcomings: some friends betray you, some just disappear, and others take your money and then disappear. We finally came to rest, newly disappointed by all the failures of friendship and desire. He then summarized all that disappointment with ordinary relationships as a feature of "the world" when he said reflectively, "This world . . . that's how Mehwî comes about: God becomes a lover; a lover becomes God. . . . You get mixed up."

This chapter began with that phrase, and now in the context of Newzad's life, its texture should become more palpable. Mehwî's poetry emerges from the same world in which Newzad lives—the world that he shared with his brother, his father, his wife, his kids, his friends, and with me as well. It was a world constituted in part by embeddedness in the human relations vulnerable to failures of various kinds, if also to enduring pleasures and satisfaction. In all those relationships, vulnerability is key to an ongoing relationship. Desire is not infinite in those relations but finds particular limits: he ought not advise his wife not to pray; he ought not prevent his brother from advising his son to fast; we both must be wary that friendships falter under the weight of poverty or self-interest. The disappointment is not only that one has not achieved infinite love. It is also that one does not always *want* that love.

The Sufi kind of mystical love is capable of overcoming or transcending even the betrayal of *kufir*, as in the case of Sheikh San'an, who left Islam and then returned to it. But the ordinary kind of desire that makes up Newzad's everyday life is one in which relations may not overcome betrayal. Ordinary relations have limits, and ordinary desire is finite. Ordinary desire, though, is not therefore separate or cut off from the mystical. Instead of showing how mystical desire builds on ordinary desire, Newzad's invocation of Mehwî shows how ordinary desire—its failures and disappointments—absorbs even the mystical aspirations of great Sufis. Paradoxically, Sufi poets such as Mehwî end up demonstrating the impossibility of transcending the pain and struggle of everyday life. For Newzad, the memory *and anticipation* of that pain cannot be abandoned but must be carried along in everyday life.

In this situation, Mehwî's poetry is not compensation but a teacher and a companion for living in a world—*this* world—where desire is finite. Mehwî helps you because he gives you "two words" to see the depth of things. This is not a solution but a new way to look at the problem. I cannot help wondering: Might ethnography do something similar? This book has not set out to offer didactic examples or teachers that might instruct readers how to behave in their own everyday lives. But perhaps ethnography may offer "two words" that allow readers to see things differently. In that sense, Newzad's evocation of Mehwî extends the earlier argument that poetry offers a language to describe paradoxical orientations to Islamic traditions. It is not that poetry makes a claim about identities and practices but rather that it expresses the texture of paradoxes that persist in everyday life and resist condensation into claims. The Epilogue returns to this idea that ethnography, like poetry, offers "two words" to see things anew.

This chapter describes two occasions on which Newzad's brother offered advice: once to Newzad that he pray and once to his son that he fast. The practice of offering advice has a long history in Kurdistan and in Islamic traditions more broadly. But the recent popularity of Islamist movements in Kurdistan and Newzad's brother's affiliation with them make these two occasions events in which the techniques and sensibilities promoted by Islamist movements came to put pressure on the life of a Kurdish Muslim who was "only Muslim on his ID card." The next chapter explores the ideas and techniques through which Islamist movements have sought to transform ordinary relationships in Kurdistan.

Chapter 4

SEPARATING FAITH AND *KUFIR* IN AN ISLAMIC SOCIETY

IN 1974, AN EIGHTEEN-YEAR-OLD GUERRILLA FIGHTER (*PÊŞMERGE*) named Necmedîn Ferec Ehmed sat in the mountains of Iraqi Kurdistan writing the name of his beloved on bullets as he loaded them into his weapon, preparing to fight Iraqi soldiers of the Ba'athist regime. He had only met the girl earlier that year, but they had traded many letters. Ironically, Necmedîn got to know the girl because her house lay between his own house and the mosque, so he passed it several times each day, picking up and dropping off love notes. At the mosque, he not only offered obligatory prayers but also received instruction in the *hucre* from a scholar committed to the Muslim Brotherhood, a transnational Islamist party that had begun activity in Iraq in the 1940s. This scholar had influenced Necmedîn so deeply that he also became a member. Necmedîn would later describe his situation as contradictory: "On one side I was giving the call to prayer; on the other side I was trading love letters; how could that be?"[1] Surely the pursuit of piety comes with its own set of paradoxes.

But Necmedîn Ferec Ehmed mobilized these paradoxes for a very specific goal. Between 1974, when he traded love letters in Iraqi Kurdistan, and 2010, when he told the story from his home in Norway to an internet-based chat group, he had become "Mela Krêkar"—one of the most influential figures in the Islamist movement of Iraqi Kurdistan. In the 1980s Mela Krêkar carried out jihad in Afghanistan, fighting the Soviets and studying with the prominent scholar Abdallah Azzam, whose more famous student was Osama bin Laden.² In 1988, when Krêkar heard about Saddam Hussein's use of chemical weapons against Kurds, Krêkar was so disturbed by the news that he returned to Kurdistan and worked at the forefront of the Islamic Movement of Kurdistan. With Krêkar among its leaders, this movement briefly carved out territorial autonomy in 2000 around the Hewraman region (near the town of Halabja and close to Iraq's border with Iran). The movement soon fragmented, especially after the US-led invasion of 2003, when the US military partnered with the PUK to annihilate the militants in Kurdistan. Some militant wings continued to operate underground, and other parts of the movement joined mainstream politics as recognized political parties. But Krêkar took refuge in Norway and carried on his fight on the internet. In 2010, when he told the story about his old love letters, he demonstrated that even though he was a prominent political voice and a famous jihadi, he was also vulnerable to the ordinary experience of falling in love.

As part of a sequence of recordings made available on the internet, this story was also part of his larger effort to mobilize ordinary Iraqi Kurdish Muslims to transform their lives. In Krêkar's view, ordinary life in Iraqi Kurdistan was saturated with moral turpitude insofar as it deviated from the vision of life given by the Quran and the hadith. This turpitude had been exacerbated by Ba'athist rule as well as the corrupt governance of the secular Kurdish parties that made up the KRG. Turning away from faith in political parties and state governance, Mela Krêkar called for a complete transformation of society to rely exclusively on the models of the Quran and hadith. Krêkar's goal was to resolve or overcome the paradox of trading love letters and giving the call to prayer. In a sense, he wanted to focus solely on the call to prayer—a call that was simultaneously a call to faith and a call to fight against any and every sign of *kufir*.

According to Krêkar, pious Muslims should first of all learn to recognize the difference between faith and *kufir*, and then they should be alert and vigilant for signs of *kufir* wherever they appeared. The vigilance that he advocates is most often directed beyond the self and toward others: toward strangers one meets in public, one's parents, siblings, in-laws, and friends. In this way, his vision stands in stark contrast to that of the Pillar Poets, whose vigilance against *kufir* had been directed toward the many tendencies within the self.

Mela Krêkar's call for transformation was part of the reformist movement that had profoundly influenced Newzad's brother. When Newzad's brother gave advice to Newzad and his children about prayer and fasting, that procedure of offering advice (*nesîhet*) falls within the wide stream of prescriptions that Krêkar offered. Also within that stream is advice about fasting and veiling that Pexshan's daughter had complained about. Mela Krêkar sought to mobilize these techniques of *nesîhet* to transform Kurdish Muslim society into a properly Islamic society: one that was built on faith because it was able to separate faith from *kufir* and enable the triumph of faith over *kufir*.

Mela Krêkar's voice is thus an essential component of this book for two reasons. First, he articulates a vision of an Islamic society that inspires aversion to Islam among those who turn away from piety. When Pexshan, Newzad, and others turn away from models of Islamic piety, they are not turning away from the model of the Pillar Poets. Rather, the vision of a total transformation that Krêkar sought was precisely what they found inhospitable and what prompted deep aversions to Islam. Second, because Krêkar articulates a doctrine of total social transformation at the level of ordinary relations, he is also the leading political theorist of this book. Mela Krêkar seeks to inaugurate a political transformation at the level of everyday interactions between embodied Muslims. He assumes that those ordinary relations have been shaped by programs of state governance, yet he does not reduce political life to the work of political parties and state governance. He instead seeks to rebuild an Islamic society from the ground up, starting with relations of friendship, kinship, and intimacy that Kurdish Muslims already share.

This chapter regards Mela Krêkar as a theorist of politics because he sees the workings of power in the microscopic details of ordinary life while introducing new criteria for the evaluation of power in ordinary relationships. Rather than the question "Do these relationships serve the interests of the public, the state, the party?," Krêkar asks, "Do these relationships accord with the divine command given in the Quran and hadith?" and "Do these relationships help faith achieve victory over *kufir*?" If the Pillar Poets had taken the relation between faith and *kufir* as a productive paradox internal to the self and one step removed from "real," historical *kafir*s, Krêkar takes the relation between faith and *kufir* as a dichotomy to be resolved at the level of social relations with the *kafir* who may be one's parent, sibling, or friend.

This chapter argues that in Mela Krêkar's thought, ordinary relationships are precisely the target for the radical transformation of the Muslim community from one that was full of *kufir* into a properly "Islamic society." This dimension of Islamist movements has been underappreciated in both scholarly and popular discourse. Many studies of Islamist movements emphasize other dimensions of their work, including the effort to shape the state institutions, public space, and civil society into distinctively Islamic forms of governance.[3] Other studies have focused on the paradigms of self-fashioning that these movements employ through disciplinary practice.[4] Yet for Islamism in Kurdistan, it is the interpersonal, interactive dimension of ordinary relationships that has been ground zero for efforts to Islamize society.

Attending to the Islamist movements' focus on ordinary relationships, other aspects of their work clearly challenge stereotypes of Islamist movements. To characterize Islamists' views on gender and sexuality as "conservative" or "traditional" is unhelpful. Such a characterization flattens out a complex set of ideas and practices. For not only does Mela Krêkar advise women to be proactive in correcting men's bad conduct; he also conveys more flexible ideas of gender roles than those usually called "conservative." Additionally, the vision of a transformed Islamic society does not include a firm boundary between the private life of the family imagined as a place of moral safety and the public life of politics. It calls for a more dynamic sensibility that is both active in relations with strangers on the street and always on guard against moral failure at home. Thus, in rejecting the notion of "conservatism," I seek to elucidate the radical transformation that Mela Krêkar sought to implement.

Finally, while that radical transformation does come with anxieties about the political influence of foreign non-Muslims, it does not require the conversion of Christians to Islam. It instead stipulates a firm boundary between Muslims and Christians in order to protect Muslim doctrine. After contextualizing Mela Krêkar within the larger Islamist movement in Kurdistan, and describing the sources on which it is based, I examine his vision of how to build an Islamic society by transforming ordinary relationships.

ISLAMIST MOVEMENTS IN KURDISTAN

The Kurdish phrases *bizutinewey Islamî* and *bizavî Islamî* are commonly used to gloss the contending projects of revival, reform, awakening, and transformation that grew particularly strong in the 1990s. They are translated here as "Islamist movement" and "Islamism" in keeping with common English usage in and beyond Kurdistan. The history of Islamism in Kurdistan, as told there, holds that Islamism coalesced into a single movement in the late 1980s. Yet that period of coalescence was brief and was followed by intense fragmentation, so it is perhaps better to refer to Islamist movements or Islamisms in Kurdistan.[5]

The movements began in the 1940s when activists affiliated with Egypt's Muslim Brotherhood began organizing in Kurdistan. There were a few vanguard intellectuals and activists in the 1960s and 1970s, but the movements gained momentum in the 1980s after the success of the Iranian revolution and alongside sustained resistance of Muslims against the Soviets in Afghanistan.[6] Thus, while the spark of Islamist movements came from Kurdistan's west (Egypt), those to Kurdistan's east (Iran, Pakistan, and Afghanistan) fanned the flame. During the 1980s, these movements in Kurdistan maintained shifting relations with political parties in a shared struggle against the Ba'athist regime. While they insisted on the sufficiency of Islam as a paradigm for governance, these movements did not see any contradiction between affirming a Kurdish identity and evoking a broader Islamist discourse. Their goal was to establish a system of governance that allowed for the recognition of distinctive Kurdish identities, not one that obliterated the differences.

After the establishment of the KRG in 1992, several Islamist factions were entangled in Kurdistan's civil war. The civil war divided the PUK, the KDP, and other parties in a struggle for land, loyalty, and resources. The civil war fractured the region geographically—and it split apart families as well—until 2003. Around 2000 a portion of the Islamist movement actually gained territorial control of a group of villages near the town of Halabja. That power was quickly challenged by the PUK, and in 2003 the PUK solicited American military support to launch a final attack on the militant Islamists around Halabja. The Islamists suffered a quick and decisive loss there.

Following that loss, more mainstream Islamist movements emerged that disavowed armed struggle and embraced formally democratic electoral politics, as the KRG sought to move past its civil war. In the two decades after the US invasion of Iraq, three main political parties called themselves *Islamî*, "Islamist."[7] These parties have sometimes worked in partnership with the larger ruling parties and sometimes as a coalition of opposition. Yet alongside these formal political parties, there is a strong strand of Islamists who identify as Salafis and disavow participation in political parties. Mela Krêkar belongs to this last strand.

Mela Krêkar's voice is thus not representative of the Islamist movement because that movement has been diverse and fragmented. Yet his voice has been profoundly influential. It stands out for its clarity, its argumentative rigor, and perhaps above all, its eloquence. Even his most staunch opponents acknowledge that Krêkar's speeches and sermons are often persuasive or even seductive. Newzad, for example, described Krêkar as a compelling speaker: "You just like to listen to him." Krêkar's speeches demonstrate a masterful command of the Quran and the hadith, the foundational texts of the discursive tradition. He is also widely read in the history of their interpretation and efforts to derive *fiqh* (Islamic law) from them. Throughout his speeches he recites these sources with ease and gives extemporaneous Kurdish translations. Furthermore, he has an equally impressive grasp of Kurdish history, folklore and proverbs, and classical poetry. He even composed poetry of his own in Arabic and Kurdish. And like other Islamists in Kurdistan, he saw no contradiction between the demand for recognition of a distinctive Kurdish identity and the aspiration to a build a completely Islamic society. Finally, his uncompromising critique of corruption in both the established Islamic parties and the secular parties earned him a reputation of being committed to a set of principles rather than merely aspiring to hold political power.

A DIGITAL ARCHIVE

When I began this phase of research in 2014–2015, I tried to interview former followers of Mela Krêkar's ideas. But understandably, most of my interlocutors were reluctant to connect an American researcher with this strand of Islamist activists. As described previously, this was a key feature of my research. Consequently, I was not able to conduct any such interviews, nor could I acquire recordings of his teachings in Kurdistan as they had been confiscated by KRG authorities in the effort to suppress militancy.

Nonetheless, hundreds of hours of his teachings were available in audio format on the internet (didinwe.net) in 2014–2015, and this chapter is a study of those recordings. The recordings were a mixture of cassette tapes of sermons that had been delivered as early as 1991 and later recordings of internet-based chats and lectures hosted in Paltalk as late as 2011. Their collection together presents a surprisingly coherent image of his ideas and aspirations. While there were certainly dramatic shifts in his political commitments—not least reevaluations of whether the current political conditions warranted armed jihad or not—the archive presents a single Mela Krêkar. This chapter reflects that singularity, foregrounding the recurring themes of his speeches.

The digital archive of Krêkar's voice draws on and extends practices of audition that have become common in many Muslim communities. Since the 1980s, sermons were recorded and disseminated by audiocassette in a way that allowed Muslims to extend the practice of audition beyond the mosque into their homes, taxis, or any place where there was a cassette player.⁸ The main condition limiting access was the language: while spliced with extensive quotations in Arabic, as well as phrases and terms borrowed from English and Norwegian, the archive is exclusively Sorani Kurdish.

Among Kurdish speakers, though, the audience reaches across a wide spectrum of religious orientations and educational levels. Krêkar often answers questions posed by Kurdish Muslims who are clearly committed to the project of revival and reform, but he also answers questions from skeptics who make plain their enmity to him and his project. These factors contributed to Mela Krêkar's prominent—if also contested—position as an Islamist in Kurdistan.

THE FOUNDATIONS OF THE AWAKENING

One sermon in the archive offers an introduction to Mela Krêkar's vision of how to transform a society of Kurdish Muslims into a true Islamic society. "Foundations of the Awakening" identifies five foundations or pillars for the process of transformation that seemed to have just begun in the late 1990s and early 2000s in Iraqi Kurdistan. Listening closely to this sermon, one can hear many of the themes common to other Salafi Islamist movements in the region during this time. One can also hear a set of prescriptions for inhabiting ordinary relationships where religious difference appears. I listen for Krêkar's descriptions of how abstract principles of the awakening are embodied in ordinary relationships. Listening in this way, one can hear Krêkar demand of his audience an ability to evaluate ordinary relationships and the events of everyday life according to a sharp dichotomy between faith and *kufir*.

Mela Krêkar's sermon on the foundations of the awakening begins on precisely this note, claiming that proper knowledge of the foundations will allow Muslims to identify "what will lead us to crass ignorance and what will separate us from it."⁹ I translate the term *jahiliyet* as "crass ignorance" because it is not simply the lack of intellectual knowledge that is at stake but the corresponding inability to behave in an appropriate, dignified manner without true knowledge.¹⁰ He goes on to elaborate the following five foundations of the awakening. A short summary of each provides a useful introduction to the essential points of an agenda that Krêkar shares with other Salafis while also highlighting the central theme of this chapter: separating faith and *kufir*.

Committing to the Quran and the Sunna

The word "sunna" means "tradition" and here refers to the traditions of the Prophet—his words and deeds as conveyed by the hadith. Mela Krêkar first describes this foundation briefly as requiring intellectual knowledge of Arabic to study both of these sources. He also describes the danger of deviating from this commitment by reference to a hadith that predicts the fragmentation of the Muslim community into seventy-three sects, of which seventy-two will deviate so far from proper Islam that they earn the fires of hell for themselves in the afterlife.[11] In this way, Krêkar links the ability to identify false pretense to knowledge of the Quran. Vigilance against false claims to Islam starts at this broad level.

Inheriting the Legacy of Sunni Scholars' Agreement on the Prophet's Sunna

Here Mela Krêkar uses an Arabic phrase that is very common in Kurdish, "ahlî sunet u ceme'at." While the phrase has a long history, Krêkar's usage refers to the mainstream consensus of Sunni scholarship over the centuries following the time of the Prophet. Implicit in the phrase is a rejection of the innovations associated with Shi'ism. In explanation, Krêkar makes this dimension more explicit by evoking a common negative stereotype of Shi'i Muslims among Sunnis in Kurdistan that portrays Shi'is as loathing the first three caliphs of Islam after the Prophet Muhammad. Krêkar specifies that one must never speak ill of the caliphs or other companions of the Prophet. He also describes this legacy as a "true moderation." True moderation, he continues, means that one does not shy from jihad when jihad is necessary, and one is not shy to repeat God's definitions of a *kafir* when the Prophet himself spoke openly and plainly of *kafir*s. Here vigilance against false claims about Islam is directed toward two concrete voices that are part of Kurdistan's past and present: the voice of Shi'i Muslims and the voices of Muslims who claim that "moderate Islam" must be nonviolent. Both of these voices, Krêkar implies, should be identified as the voices of *kafir*s.

Adopting an Uncorrupted Doctrine

Mela Krêkar devotes most of the sermon to elucidating this third foundation. He begins by clarifying what the term *'eqîde* means—a clarification that is as important for English audiences as it was for his Kurdish audience. While it is difficult to translate it into English by any single word other than "doctrine," Krêkar reminds his audience that it does not refer only to a set of statements about God, God's revelations, and the cosmos. In fact, *'eqîde* is inseparable from governance (*hukim*); that is, it is inseparable from political authority. As he states on many occasions, he considers it impossible for a Muslim to truly believe in the unity of God and the Prophethood of Muhammad (traditionally "doctrinal" statements) without also accepting the form of governance that the Quran and hadith offer.[12] To separate "doctrine" from "action" is therefore to corrupt "doctrine." One section of the sermon makes this clear:

> It is on the basis of faith and the governance of faith that a Muslim knows how to separate the truth from nonsense [*heq u batil*], knows how to distinguish a Muslim from a *kafir*, and knows how to implement the legal judgments about faith and *kufir*.[13]

In this sentence, Mela Krêkar builds a seamless connection between faith, knowledge, and social relations. Having faith inspires one to know how that faith requires one to live, and that knowledge of how to live extends to everyone one encounters in everyday life. This statement projects an image of a Muslim as one whose knowledge about faith and *kufir* makes them vigilant in every interaction with others. The very next sentence gives an example of how that knowledge works through what this book calls ordinary relationships. In this case, he speaks of family relationships, and Krêkar takes the example of a father-in-law who is a properly faithful Muslim and whose son-in-law is a Muslim-turned-*kafir*:

> So if a man has fallen into *kufir* and he refuses Islam in every way, it is not permissible for his wife to remain with him, it is not permissible for his children to remain with him, it is not permissible for all his wealth and possessions to remain his own, it is not permissible for him to be washed and wrapped [for a Muslim burial] when he dies, [and] it is not permissible for him to be buried in the Muslims' graveyard. Given these requirements, if a father-in-law knows that his son-in-law has become like this, has become a *kafir*, then he does not allow him to go and commit adultery with his daughter. The man thinks she is his wife, but his father-in-law knows that they are *haram* to one another.[14]

This offers a stark picture of the extent to which Krêkar expects Muslims to go in exercising the knowledge that separates faith from *kufir*. The background for this is the legal doctrine common among Muslim scholars in and beyond Kurdistan that a Muslim woman may not uphold a marriage contract with a non-Muslim man.[15] That includes both non-Muslims such as Christians and Jews and Muslims who have become *kafir*s.

This passage is remarkable because it demonstrates Mela Krêkar's assumption that commitment to the Quran and hadith will not necessarily "keep families together." It may also require separating them if they are afflicted by *kufir*. This is one reason that the stereotypical portrayal of Islamism as demanding that Muslim husbands exert unbridled authority over their wives is not representative. Others can intervene in that relationship if and when they see *kufir*. Krêkar concludes the discussion of this point by reminding his audience that this is not something simple and straightforward that can be found by reading the Quran independently. Rather, the judgments in question result from hundreds of scholars who have written hundreds of volumes on the topic over the centuries. But he has powerfully illustrated the point. The relation of marriage is one example of an ordinary relation where the separation of faith from *kufir* requires constant vigilance over everyday life.

Following the Path of the Prophet

Mela Krêkar explains that this means making the Prophet and the Quran the sole foundation of all judgment, in all matters of life. He then cites the fourteenth-century scholar Ibn Kathir, who says in effect that anyone who has apparently become a Muslim yet remains skeptical about the judgments that issue from sharia is not to be counted among the Muslims. This fourth foundation is quite close to the third insofar as both insist that awakening requires complete acceptance and adherence to the judgments of sharia. And like the third, it keeps the specter of the *kafir* at the center of knowledge.

Following in the Path of the First Generations of Muslims

Here Mela Krêkar refers to the first three generations of Muslims who lived in the years following the Prophet. These generations are commonly regarded by Sunni Muslims as having stayed close to the habits and conduct of the Prophet himself. Like other Salafis, Krêkar regarded the lives of these few generations as marking an outer limit for innovation: anything that was not practiced in these first generations counts as an innovation and should be condemned. Conversely, everything practiced then is worthy of imitation. Interestingly, though, as Krêkar describes these generations, he also describes the virtues of the old traditions of scholarly study in Kurdistan, which had their home in the *hucre*. He mentions that until the colonial apparatus began its destruction of the *hucre*, young students were able to acquire virtues by imitating senior scholars who were themselves imitating the first generations of Muslims. Yet in the present moment, those institutions had been severely weakened. Thus, for contemporary Muslims to wake from their state of crass ignorance (*jahiliyet*), they should turn to the example of the first generations of Muslims.

In sum, the sermon that identifies the five pillars of the "awakening" revolves around the capacity to separate faith from *kufir*. The source of that separation is ultimately the Quran and the hadith of the Prophet. Muslims must study the Quran and seek to imitate the Prophet in every aspect of their lives. Yet the more precise knowledge about how to separate faith from *kufir* requires adherence to the models of the first generations of Muslims and the detailed study of scholarship produced by many generations of Muslim scholars.

If the example of family relations as the place of transformation gives a hint about the method he imagines for facilitating the awakening, it raises several questions. What is the role of state institutions in this awakening? How precisely does Krêkar envision ordinary relationships contributing to the awakening? These two questions guide the remainder of this inquiry.

A POLITICS BEYOND STATE OR PARTY

Mela Krêkar answered the first of these questions loudly and clearly: the awakening should have nothing to do with the state or political parties. Throughout his speeches, Krêkar decries the effect of twentieth-century political parties as having deformed the reasoning, conduct, sensibilities, and goals of human beings. He asserts that political parties have produced their own form of human being, one that teaches obedience to other human authority rather than a divine authority, and one that separates means from ends, allowing people to kill others unjustly in the name of the party. As he once put it, the reasoning of the political parties insists on power first and truth second. The result is inevitably oppression. When Krêkar speaks of the form of reasoning characteristic of the political party (*'eqliyetî hizbayetî*), he frequently evokes the example of the assassination of Heme Reşîd. Heme Reşîd was not a particularly famous or influential figure, but he illustrates what can happen to ordinary people caught up in party politics. Here Krêkar refers to the political party as "they":

> There was a fellow named Heme Reşîd. They said that he was responsible for many bad deeds and he should be killed. Then they said, "Okay, bring him and kill him." They brought him and killed him, and then they said, "Oh, no, that

was not Heme Reşîd. The one we wanted to kill is still out there. Go get him." So they went and got another Heme Reşîd and strung him up. Then they said, "No, this was his son; it was not him. Go get the father." So they went and brought another Heme Reşîd and killed him, too. This is true, it happened in Kurdistan, and it was revolutionaries who did it! They killed three Heme Reşîds, and the real one was still alive. That is power without truth [*qwote bebê heq*].[16]

Krêkar frequently evokes the example of the three Heme Reşîds to prove the necessary failure of any "revolution" based on a power that was separated from the truth of the Quran and hadith. Even though he often celebrated the progress of Islamists as a "movement" (*bizutnewe* or *bizav*), he very rarely called it a "revolution" (*şoriş*), precisely, it seems, because revolutions are the domain of political parties and states. Islam requires truth first, Krêkar insists, and then it exercises political power.

The disavowal of political parties and the state means that the Islamicization of society cannot take place on the temporal scale of a quick seizure of power. A few minutes later in the same sermon, Krêkar specifies a timetable for establishing power. He uses the example of someone who wants to practice medicine but first must study for six years. It requires patience: "Change in our society—let it take ten years! Why should we rush? . . . Let the people first want an Islamist; then whichever [Islamist] gains the power, let them have it."[17]

To make an "Islamic society," one must denounce the form of being prescribed by political parties and, by extension, the modern state, and become an "Islamic human."[18] In seeking a mode of transformation that avoids replicating the failures of political parties, Krêkar seeks to identify a substrate of humanity that is "suprapolitical" in Faisal Devji's sense that it transcends the given categories of political action in order to achieve freedom.[19]

To recall Shahab Ahmed's distinction between prescriptive authority and the authority to explore, the form of knowledge that separates faith and *kufir* evidently falls on the prescriptive end of the spectrum. Speaking within the genre of the sermon, Mela Krêkar is exercising a "license to prescribe to another."[20] But two points about this prescription are crucial for those who, like Pexshan and Newzad, turn away from piety. First, this prescriptive call seeks to ground itself *exclusively* in the authority of the Quran and hadith. That is, Krêkar's disavowal of the structures and mechanisms of the political party mean that his call to piety is not cast as a call from the state to the citizen. It is a call to piety couched as resistance to the corrupt forms of governance that are so familiar to Iraqi Kurds.

Second, if in this case a preacher mediated the call to piety that the divine speaker directs to a human audience, then this preacher also enjoins his audience to acquire the knowledge and authority to prescribe for others. As the next section shows, the call to piety in the 1990s and 2000s in Iraqi Kurdistan did not merely come from *hucre*-educated elite scholars. In fact, Mela Krêkar sought to mobilize Kurdish Muslims who were quite young and *not* educated in institutions of Islamic learning. This means that the call to piety comes not only from authoritative preachers who speak from on high but also from friends and family who speak up-close.

HOW YOUTH SHARE KNOWLEDGE

Rather than rely on political parties or a government to disseminate knowledge, Mela Krêkar relied on the work of one group of Kurdish Muslims who were particularly receptive to his ideas: youth. Throughout his sermons, speeches, and conversations, Krêkar assumes that youth constitute the vanguard of the awakening and that their enthusiasm for awakening is also an enthusiasm for knowledge. He understood modern technology as an asset for the youth's search for knowledge, and he often emphasized that the circulation of books and cassettes that had accelerated in the 1990s was a positive development. As he put it, it was now possible to collect more knowledge in an armful of CDs than was available from a hundred senior scholars in Kurdistan. Because youth were proficient in the acquisition of that kind of media, they also become proficient in the knowledge that it contained.[21]

However, the emergence of youth as a kind of intellectual vanguard led to problems within families. Disagreements appeared between youth and their parents. Such problems were at the heart of a question posed to Mela Krêkar during a radio interview around 2000. The interview took place in the village of Xurmal, one of many villages near Halabja that were under the authority of the Islamists at that time. The interviewer asked, "Today there are a lot of youth who have problems with their homes, with their parents, or with their relatives. What is your advice for them?" Krêkar's lengthy answer deserves careful attention because it contains a description of a family environment in which the kind of religious difference at the heart of this book becomes a problem. His answer prescribes a mode of conduct for pious Muslims to engage that difference.

Krêkar begins by generalizing the problem and locating it in a unique conflict between the generations. He describes these problems as "natural" (*tebî'î*), saying that "ninety-nine percent of youth will have these problems."²² He goes on to describe how the knowledge available to contemporary youth differs from the knowledge available to the previous generation. The previous generation relied on the authority of preachers and religious scholars, but today youth are able to become experts on the science of hadith themselves. Thus, "this generation is more intellectually enlightened [*roşinbîr*], and it will be that way from this generation forward."²³ He then repeats his claim that this kind of conflict is something all Muslims in the movement will face.

Turning to a prescriptive mode in which he offers advice about how youth should conduct themselves, Krêkar answers the interviewer's question directly by identifying two modes of interaction that youth should take up with their families: gentleness and patience.

> So youth should conduct themselves gently [*be nermî*] with them. That does not mean that when you learn a hadith, you immediately convince them.... The problem now is that youth are very radical [*tund u tîj*] in the implementation of these things. When you learn something new, it's not necessary to immediately convince everyone else of it, not your relatives—especially not your parents. Your parents say, "I've been praying this way for years!" So how can they change it immediately?²⁴

The example of prayer that Mela Krêkar evokes suggests that the knowledgeable youth in question has conflicts with parents who are largely committed to prayer. Yet in the next moment, he addresses an even wider gap between youth and their parents, which resembles the kind of difference that appears between Muslims who take up their prayers and Muslims who may neglect their prayers without regret. Here he addresses the difference between pious and impious Muslims by advising the pious young man:

> The solution is not to run away. On the contrary, he should stay there, be patient with them, kiss their hands every day, with respect and admiration. As long as they pray—but even if they drink liquor—he is obliged to stay with them so that he can slowly have an influence on them.²⁵

Krêkar here draws on a general assumption throughout Kurdistan that a commitment to prayer is a basic indication of an aspiration to be a proper Muslim and that drinking liquor is a prominent indication of the absence of that aspiration. So when Krêkar states that the patience of the knowledgeable youth should extend to those who drink liquor, it is a strong statement meant to include those who appear to be "beyond the pale," which would apply to those who drink as well as those who do not drink but also do not pray.

Mela Krêkar then recites a few lines of the Quran that address relations with one's parents and renders them into Kurdish, which I translate into English: "If they are among those who deny God's unity in word or deed [*muşrik*] and if they invite you onto the path of denying God's unity [*şirk*], then do not do what they say but remain with them as friends, living together."[26] In other words, when pious Muslims find that their parents are neglecting Islam in some fashion, Krêkar reminds them that the Quran itself advises them to stay with their family, to behave kindly toward them.

Krêkar's next comment also connects to Chapter 2 because it illuminates his position toward a range of Sufi practices that were quite common in Kurdistan. Though Krêkar does not malign poetic tropes of lover and beloved, he was strongly opposed to a range of other practices associated with Sufism in Kurdistan. One such practice is offering a supplication that is addressed to the ninth-century saint Abdul Qader Gaylani (rather than directly to God). At the end of their prayers, or in the course of daily life, many Kurdish Muslims may offer supplications to the saint who, in turn, will offer persuasive supplications to God on behalf of others. Mela Krêkar understands those practices as attributing powers to a human saint that in fact belong exclusively to God. Those who offer prayers to the saint thus implicitly deny one dimension of God's unity and commit an act of *kufır*. Like other Salafis, he loathes this practice.[27] Yet his prescription for how pious Muslims should respond to what he regards as blatant acts of apostasy is noteworthy because it prescribes *patience*:

> It is obligatory to love one's mother and father, and at the same time we love them, we must be patient with them so that we can slowly correct their mistakes. Especially in the matter of doctrine [*'eqîde*]. For thirty or forty years, your father has been calling out to Abdul Qader Gaylani. In order to correct him, you have to be patient with him for thirty months. He did that for thirty years, so you go with him for thirty months so that you clarify things for him with kindness—with kind speech and proper evidence.[28]

Clearly the point of suggesting that youth "go with" their father for thirty months is not to set a limit to that striving but to suggest that one should "go" for a long time. Krêkar emphasizes kindness as the definitive feature of one's conduct with kin who have "incorrect" habits.

Alongside kindness he places "proper evidence," which shows that ultimately persuasion is an intellectual process. The paradigm for the relation between pious youth and their unawakened family is an argument that relies on the Quran and hadith. While Krêkar himself was fond of poetry, writing it himself and reciting it on occasion during his speeches, it is noteworthy that the paradigm he offers here for growth as a Muslim is not one that emerges from the paradoxical sensibility of the Pillar Poets but one grounded in the derivation of clear claims about proper practice from the Quran and hadith. Ultimately, it is still knowledge that separates faith from *kufir*, and thus it is knowledge that provides the foundation for the awakening.

This interview demonstrates that while the Islamist movement in Kurdistan was at the peak of its revolutionary momentum in 2000, it was responding not only to the military and political strategies of how to conduct itself in relation to secular parties but also to the equally political question of how the awakening would appear in intimate relations between parents and adolescents. At the heart of those relations is a tension between pious Muslims who call others to piety and those who are averse to the call.

Another story early from his own life illustrates how this call to piety is intertwined both with other intellectual traditions of argument in Iraqi Kurdistan and religious difference within families. In the course of telling his life story, Mela Krêkar includes the tale of one of his Islamist friends who had invited him to his house in 1984 to speak with his sister. The friend was concerned because his sister was a communist, but Krêkar was eager to engage with her and insisted that he could do so politely. Krêkar describes the first moments of meeting this communist woman as one of admiration: like all the communists, he noted, she was humble in her conduct and not to be criticized for her ethics (*exlaq*) even if she was a bit intellectually arrogant. But at the same time, he noted that she had done a lot of reading and was well educated in politics. In their first meeting she told him that she had not been able to find a copy of the *Communist Manifesto* itself, and in the spirit of informed intellectual debate, Krêkar promised to bring it to her. He did that for their second meeting, and Krêkar reports that he stayed up all night talking about "Islam, politics, and Kurdish identity [*Kurdayetî*]" with the woman, her Islamist brother, and their mother.[29] Eventually, the woman learned to pray, she became an Islamist like Krêkar, and he married her. And notably, unlike many prominent Islamist men who married several wives, this woman was to be Krêkar's only wife.

This story is important not only because it reveals that Krêkar's wife had been a communist. It also reveals that the method of recruitment and the commitment to intellectual debate and agonistic respect for one's opponents were elements of political action that both Islamism and communism shared in common in the 1980s. Furthermore, these features of ethical conduct and political debate were not merely matters of public debate in newspapers but matters of ongoing concern in the context of family life, where different orientations to Islam were gathered under a single roof.

The examples of the father-in-law relating to his daughter and son-in-law, youth relating to their parents, and an Islamist relating to his communist sister each suggest that the type of ordinary relationships in which Mela Krêkar envisioned the work of awakening were primarily relations of kinship, revolving around family units. This mode of disseminating knowledge and awakening Kurds to the call of piety has been seen throughout the daily lives of Pexshan and Newzad. Perhaps most evidently, it can be seen in Newzad's brother's patient invitations to Newzad that he pray and in his subtle encouragement to Newzad's children that they fast. In offering these simple forms of encouragement, Newzad's brother was "going with" Newzad. Newzad's brother was exercising patience in the hope that one day Newzad would see things clearly and take up his duties as a Muslim. Chapter 5 examines the experience of a father whose daughter goes with him, showing patience and kindness in the face of his reluctance to pray.

FLEXIBLE ROLES IN MARRIAGE

But how does Krêkar speak of the Muslim family more generally? And how does he understand the relation between the family and other kinds of ordinary relationships? Mela Krêkar often emphasizes that the family (*xêzan*) has a central role to play in the awakening. Evoking modern metaphors, he often describes the family as "the first stone in the foundation of the Islamic society,"[30] and in his view marriage is essential to the family. This is perhaps unsurprising in itself. Yet in describing what the family should look like, the stereotype of Islamists as holding conservative views fails to capture his perspective for two reasons. If by conservative one understands a commitment to established gender roles and an aversion to change, then Mela Krêkar is anything but a conservative since he calls for radical changes to the life of the family. And if the family is often understood in Islamist movements as an essentially private rather than public domain, then Krêkar again breaks the mold.

Concerning marriage, Krêkar is quick to denounce contemporary ideas of romance and "love at first sight" as destructive for families. Perhaps predictably, he claims the evidence of his own experience as a refugee in Norway observing Norwegian marriages to assert that marriage is an unstable institution there. For example, he describes divorce as being so common in Oslo that when men and women marry and move into a home together, each of them brings one bed, six plates, and four forks so that when they divorce, they can easily split their property and take it to their next spouses. Krêkar insists that a proper Islamic marriage is worship (*xudaperestî*). He defines a proper marriage as built on consent of two individuals to marry with the support of both of their families, and Krêkar assumes it is natural that couples will have children.[31] These elements are consistent with the image of companionate marriage described previously. Furthermore, Krêkar draws on an established critique of the prevalence of divorce that many reformers in Iraq have called a "marriage crisis" since at least the 1940s.[32]

At the same time, several features of Mela Krêkar's speech complicate this common image of marriage and family. First, while Krêkar assumes that married couples will produce children, he specifies that the authority of deciding about how many children to have should be distributed between men and women. He says that 60 percent of the choice should belong to the woman, since she is the one who will suffer in the process of childbearing.[33] Thus, contrary to the assumption that the father is the locus of authority and decision-making regarding reproduction, Krêkar envisions a reproductive family in which the mother's decision is primary.

Second, while Mela Krêkar takes it for granted that sharia requires a man to work outside the home to obtain a living and support his family and does *not* require a woman to do the same, those prescriptions do not mark the limits of gendered difference. Mela Krêkar's own life story is illustrative. In March 2010, Krêkar had been living continuously in Norway for six years, with sporadic jail terms and periods of house arrest after being charged with inciting terrorism and threatening Norwegian politicians. In a series of ten consecutive meetings on Paltalk, he devoted eleven hours to telling his life story and then answering queries from those present in the chat room. Someone asked, "Did your wife ever feel tired or exhausted?" He replied: "Naturally, I called her and asked her, and she said, 'No, I was never tired; I did it all for God's sake. And because I did it all for

God's sake, I don't think it was anything beyond the usual.'"[34] He recounts some details of their marriage contract,[35] and then he describes his wife:

> And thanks to God, by the mercies of God, for me, she was both a wife and the man of the house. And you know, in these last years, these last seven years, she has been the one to go out and work. As for me, in this democratic country that is [supposedly] the peak of human rights, I am sitting at home like someone who is disabled. She is the one who provides for us.[36]

The wife of the jihadi, thus, became the "man of the house" while her husband was fighting or while he was under house arrest. He goes on to praise how his wife contributed to jihad, how she endured difficult times, and how she sought to protect him when he was at home and under the surveillance of the Norwegian government and in danger of assassination. While he considered it less than ideal that his wife work to support the family, the violation of rights did not occur when she worked but rather when the Norwegian government prohibited him from working.

Thus, if certain dimensions of Krêkar's vision of gender roles evoke common divisions of labor, calling them "conservative" overlooks the fact that a reversal of those gendered divisions is possible. That reversal is not a tragedy or a violation of women's "nature,"[37] but it is a testament to the fact that, as he puts it a few sentences later, a "Kurdish wife is a citadel for her husband." For Krêkar, Muslim women's capacities are not limited to domestic child rearing but include intensive labor and jihad itself. This is not to say that Mela Krêkar will find allegiance with feminists, only that the fault lines of their disagreements would not boil down to fixed gender roles or women's abilities. He seems to approach a conclusion to praising his wife when he says, "Certainly, if it was not for my spouse, I could not have become the Krêkar who I am."[38]

Yet in the very next breath, he adds another relative to the list of those who made him the "Krêkar he is"—his brother:

> That is the first one, and the second supporter is my brother Khalid, who for thirty-six years has been like a brother and a friend and an adviser, and he has not put off anything [that I've asked of him]. If I were a bird, they were my two wings, and I don't distinguish right from left wings.[39]

Krêkar describes an image of family life that revolves around companionate marriage. But the picture of that marriage is not a husband and wife considered in isolation. It is a husband and wife who thrive with the support of the husband's brother. Again Krêkar evokes a relationship that resonates with Newzad's experiences. For Newzad, too, his companionship with his own wife was not something they enjoyed in isolation but something that transpired in conversation with and in the company of his brother. In-laws can serve as either supporters or threats. In either case, Krêkar's description of family relations in particular resonates with the picture of ordinary relationships more generally that this book has sought to offer: ethical lives and religious orientations in Kurdistan are discernible when considered as part of ordinary relationships that make up everyday life.

WITHIN AND BEYOND THE HOME

One notable feature of much Islamist thought across the Middle East is the vision of home as a sacrosanct domain, a place where Islam can thrive in contrast to public space, where secular states threaten Islam. As Ellen McLarney has shown in detail, Islamist activists in Egypt have borrowed this division of public and private from secular liberalism. It is a distinctive feature of secular liberalism to insist that women, family, and religion belong together as a "private" domain that ought to be autonomous from the state's efforts to guard "public interests." So when Islamist movements take for granted the domestic space of the home or the particular form of kinship that is heterosexual companionate marriage and make that space a "foundation" for an Islamic awakening, they end up putting a liberal category to work for Islamist goals.[40] This raises a question of the "relationships between relationships" in Krêkar's speeches and sermons: How are family relations like or unlike other ordinary relations? How, for example, does Krêkar describe relations between strangers in public?

The family is not a uniquely sacred or private space for Mela Krêkar in the way that it is for liberalism. Family relationships are a place of vulnerability rather than of moral safety or security. This is partially evident from the descriptions in which Krêkar assumes that families will include Muslims who hold different orientations to Islamic traditions. Parents are not necessarily reliable guides in the moral education of children. As in the verse of the Quran that he cited, parents may invite children onto the path of *kufir*, and it is the responsibility of children to decline that invitation while remaining "friends" with their parents.

Another reason that families cannot be assumed to be moral safe spaces is the particular threat of illicit sexual activity (*zîne*) that they harbor. Scenes from inside the home illustrate his point concerning illicit sex. Principally, in-laws—the sibling's spouse and the spouse's sibling—pose the greatest threats. Krêkar repeatedly advises that women refrain from breast-feeding in front of their brothers-in-law and that both men and women should take initiatives to avoid being in the room alone with others.[41] Furthermore, he suggests that there is a moral disaster (*fitna*) lying in wait anytime people share secrets about sexual relations beyond their spouses. If either husband or wife has a problem with the other, they must not reveal it in the household where brothers and sisters may learn about it.[42]

In regard to public space, Krêkar condemns the ease and accessibility of sex work that he witnessed in Europe. But in his address to Kurdish audiences, he generally assumes that the public availability of sex workers is not a threat to Muslims individually, and he does not advise them on how to respond. For Mela Krêkar, the greatest anxiety about sexuality among Muslims was not tied to the regulation of women's sexuality in public but appeared in the possibilities of illicit sex that lie within domestic space.

The stereotype that Islamist movements are especially concerned with regulating women's conduct in public and confining them to private space is a prominent feature of public discourse in Silêmanî, as it is around the world. In Silêmanî, it is often connected to the idea that during the 1990s, Islamists encouraged youth to hide in the alleys of the city and attack women whose legs were exposed by a skirt with a rubber-band gun, shooting thumbtacks or needles, or even by throwing acid.[43] Yet, as if he were responding to that stereotype, Mela Krêkar reverses the roles of the police and the policed in the following example:

> Muslim women are not simply soft and supple [*nerm u niyan*] when it comes to ethics and conduct [*edeb u exlaq*] since they have been raised on the ethics and conduct of the Quran. So it is necessary for Muslim women—it is incumbent on us, on our Muslim sisters!—that [whenever] someone appears in the alleyways with a question mark on his morals, go and threaten him [*hereşey lê bike*], offer him advice [*nesîhet*], threaten him with the resurrection [*hereşey qiyametî ke*], make him fear God![44]

When he speaks of someone who appears "with a question mark on his morals," he refers to men of poor conduct who follow women or catcall them. Krêkar instructs women to reprove men who act this way. He specifically critiques the idea of women as "soft" and suggests that the ethics of the Quran does *not* authorize "soft and supple" conduct in these circumstances. Women's appearance in public required no explanation or regulation, and they are instructed to police men's wayward sexuality.

Krêkar challenges a simple division between public and private space in other ways as well. In a sermon from the year 2000 that was given in Hewraman while under Islamist control, he identifies the task of child rearing as the topic of the sermon. Then, in a breathless staccato, he offers a short inventory of famous jihadis in and beyond Kurdistan who are the types of Muslim children that his audience should seek to raise. Line breaks offer a visual aid to help readers imagine the pacing of his speech and its poetic structure:

> My sermon is especially for the Muslim sisters to know how they should
> raise their boys and girls—
> how to raise them to give the sense of responsibility like that of Abdul-
> lah Azzam,
> how to build up within them the courage of confrontation like Osama
> bin Laden,
> the courage to speak … like Omer 'Ebdulrehman,
> to become like bees in their operations,
> like Anwar Shaban and Abu Talan;
> how to bring them up on the piety of Mela Şerîf,
> on work and commitment of Kak Şwan …
> on the purity of heart of those martyrs who gave their blood for *these*
> people of Islam.[45]

With this framing, and assuming that the raising of children happened in the household, one may expect a sermon that identifies modes of conduct unique to the home. But the sermon offers nothing of the sort. Consider the following sequence of advice. He says that Muslims should not be content, as they were in the 1970s, to simply learn the proper way to recite the Quran and memorize a few hadith. They should reestablish Islam through an extended struggle based on continual intellectual development. They must acquire an extensive knowledge of law and doctrine (*fîqh* and *'eqîde*), as well as knowledge of Islamic history. They must conduct the necessary disciplines (including prayer and fasting) to ensure the victory of divine unity (*tewhîd*) over polytheism (*şirk*), the victory of faith (*îman*) over apostasy (*kufir*), and the victory of piety (*teqwe*) over desire (*hewa*). Finally, they must exercise three particular virtues: the *patience* to make do in the short term by learning from books and cassettes, since most of the best scholars are in jail; the *courage* to sacrifice themselves in jihad as necessary; and the *initiative* to seek out knowledgeable Muslims who can clarify questions of law and doctrine.[46]

This long list of tasks for radical change is striking because even though it was framed as advice to Muslim women on how to raise properly Islamic children, nothing is flagged as unique to the family or even to the domestic space of the home. These conditions for raising Muslims do not have any necessary home where they belong; rather, they percolate throughout social relations and do not respect divisions of private and public. Even if he began by addressing Muslim women, he described the task of raising proper Muslim children as a task that all Muslims—not exactly families and not only mothers—share together. As the next section shows, building an Islamic society requires the participation of strangers in public.

GIVING ADVICE IN PUBLIC

Mela Krêkar frequently describes Muslims engaging one another through the practice of *nesîhet*. This Arabic term is frequently used in Kurdish in the way that "advice" is used in English. In a landmark study of this practice in Saudi Arabia, Talal Asad has shown that *nesîhet* is a concept and practice of "morally corrective criticism" or "moral advice." *Nesîhet* cuts across liberal distinctions of public and private because it can act as both a form of critique directed at institutional powers and an invitation to moral improvement. It can be conducted in an exclusive, one-on-one encounter, or it may take the form of an open letter addressed to the king. What is essential to the practice is not where or how it is carried out but the attitude and sensibility one embodies: one should possess proper knowledge of correct conduct, and one should share this knowledge in a spirit of kindness and gentleness.[47]

Krêkar offers two examples of *nesîhet* that bear on the question of how Muslims may relate to other Muslims beyond the purview of family relations. The first demonstrates the extent to which Krêkar would like to incorporate modern modes of technology and surveillance in his effort to wrest power away from the modern state and put it in the hands of Islam. In one passage, Krêkar describes a Kuwaiti group's practice of giving *nesîhet* as exemplary:

> When someone contravened the divine law [*şer'*], they would go and print it out on paper from a computer—just like the papers that traffic police use—and they would put it on the windshield of the car. The fellow thinks that he got a traffic ticket, but he looks at it and sees that it is *nesîhet*.[48]

In the passage that follows, Krêkar goes on to explain that one must bear in mind that what seems to be a contravention of law may have extenuating circumstances that mitigate one's guilt. Who knows what kind of argument the fellow had before leaving home that day, and who knows what kind of financial pressure he was dealing with when he made that mistake? By refraining from judgment, Muslims who offer *nesîhet* not only protect their own souls from the arrogance of judging others, but they also mitigate the affective state in which they offer the *nesîhet*. This, in turn, increases the chances that it will yield a positive result, since those who receive *nesîhet* are more likely to benefit from it if they are not humiliated by the procedure itself. Krêkar requires that Muslims refrain from rushing to judge their fellow Muslims, and at the same time he invites them to a vigilant observation of public interactions that separates faith from *kufir*.

A second example recalls the experiences of Ramadan that Pexshan and her daughter described. According to Pexshan's teenage daughter, who did not cover her head with a scarf, Ramadan was a time when other Muslims would more readily express their expectation that she wear a scarf and so become a *muhejebe*, embodying Muslim virtues in a more comprehensive way. On one occasion, Mela Krêkar indicates that precisely this kind of advice counts as *nesîhet*, instructing Muslims to encourage those who wore the scarf during Ramadan to also wear it during the rest of the year:

> Ramadan is a period of cleansing and purification; more people come to Islam, and it is easier to speak with them and encourage them in Islam; anyone you see who has a scarf over their heads, with a long jacket and [modestly dressed], [you see that they] have the love of God in their hearts; we can express a special love for them. But it is necessary to advise them as well [*nesîhet*]; so you should ask them, "Why won't you become *muhejebe* [year-round] if you are [already] fasting?"[49]

Krêkar then imagines a scenario in which the woman receiving that advice responds: "The woman says, 'But those who are *muhejebe*, people don't go and ask for their hand in marriage; I'm afraid that I won't get married. Some people at the office don't like it if a woman is *muhejebe*.'"[50] Krêkar's response to this hypothetical objection is to emphasize that one's husband has been decided by God, and this is not a decision that can be undone by wearing a scarf. By imagining this sort of interaction in a sermon, Krêkar provides an example of the kind of conduct that is suitable to the performance of *nesîhet* with complete strangers one encounters in public. The "adviser" keeps a cool tone, allows those receiving advice to explain themselves, and then offers in response a reasoned reply that invites the woman to demonstrate faith in God's appointment of a husband as an extension of faith in general.

For Mela Krêkar, the heart of the Islamic awakening is a knowledge that separates faith from *kufir* in the practical details of ordinary relations. He anticipates the temporal arc of the awakening as a long process: it cannot be accomplished through the usurpation of power that political parties usually seek but must allow truth to precede power. The process depends on offering *nesîhet* in a range of ordinary relationships: from youth to their parents, among in-laws, and between strangers in public. This is not a conservative view of family relations but a radical transformation of them. Neither does this view keep family relations contained in a private domain alongside women and religion. It is a comprehensive vision of what Krêkar calls an "Islamic society."

Yet the Islamic society is not composed exclusively of Muslims. If Krêkar calls Muslims to vigilance toward the appearance of faith and *kufir* in the lives of other Muslims, then what sort of conduct does he expect of them in their relations with those who are not Muslim? Given the centrality of non-Muslim figures of thought to the Kurdish poetic tradition of the nineteenth century, and given the productivity of imagining oneself—or one version of one's self—as a Zoroastrian or Christian, one must wonder what kind of relationship Krêkar envisions between pious Muslims and Christians in contemporary Kurdistan.

THE RIGHTS OF CHRISTIANS AND JEWS

Mela Krêkar and the Pillar Poets share several assumptions about how Muslims should relate to non-Muslims. They assume both the ascendance of Islam and ongoing relations with Christians and Jews. But Krêkar shares much more in common with the twentieth-century Kurdish poets who were anxious about the incursion of foreign Christians. The poet Narî had been concerned that "Kurdistan would become a church," and he had praised an Armenian Christian girl who converted to Islam by regarding her as the forefront of a battle against the English and French, in which "Imam Ali is your comrade facing the foreigners."[51] Two excepts from Mela Krêkar's sermons illustrate how his call for radical transformation mobilized a difference between Muslims, on the one hand, and Christians and Jews, on the other.

One passage that touches on this theme is interesting for the way it recalls Newzad's descriptions of Imam Ali. Mela Krêkar relates a slightly different version of the same story, referring to Imam Ali as Ali Ibn Talib:

> There was a Jewish fellow who insulted Islam. He insulted the Prophet of God (peace be upon him). Ali (may God accept him) attacked him and threw him to the ground; he drew out his sword, and then the man underneath him spit on Ali. Ali (may God accept him), got up off him. The Jewish man thought it was strange, but Ali explained things, and he said, "My first anger is for God, and my second anger is my own."[52]

Following this anecdote, Krêkar speaks for almost ten minutes on contemporary examples of Muslims who were fighting in jihad yet acted with kindness toward their enemies. The point of these stories was that even in conditions of war, it was not warranted to execute Jews or Christians *because* they were Jews or Christians. In another sermon he repeats this point and recites the hadith that "if anyone kills one of those who have taken a treaty with Islam (a *dhimma* [Ar.], which is to say, Christians and Jews), then the scent of paradise will be kept from him for seventy years."[53] In Newzad's telling, this story had been evidence of Imam Ali's "peace-loving" nature, but for Mela Krêkar, it is evidence of a deep sense of justice and humility that animates Imam Ali's courage in fighting jihad. Through this story and the hadith, Krêkar paints a picture of an ascendant Islam that recognizes the rights of Christians and Jews. In the sermons that I have been able to study, Krêkar never speaks disparagingly of the native Christian populations in Kurdistan. He emphasizes that Muslims can and should live peacefully alongside Christians, affording Christians their own freedom of religion.[54]

At the same time, Mela Krêkar emphasizes differences between Christianity and Islam. In discussing these differences, it is not for the purpose of interreligious dialogue but with the goal of protecting what he considered an uncorrupted *'eqîde*—doctrine intertwined with action. As one sermon illustrates very clearly, Krêkar's descriptions of Christians is mobilized to correct the practices of Muslims and sharpen their knowledge of what separates faith from *kufir*.

The sermon, apparently from December 1999, begins by lamenting all the money European countries will waste on fireworks for the occasion of the New Year when there are still people in the world who die of hunger. Within Kurdistan, he states that many will be imitating European Christians in this way, but using the word *multezîm*, he states unambiguously that "for the committed Muslim human [*însanî muselmanî multezîm*], it is not permissible to celebrate the first of January 2000."[55] He goes on to specify that it is not permissible for Muslims to attend parties at their own house or the houses of others or even to buy new clothes for the occasion. He then prescribes the proper mode of addressing Christians during this time, speaking generally about the New Year as the time of year when Christians also celebrate the birth of Jesus. Krêkar speaks of the Kurdish phrase *cejnit pîroz bêt*, which colloquially could translate to English as "happy holidays," but the literal meaning is closer to "may your holiday be sacred/blessed." Krêkar makes a short argument about the implications of "sacralizing" a Christian holiday with this phrase:

> It is not permissible to say to a Christian "cejnit pîroz bêt"; it is better to say "salêkî xoş" [Happy New Year], or "hîwadarim salî dehatut xoştir bêt" [I hope next year will be even better for you], or some polite expression of that kind. But it is not permissible to say something to them that falls in the category of sacralizing [*le sîxey mubarek bun*], because if we sacralize that holiday, then it means that we have called the Quran a lie, where God said that Jesus was not killed, but they [Christians] consider Jesus to have been crucified.[56]

The logic animating his argument here conflates the Christian celebration of Easter as the resurrection of a crucified Jesus with Christian celebrations of Christmas as the season of the birth of Jesus. Krêkar reasons that if a Muslim acknowledges that celebration as holy or sacred (*pîroz* in Kurdish and *mubarak* in Arabic), then they have granted legitimacy to the doctrines behind it—that is, the doctrines that Jesus was crucified (Easter) or born as the "son of God" (Christmas). To acknowledge the legitimacy of those doctrines would be, in Krêkar's phrase, to call the Quran a lie. His solution is the phrase "I hope next year will be even better for you," which is awkward and stilted in Kurdish, sounding almost as if it were translated from a foreign language.

Krêkar's sermon did not mention efforts to prevent or constrain Christian celebrations, but he sought to completely curtail Muslim participation in Christian celebrations by deriving doctrinal conclusions from that participation. Precisely because doctrines and actions were so deeply intertwined in his view, he compared Muslim participation in a Christian celebration to what his audience would consider a radical act of *kufir*: calling the Quran a lie. In this case, Krêkar's evocation of Christians' *rights*, in the legal sense, was part of a larger effort to persuade Muslims of what was *right*—in the sense of what fell within the bounds of faith and rejected *kufir*. The difference *between* religions (Islam and Christianity) was thus crucial to mobilize a difference *within* Islamic tradition (between acts of faith and acts of *kufir*) and inspire Muslims toward faith.

In Krêkar's vision of an Islamic society, the key principle for regulating relations between Muslims is the definitive knowledge of what separates faith from *kufir*. The arena in which that knowledge works is that of ordinary relationships: both family relations and the relations between Muslim strangers that make up public space. If the Pillar Poets' route to piety was to ask themselves whether they were *kafir*s and to open up a route back to piety that may pass through Christianity or Zoroastrianism, then Mela Krêkar's route to piety requires constant vigilance over others, a constant readiness to call others away from their *kufir* and back to faith. And if the Pillar Poets found the co-presence of faith and *kufir* a paradox that was productive of striving, Mela Krêkar saw a deep dichotomy between faith and *kufir*: a battle that it was every Muslim's duty to wage against *kufir*. In waging that battle, though, Krêkar made the pursuit of piety much more difficult for Muslims such as Pexshan and Newzad.

The presence of different religious orientations within a single family is understood as given in contemporary Kurdistan, and the question of how to address those differences is raised over and over again. Mela Krêkar proposes one response to the question. His voice is a loud one in the field of religious discourse in Kurdistan. Yet from the perspective of the ordinary relationships of everyday life, his voice is one from a broad spectrum that includes other revivalists, other ways of being pious, and other ways of imagining and describing religious difference. The recurrence of the question of religious difference within families in Kurdistan both constrains every family to answer it in some way and affords them some degree of freedom and creativity to find or forge their own response. As Magnus Marsden has suggested, the study of "so-called revivalist Islam" should also address the "multiple types of resistance it generates."[57] The next chapter examines other responses to the question of religious difference at home, which constitutes a form of resistance or dissent to Mela Krêkar's call for transformation.

Chapter 5

PLEASURE BEYOND PIETY

Religious Difference in Domestic Space

ADDRESSING HIS DAUGHTER, SHADMAN SAID, "DON'T SPEAK ABOUT God and the Prophet with them." We were sitting in his home where I was their guest for lunch. His daughter was preparing to visit a friend's home in the afternoon, and although Shadman had no objection to her visiting the friend, he added this small piece of advice couched within a broader discussion of how she would go and when. Later in the afternoon as we sat together in his study, he explained to me the context of his advice. His daughter had been friends with the children of this family since she was young. Even in the early 1990s, this family had Islamist tendencies, and Shadman regarded them with suspicion. But, he said, why should that prevent children from playing together? As time passed, though, the children became more *tundraw*—more intense or more radical—like their parents. Now his daughter still visited them and savored their old friendship. But these visits left Shadman anxious about the influence they would have on her. He described the friends by saying that their conversations were always about "separating *haram* and halal." He added, "Other than this, they don't have anything to talk about."

As they appear on the written page here, translated into English, the words "Don't speak about God and the Prophet with them" may appear to be a stark command or an imposition of authority. Lingering in the background was some disagreement, as his daughter may be inclined to speak about God and the Prophet with them while Shadman thought it was best not to. Yet in the context of the conversation, they were merely a footnote to the discussion of the people whom she would visit, who was at the house these days, who had gotten married, who was working where now, how his daughter would get there, and how long she would stay. In other words, Shadman's words were more advice than commands about how his daughter ought to live. Even if these words indexed a difference between them, they were part of a broader interaction in which there was an implicit agreement on more mundane details about what to do for the afternoon.

These kinds of interactions were precisely what preoccupied Mela Krêkar because he understood them as the arena in which Islamic awakening was either carried out or delayed. Krêkar worked from the assumption that the moral formation of individuals took place in relationships over a long period of time, through the accrual of small events, small gestures, and advice. This chapter continues the task of examining how religious orientations emerge in everyday life through small gestures embedded in ongoing relationships. Previous chapters have focused on the fault lines, potentials for conflict, and experiments that appeared in the lives of Pexshan and Newzad. Shadman's relationships also include similar features. But the interactions that I heard about and witnessed between Shadman and his family offer an important reminder that alongside the potential for pain or conflict lies great potential for pleasure and joy—even among those with quite different orientations to Islamic traditions. Thus, different kinds of pleasure and joy offer an important lens through which to think about the relation between Muslims who take up a path to piety and Muslims who turn away from it.

Essential to the task is to attend carefully to the small acts—small events, small gestures, small pieces of advice—and the way that actors themselves describe those acts. The question of how to describe small acts in particular, and religious orientation in general, is not only the task of ethnography. It is a task that saturates everyday life and ordinary relationships in which Muslims engage others across shades of difference in their orientation to Islam. In order to render the *texture* of these small acts, it is necessary to focus in close detail on how relationships unfold in time. So rather than isolate a single small act that I witnessed in the lives of different interlocutors, I focus on a series of small acts that unfold within a single set of relationships, which all revolve around a single individual.

By attending to the way that Shadman and others describe both their own religious orientation and that of others, I consider questions that connect the study of Muslim ethics to a broader anthropology of ethics. Much recent work in the anthropology of ethics has touched on the question of how ethics are described. Some have insisted that ethics can be described abstractly, as "relatively fixed statements about what is good and bad."[1] According to this view, clear claims are at least implicit in ethical life. If people themselves do not always make those claims clear, then it can become the work of the anthropologist to make people's implicit ethical orientations into clear or "fixed" statements.

Another view of ethics insists that people do not demonstrate ethics only when they make prescriptive statements or explicit claims. Even though such statements often occur in particularly dramatic moments, Veena Das writes that people "get the feel of the rightness of certain actions or pronouncements only when [they] can take these dramatic moments and integrate them into the flux of everyday life."[2] In this sense, statements about how Muslims should behave toward non-Muslims, for example, may make sense to people only when they are part of an unfolding story in their daily lives. This view resonates with Sandra Laugier's account of texture as "an unstable reality that cannot be fixed by concepts, or by determinate particular objects, but only by the recognition of gestures, manners, and styles."[3] Rather than attempt to solicit or deduce propositions from Shadman's speech, I reach beyond propositional statements to describe the texture that appeared in the "flux of everyday life" where Shadman and his family described one another's gestures, manners, and styles. Small acts—as small as a meaningful silence or a choice of words when describing others—can illuminate ethical orientations both to others in one's life and to Islamic traditions more broadly.

The chapter also draws a critical eye to the role of pleasure and joy in these small acts. Scholarship on the theme of pleasure has usually focused on sexual pleasure, but I examine the joyful character of experience beyond sexuality and provide a new way to think about the politics of pleasure beyond the regulation or exploitation of sex, where pleasure frequently appears alongside the analytic of domination. At the same time, the focus on pleasures that persist in relations characterized by different orientations to Islamic traditions shows how some Kurdish Muslims are able to sustain those relations in a spirit of receptivity and accommodation.

DESCRIBING RELIGIOUS ORIENTATION

Shadman had found security and comfort in an upper-middle-class lifestyle after 2003. He kept company with a group of intellectuals who often worked, as he did, in a shifting combination of journalism, literary criticism, creative writing in various genres, and translation. But unlike other intellectuals I knew, Shadman spent less time in the public settings I frequented. Home was his favorite place to be, and he regularly invited me to join him there. I met with him in his home and the homes of his relatives in Silêmanî and Hewlêr, usually spending several days a month immersed in their life over a period of more than a year. I slept in his study, ate with the family and the regular stream of other guests whom they hosted, and visited other families with them. I eventually entered and left the home freely, even in Shadman's absence.

When we spoke alone together, I often scribbled notes that I would then expand from memory when typing them up that night or in the following days. These typed notes were interspersed with accounts of short interactions I had or witnessed with his family. While those interactions felt incidental at the time, they have become essential to my account because they include Shadman and others in his household describing how they related to one another and to Islamic traditions.

Shadman's mother was frequently at the house when I was there. She had been pleased with him as a child, he once told me with a hint of irony, because he went to the mosque every morning to pray and stayed much longer than was necessary. She had called him "light" (*nuranî*), a term usually reserved for saintly figures who reflected the light of divinity toward those they encountered. His mother's description of his former self was in part a description of something that she valorized and admired. The irony was that Shadman no longer prayed or fasted. Furthermore, he did not exhort his children to practice these disciplines.

At the beginning of Ramadan, I once asked his daughter who in the household would be fasting, and she replied matter-of-factly, "All of us." Then a moment later she added, as if to keep me from forgetting the obvious, "except for my father . . . he doesn't listen."

The expression she used, *gwê nadat*, translates literally as "he does not lend an ear." It can indicate either discernment in disregarding what is insignificant (as when one ignores bad advice) or stubbornness or carelessness (as when one ignores good advice). More generally, it can refer to one's approach to a broader state of affairs, as when one does not worry or preoccupy oneself with something. During my fieldwork, the phrase was a common description of some Muslims' orientation toward Islamic traditions, and it was exactly how Newzad's wife described his relation to Islam. The idiom of "not listening" describes a person's orientation to Islam with the image of closed ears, a distracted or inattentive body. The idiom indicates that although one sees oneself as a Muslim and acknowledges the obligations to pray, fast, and abstain from alcohol, one shrugs them off. But it does not diagnose that *shrugging* gesture—a turn away from piety—in specific terms of deficiency in faith or belief. Thus, the idiom could express praise, disappointment, condemnation, or matter-of-factness; or it could encompass all these possibilities, settling on none. In this ordinary conversation, his daughter's description of Shadman's relation to Islamic traditions appeared ambiguous to me but without a trace of condemnation. It was as profound as it was subtle.

The image cannot be translated into a clear proposition or statement of belief. To do so, one would have to answer questions such as these: Who or what is not being listened to: the Quran, or God, or all religious requirements? How temporary or permanent is this not listening? The usefulness of the idiom derives in part from its not asking those questions. "Not listening" is a description of Shadman's relation to fasting that provides a picture of his relation to Islamic traditions not as his own declaration but from his daughter's perspective.

The subtlety of his daughter's description sharply contrasts with the other, more charged terms such as "secular" or "atheist" that were available to her. Those charged terms had been inflected with acrimonious political debate and violence in Kurdistan's recent history during and after the civil war. After Islamists entered mainstream politics, they invested heavily in media institutions that allowed them a prominent voice in public debate. There was a familiar cycle of debate that staged an opposition between Islamists and secularists: Islamist activists claimed that the public speech of secularists was injurious and leveled accusations of apostasy (*kufir*), diagnosing signs of *kufir* in ways that resembled Mela Krêkar's instructions. Islamist activists and preachers appeared on television and grouped together secularists with those who do not pray or fast as atheists (*mulhîd*), apostates (*kafir*), or irreligious (*bêdîn*) or described them in other terms intended as insults. In response, secularist activists often doubled down on their right to free speech and characterized the Islamists as authoritarians who call their political enemies apostates. I heard these terms of public debate through television programs projected into the domestic space of Shadman's house.

Against that background, the stakes of Shadman's daughter's description become clearer. When she said that her father does not listen, she indicated that he neither fasts nor aspires to fast. Yet she also refrained from criticizing him for it. She had described and acknowledged her father's orientation without allowing the acrimony of public discourse to determine or co-opt it—a small gesture that cannot be taken for granted.

THE APPLE OF BELIEF AND THE DARK HUMAN

The image of "not listening" resonates with Shadman's own descriptions of his religious orientation. One day he asked me how my research was coming along. I told him about the sense of contradiction that I had noticed when some Muslims in Kurdistan talked about Islam in their life. They claimed not to believe but still found Islam in their lives. To my surprise, many of them regarded that as a problematic contradiction. Responding to that idea, Shadman spoke slowly and allowed me to scribble his words in my notebook. Using the Kurdish word *bawer*, which is very close to the English "belief," he said,

> Belief is like an apple. If you throw away one, the tree is still there! In our society it [belief] has become like this: it has become a part of the system of ideas [Ar. *afkar*] so that even if you don't have belief, your ideas still have the same appearance [*şêwe*]. You see, there are some beliefs that become a part of the conduct [*siluk*] of society. They become so widespread that they can't simply be pulled up and thrown out.

In the ensuing discussion, he mentioned the idea that it becomes a matter of a physiology. He said that Islam is "in the blood," like "meat on our bones":

> You can say, "I will stop eating meat," but the fact is that after thousands of years of human history, this human body we have now has come about because humans have been eating meat! Things don't come to an end so easily. So [even if] a man says, "I'm not Islamic," Islam is still in his body. And I think that religion is still a part of humanity.

The end of that conversation captured his point succinctly. Using the term *dîn* to refer to Islam specifically but also "religion" more generally, he said, "My point is that being cut off [*dabiran*] from *dîn* is hard; it is difficult. You can't say 'It's over!' and have it over. The world is a religious world. Our entire understanding of the world is religious."

Shadman's description of belief drew on some familiar themes but also offered a new perspective and a provocative metaphor. Two important points about belief and its disavowal are necessary to appreciate the subtle innovations of Shadman's descriptions. First, belief is a central component of Islamic traditions, and a commonly recited hadith of the Prophet known as the hadith of Gabriel illustrates that centrality clearly. The hadith actually describes *îman*, or faith, which often should be regarded as distinct from the English idea of belief, but for the purpose of understanding the hadith and Shadman's speech, it will suffice to say that both faith and belief as described here involve confident affirmation of a truth.[4]

In this hadith, the angel Gabriel appears in disguise and asks the Prophet Muhammad, "Tell me about *îman*." The Prophet responds, "*Iman* means that you have faith in God, His angels, His books, His messengers, and the Last Day, and that you have faith in the measuring out, both its good and its evil."[5] This hadith enjoins Muslims to affirm the singularity of God, the existence of angels, and the various revelations that God has sent and the messengers who brought them. It also enjoins them to anticipate the resurrection and judgment (the Last Day) and to acknowledge and accept God's authority to decree good and bad for humanity. Thus, faith or belief encompasses affirming and acknowledging all these things.

What happens if a Muslim does not affirm one of those elements? And how does one know if a Muslim does not affirm one of those elements? This is the second point of context, for Muslim scholars in Kurdistan have considered faith a state of being in which three aspects of one's being complement one another: a condition of the heart is expressed by the tongue and realized in action.[6] There is a range of ways to respond to a Muslim when one of those three aspects does not match the others—when one loses faith in one's heart, speaks in a way that denies the elements of faith, or acts in such a way as to suggest that one of those elements is not true.[7] For example, in extreme cases, some scholars may prescribe execution for a Muslim who publicly denies having any faith or invites others to deny faith. Without deciding anything at all about the condition of that Muslim's heart, the denial of faith with the tongue may be judged to demand that punishment. However, in most cases scholars would encourage a kind response, hoping that wayward Muslims who question whether they have faith in their hearts or who do not follow up on that faith by praying will repent. Thus, a seeming disavowal of an article of belief is rarely taken as absolute or binding.

In this context, Shadman's description of belief echoes this last approach insofar as he separates the matter of speaking about belief from the matters of *having* belief or acting in belief. He says that even if one disavows faith with one's tongue, belief may still be present in one's actions. Yet rather than insist that the presence of belief in one's actions is an expression of the heart, Shadman describes two other dimensions of human experience that can produce belief in behavior.

The first is the role of "society" and history, which he compares to a tree: even if the individual claims not to have belief, the tree of society will continue producing belief all around the person. To extend Shadman's metaphor, even if one throws out the apple of belief, one cannot thereby escape the shadow of the apple tree, which continues to produce belief all around one. A second dimension is the physiology of the human body, its blood and bones. He described Islam as being *given*, taken for granted, in the same way that bodies often are. Contrary to the idea that human beings can fashion themselves as moral beings in accordance with their own will, Shadman emphasized the resilience of the body as a place where religion endures despite efforts to change it. Thus, both society and the body are thoroughly religious, no matter what one says or does to try to change that. Not even a declaration of unbelief could change that constitution. As he put it, "You can't say 'it's over' and have it over."

Shadman cast doubt on the sufficiency of abstract claims about belief to give a proper picture of religious orientation among Muslims in Iraqi Kurdistan. In this short exchange, he had spoken as a Kurdish Muslim, but he had adopted a philosophical or sociological register for describing the lives of others. As provocative and memorable as this conversation was, it left me curious about how he might describe the dynamic of speaking and doing in his own life.

The day after that conversation we sat alone in his study talking. I borrowed his own turn of phrase to ask Shadman about the extent to which he considered himself "cut off from religion." "It is not so important to me to say that I have quit Islam [*wazm le Islam hênawe*]," he said. "I didn't decide that I will never fast or that I will never pray. But I simply never felt that I needed to do it. I never had the feeling [that] 'right now, I should go pray.'"

His relation to prayer is not an active disavowal but a lack of active pursuit. He hears the call to prayer, but he does not hear it echo in his soul, and thus he does not listen. In the very next breath, though, he gave a picture of his own religious orientation as constituted through engaging with intimate others. He answered my question about his relation to religion in part by describing his relations to others:

> Of course, prayer and fasting have a place in my family. My daughter prays, and it is very important to her. And my wife prays, and they fast. But my fam-

ily was not built on this, that I could say, "You should believe as I do." So God exists [*bunî heye*] in my family, and prayer exists in my family. Here, there is an Islamic atmosphere [*feza'êkî Islamî*] that I am never opposed to. There are even practices [*çalakî*] that are present in my life. When they fast, I help them, and I eat with them when they eat. I celebrate the holidays with them. I visit the cemetery with them. If I decide to oppose *dîn* [Islam], then I should give up all of those things! I should say that there should be no prayer in my house. How could I? Those who say that they have no *dîn*, they can't participate in anything. None of the rituals of society. If you become this kind of person, then you become a dark human [*însanêkî tarîk*].

Shadman's description of his family as "not built on" instructions about what to believe puts this chapter's opening scene into relief. If his words to his daughter were not explicit instructions, they were at least a form of advice. But the difference is crucial to Shadman, since forms of advice and encouragement (or discouragement) still find a place in a home where different orientations to Islam appear next to each other.

I pressed the question of the relation between religion and belief briefly, asking him if he might consider himself to be religious but unbelieving. The question opened a pathway for him to revise or expand his earlier description of belief, but his response suggested that his view of the matter was clear and consistent. He thought this was not a good description:

To say that I don't believe—well, if I really didn't believe, then why not tell them not to bury me as a Muslim? I can *say* that. I can *say* that I don't believe, but speaking is only a small part of the depth of human beings. And the practice is still there, even if I were to say with my mouth that belief is not there.

Opposing Islamic practices is not feasible for Shadman. The reason he offers for this is provocative. He does not describe a fear of rejection or persecution but rather an aversion to self-imposed isolation. The "dark human" here is a lonely figure that obscures and impedes relationships, one that stands in contrast to the "light" of saintly figures that Shadman's mother had seen in his younger self. In describing how Islamic practices have a presence in his and his family's lives, his participation in the "rituals of society" is not the work of pious moral striving but rather the ordinary work of sustaining relationships in the household. This participation involved activities like visiting the graveyard with his family, a common activity in Kurdistan.

Thus, the ritual disciplines and everyday life are proximate but not identical in their household. For the family's practice of the disciplines of prayer and fasting were as much a part of ordinary life as was Shadman's nonpractice. Without practicing, Shadman was still present and could thus participate in the life of others as they practiced. It was in that sense that he could say that the practices were still present no matter what he *said* about belief. An instrumentalist explanation of how Shadman participates in Islamic rituals may suggest that he used religion to keep up relationships. But the metaphor of Islam as an apple tree disrupts that interpretation. In that metaphor, Islam is part of the atmosphere—the very air that one breathes—not something that one could manipulate at will. The house is filled with disciplinary practice, but individual ways of relating to that practice diverge sharply.

Here again the difference in orientation appears between pious Muslims and those who do not listen. Declarations of belief or unbelief do not neatly capture this difference. Just as important, such declarations do not capture the ways that Shadman and his family acknowledge their own differences. Instead, the descriptions and expressions that appear in this family demonstrate a complex range of relations to Islam. Even if Shadman does not listen, both Shadman and his family show and describe that religious orientation carefully, and Shadman emphasizes that his relation to Islam is inseparable from his relation to his pious Muslim kin. Showing care in how they describe themselves and one another is one way that they sustain ordinary relations. In their descriptions of his orientation to Islam, both Shadman and his daughter privilege showing and engaging over knowing or saying.

These descriptions illustrate how ordinary relationships characterized by religious difference reshape the theological claims about belief. Within the bounds of the discursive tradition, Muslim scholars had derived those claims from the foundational text of the hadith. Without challenging or reforming theological claims, and without attempting to depart from the discursive tradition, these scenes from everyday life show a great deal of accommodation of the persistent reluctance to pursue piety.

Chapters 1 and 3 both demonstrate how the prospect for conflict was interwoven with everyday life in families that include both pious Muslims and those who "don't listen." Perhaps because I was attuned to the prospect of conflict and division, an invitation to think more carefully about pleasure took me by surprise. The invitation came not from Shadman but from a friend of his whom I will call

Hama. Although I met Hama only once, he issued a dramatic invitation to think about pleasure that became a turning point for my thinking about Shadman and his household.

HAMA'S OFFER OF PLEASURE

One day I found myself in the car with Shadman driving to downtown Hewlêr. Along the way, we picked up Shadman's friend Hama. Shadman first told Hama that I was interested in classical Kurdish poetry; then, after routine greetings, Hama adjusted his tone of voice so he sounded frank and sincere. "Which poet do you enjoy most?" he asked.

People often asked me this question during my research in Kurdistan, but it usually followed a longer conversation in which we had tested each other's broader knowledge of classical Kurdish poetry before discussing our preferences. In contrast, Hama had cut to the chase. I interpreted his query as a test, but a test of my passions rather than my memory. He had emphasized the word "enjoy" (*hez lê bun*) in such a way that I felt that he was saying, "If you tell me which poet you love the most, I'll know what you're capable of." Rather than challenge me to prove my intellectual virtuosity by reciting rhyme schemes or recognizing a turn of phrase from a line of poetry, he wanted to know what pleasure I found in my study.

I answered by naming Mehwî, whose poetry from the nineteenth century is renowned in contemporary Kurdistan as a beautiful example of Kurdish Sufi poetry. (He was Newzad's favorite as well.) When Hama asked why, I said that I found in his poetry a picture of life as an ongoing struggle beset with suffering. Hama acknowledged Mehwî's greatness but insisted that Nalî—another Kurdish poet, who preceded Mehwî by a few decades—is more enjoyable: "There is a flavor [*lezet*] in Nalî! For me, it's very different from Mehwî. When I read Nalî, I enjoy it, but Mehwî is different. Mehwî works on your soul and psyche [*roh u nefs*], and it tires you."

In the conversation that ensued, Hama said he considered himself a "religious person" (*şexsêkî dînî*) and was committed to the disciplines of prayer and fasting, setting himself apart from Shadman. He went on to describe Nalî's effect on him: "After reading Nalî, I see the world in a different way. I see more of the beauty of the world." He illustrated this by saying that after reading Nalî's poem about donkeys, he sees donkeys in a new way, and after reading Nalî's poem about the *hucre* (the room for study in a mosque), he sees the *hucre* in a new way as well. He then elaborated by referring to the Iranian poet Sohrab Sepehri: "It's just like Sohrab Sepehri says: 'Wash your eyes to see the world!'"

Hama and I parted ways after that, but in sharing with me the pleasure he found in poetry, he had made me an offer of pleasure. It was an offer to take pleasure in poetry and to let that pleasure affect my vision or my way of being in the world. And indeed it has. Or at least it has affected my understanding of Shadman's world. Thinking about the role of pleasure and poetry, I began to see how they intertwined in Shadman's life.

PLEASURES OF SUFI POETRY

Shadman was particularly fond of citing fragments of poetry in conversation, and he would frequently fill a lull in the conversation with a spirited poetry recitation. He had memorized hundreds of couplets of Kurdish poetry and was familiar with the biographies of Kurdish poets and other Sufi figures. The night before he introduced me to Hama, Shadman and I stayed up late reading the following poem by Mehwî:

> In speaking of sorrow and grief, why don't I open my lips?
> blood from a broken heart billows from my breast to my lips.
> How it grieves me that like a child I put a flame to the page
> whenever I hold a pen to write my heart's dismal script.
> As long as the tongue works, seize the chance to pray today,
> the loose-tongued will be tongue-tied tomorrow; your lips will constrict.
> Of the truth only True! and of lies I have always said Lies!
> if they crucify me like Mansur, True, True, I'll insist.
> Set flame to the flower, let the nightingale turn and burn like a moth
> if the garden is charred, still I'll visit and sow my secrets in the wind.
> Tomorrow come to see my execution, I gave my word when she gave hers
> but I cannot keep my promise if she never keeps our tryst.
> I said, "If you understood Mehwî, would you abuse him like this?"
> she said, "If he understood at all, why ask angels and men to keep a tryst?"[8]

Here is the sense of the poem I gleaned from my conversation with Shadman, who interpreted the beloved in the poem as feminine. The pain, sorrow, grief, and agony of Mehwî fill his chest like an ocean of blood that would spill out of his mouth if he began to speak of them. Whenever he takes up a pen to write of his grief, the grief is too much for the page to bear, and it goes up in flames—who but a child would burn paper this way? Still he takes the opportunity while he is alive to beseech the favor of God since Judgment Day is imminent. On that day, the chance for supplication will pass, and those who spent their words foolishly will be silenced. One who holds on to the truth as desperately as Mehwî must be prepared for a martyr's death, like the one suffered by Mansur Al-Hallaj, a ninth-century Muslim mystic who was executed for uttering the apparently blasphemous phrase "I am the truth." The bitter prospect of such a death and the surging grief in his breast turn a beautiful flower into a flame, so the one who sang to his beloved as the nightingale sang to the flower becomes a moth that perishes in the flame. In such grief, death appears as a reprieve, and Mehwî prepared himself for that death when the beloved promised to deliver him to death. But the promise of a simple end was never kept, and the beloved refuses any promise of being united with Mehwî, since union is impossible between creatures as different as humans and angels (or "fairies").

Shadman described the labor of helping me understand Kurdish poetry in several ways. It was a matter of hospitality to a foreigner in Kurdistan and a guest in his home. It was also a matter of what he called "national duty" because Kurds were so poorly understood outside Kurdistan that he felt compelled to work with foreign researchers to help redress this problem. But when we reached the end of the poem that evening, Shadman's first words invoked none of these things. With a sense of awe, he said simply, "Wallah xoş bu!" A colloquial way to translate this phrase is "By God, that was great!" But attending to the sense of the Kurdish word *xoş*, a better translation would be "What a pleasure!"

The pleasures of the poem include the beauty of its rhyme and rhythm in Kurdish, as well as aspects of wordplay such as the repetition in the third couplet of "tongue" in Kurdish and Persian (*ziman* and *zuban*, respectively). The pleasures of the poem also encompass images of violence and discipline that may not initially seem "pleasing." At the heart of the poem lies the image of a violent execution, which appears to the poet as a reprieve from the suffering he must endure. This reflects the Sufi path to morally reforming the self, which requires the disciplined capacity to endure pain. Through the duties of prayer and fasting, the supererogatory performance of those duties, and the submission of oneself to a master, the carnal self is dissolved and the truer self is allowed to persist in the company of God.

By studying Sufism in Kurdish poetry, I had become attuned to these dimensions of struggle and suffering. But Shadman emphasized the pleasure of the poem, echoing Hama's idea that this pleasure was central to the experience. For along with the violence and discipline came pleasures—of visiting the garden even if it had been burned, of knowing the truth with such certainty that one could give one's life for it, and of course the pleasure of love itself. Most of these features are broadly characteristic of much Sufi poetry in and beyond Kurdistan, although Mehwî is unique among the poets of Kurdistan's classical tradition in his ability to condense and arrange them in the Kurdish language.

Describing a very different context where audiences respond to poetry, Steve Caton has suggested that when Yemeni tribal audiences acknowledged the beauty of a poem, they participated in a particular kind of tribal politics. When the North Yemeni tribal audience allowed itself to be impacted by the beauty of a poem, they did so within a relation of power that contributes to extending the aesthetics of the particular political form that is tribalism: "By listening to this poem, by being moved by its beauty and persuaded by its message, the audience is admiring a part—a very important part—of tribalism itself."[9] Thus, the beauty of a poem may be inseparable from the wider categories of thought and politics in which they make sense. If to Caton's interlocutor, the beauty of the poem was attached to the political life of the tribe, the beauty of Mehwî's poem for Shadman was attached to the wider category of Sufism. So what is it about Sufi poetry and Sufi figures that Shadman admired?

In the same conversation in which we sought to mark the limits of belief, he went on to describe his own relationship to Sufi figures. Here he took as examples Mehwî and another Kurdish poet, Mewlewî (1806–1882), who was renowned for poetry that linked Sufi thought and practice:

> I see depth in religion. That depth is very wonderful to me. The kind of person whose soul is satisfied [*qen'etêki rohî*] in Islam is wonderful to me. Those kinds of men are Mehwî and Mewlewî and the great Sufis. I kiss the hands of such a man. I kiss his hands because he has been able to put such a distance between himself and the filth of the world. He lives in a dialogue of the soul.

Here, Sufi figures appear as paradigms of satisfaction since their souls are pleased or "satisfied" by their commitment to Islam. A manual of Sufi thought written in Kurdish in the 1980s associates the word that Shadman used—*qen'et*—with *reza*, which it defines as "acceptance, pleasure, and satisfaction."[10] Through their commitment, they have overcome any desire for material gain and separated themselves from the corruption that Shadman called "the filth of the world." Shadman described his attraction to these figures through the image of his kissing their hands. Kissing the hands of an exemplary person in Kurdistan is a common practice done to many kinds of authoritative figures. The gesture may express admiration, deference, respect, or love. It may also indicate personal attachment to the seniority, learning, or insight of the one whose hand is kissed.[11] It is also widely practiced toward religious scholars and sheikhs but a practice that inspires revulsion among secularists, who perceive it as an expression of unreflective submission.[12] By describing his admiration of these figures through this gesture, Shadman not only snubbed a popular secularist attitude but also showed one of the ways that gestures common to Muslim life in Kurdistan are still a part of him. Shadman named two Kurdish poets as exemplary Sufi figures, illustrating how Sufism and poetry are inseparable, and often interchangeable, when discussing the history of Kurdish poetry.

Kurdish poets draw from and contribute to a larger Sufi tradition in which poetry and anecdotes from the lives of the great Sufis comingled. Of the many anecdotes featuring "great Sufis" that Shadman shared with me, two relate to the themes of this chapter. The first addresses a question of religious difference—in this case the difference between Jews and Muslims. The anecdote refers to Kak Ehmedî Sheikh (1795–1888), who is one of the most prestigious Sufi figures in Kurdistan, mentioned earlier as having arranged a marriage between his son and a Christian woman. His grave in Silêmanî is still a site of pilgrimage, and his collected letters are available in bookshops.[13] In my own paraphrase: Kak Ehmedî Sheikh was sitting in the Great Mosque in Silêmanî. A Jewish merchant had been doing business in the area and visited Kak Ehmed frequently. Kak Ehmed never asked this man about his religion. But one day, one of Kak Ehmed's companions asked the Jew, in view of the Jew's good moral character and good relations with the Kak Ehmed, why he would not become a Muslim. The Jewish merchant answered by contrasting the majority of Muslims with Kak Ehmed himself. "If Islam is what they do," he said, "then I have no need for it. If it is what he does, then I have no strength for it."[14]

The anecdote describes an important virtue but does not give it a name. Perhaps it is one of what Charles Hallisey calls "nameless virtues," which persist alongside the explicitly named and debated virtues but are illustrated more often than they are defined.[15] Strictly speaking, the virtue belongs to the story itself, not to any name or keyword that may be derived from the story. And the story, like the virtue, is one that prizes indirection, indication, and subtlety rather than straightforward claims or statements. For brevity's sake, we can refer to the virtue of the story as the virtue of not asking.

The virtue of not asking is what Kak Ehmed exercised by not asking the Jewish merchant about his religion or inviting him to become a Muslim. And the virtue of not asking is precisely what is missing in Kak Ehmed's poor companion who asks the Jew why he did not become a Muslim. Ironically, that query placed the companion among the Muslims whose religion the Jewish merchant does not need.

The anecdote foregrounds a tendency widely available to Muslims and non-Muslims to affirm religious plurality in Ottoman societies. Chapter 2 explains at great length what Aron Rodrigue has described more succinctly: "In the Ottoman context, the radical affirmation of difference entailed acceptance and toleration but also discrimination."[16] That is, "acceptance and toleration" were crucial to allowing Muslims, Jews, and Christians to coexist, but "discrimination" meant that Islam was still considered the superior religion. In this anecdote, the Jewish merchant appreciated the virtue of not asking about another's religion, but it was a pious Muslim who exemplified that virtue. The affirmation of difference appears as an Islamic virtue even if not all Muslims share it, so the natural superiority of Islam goes unquestioned. Many anecdotes that Shadman shared with me privileged a similar tendency to "radically affirm" religious difference. For Shadman, these stories and the Sufi poetry that accompanied them were a point of attraction to Islam. He described that attraction as a capacity to see depth in religion, and he named his own feeling as wonder at the pious Sufis who found satisfaction for their souls in Islam. In this sense, Shadman could acknowledge the pleasure that many Muslims find in the disciplines of piety.

A second anecdote relates to the question of the relation between speech and action in Muslim ethics. Unlike the first, this one comes from his own experience, and it describes the work of not a prominent Sufi figure but an ordinary, unnamed man in Kurdistan who demonstrated the virtue of the Sufis. As Shadman told the story, when he was young (and still luminous in his mother's eyes), he would pray at the mosque every day. He was the only boy who would pray there with a group of older men first thing in the morning. One day it was raining quite hard, and when he reached the mosque, his shoes had become muddy. He left them in a muddy state at the door to the prayer room and went about his prayers. When he left, he saw that an old man had cleaned Shadman's shoes, "without saying a word."

The old man's actions demonstrate the virtue of humility in a special way because it is quite common that younger boys are expected to clean the shoes of their fathers, grandfathers, or other elderly men. When the old man cleaned Shadman's shoes, it was an extraordinarily kind and humble gesture. It is not clear that this particular old man was necessarily a practicing Sufi, but in Shadman's narrative, he demonstrated the paradigmatic Sufi virtue of humility. By exercising this virtue silently, without seeking credit for himself or explicitly asking Shadman to follow his example and keep his shoes cleaner, he demonstrated yet another degree of humility.

When Shadman told this story, he added in conclusion, "If all Muslims were like that, I would never have quit praying." This final comment demonstrates deep disappointment in the ways that other Muslims behave. Shadman's sense that Muslims' bad conduct has corrupted Islam and made Islamic practices less habitable resonates with the descriptions that Newzad and Pexshan offered of both early Islamic history and recent events in Kurdistan, which were full of killing and bloodshed. Yet at the same time, Shadman's description of the old man's deed clearly demonstrates his lingering admiration of Sufi figures.

Thus, for Shadman the pleasure of poetry includes the sensorial and intellectual pleasure of a poem's sonorous beauty, its wordplay, and paradoxical images. Engaging Sufi figures through poetry and stories gives him the moral pleasure of encountering Muslims who are devout in their disciplines and who demonstrate the virtuous ability to affirm religious difference, often without announcing it as a virtue at all.

THE PLEASURES OF HOME

Home was above all a place of pleasure for Shadman. Many of the men in his age cohort whom I met had a more ambivalent attitude toward the home. Echoing stereotypes of gendered space, many men said that they would become anxious or annoyed (*bêtaqet*) if they spent too much time at home. Shadman was the opposite, and he often delighted in explicitly rejecting that image of a man who cannot inhabit domestic space. He described his time in domestic space by saying "pêm xoşe" (it pleases me).

Pleasure was palpable in some of the small acts that permeated everyday life. Shadman was quick to praise the intelligence of his children, taking obvious delight when they answered my questions about the Kurdish language or when they asked questions about English that showed their ability to learn. He was even quicker to praise his wife for her prowess in cooking, hosting guests, and running the household. "My wife is remarkable!" he said on dozens of occasions. One day I was there as they were cleaning up the house together and washing their car. Water was often in short supply during these years due to the ongoing crisis of water and electricity that the KRG could not solve, but on that day there was enough water to wash the car. Shadman bragged, "I can wash a whole car with just one pail of water!" I expressed my surprise, but his wife overheard him and quipped back, "That's true; he can; he learned it from me." They both burst out in laughter, and this was a quite typical dynamic between them. These were some of the ordinary pleasures that Shadman found at home.

These ordinary pleasures also included the pious pursuits of others in his family. During Ramadan, for example, everyone in his family but him fasted. When we sat down together for dinner when they broke their fast, he would praise his children for their determination and self-discipline. When I joined them for an evening in town and everyone was rushing to get out the door together, his wife might get to the door and say, "Wait, let me pray first." Standing at the door, Shadman would answer her without any impatience, "Go and pray!" These small acts were part of a broader style or manner in which he engaged others that demonstrated an attitude of accommodation and conviviality. In this way, the pleasures that his family found in piety were also a part of Shadman's life. Without pursuing piety himself, his passive, receptive stance toward its pursuit was inseparable from the pleasures he found at home.

AN ETHOS OF RECEPTION

The attitude that pervaded Shadman's descriptions of Sufis illuminates the resemblance between the pleasures of poetry and the pleasures of daily life for Shadman. Shadman did not explicitly describe poetry as didactically teaching this attitude, nor did he, like Hama, say that the pleasure of his encounters with others was a consequence of his engagement with poetry. He did not establish the explicit analogy between poetry and life that Newzad articulated, and such an analogy would have been loose since no one in his family, to my knowledge, was committed to the disciplines of the Sufi path as were the poets whom he admired.

Yet the sense of admiration and attraction that Shadman showed toward Sufi figures' virtue and self-discipline is comparable to his admiration of his family's piety and self-discipline. Even if it is not a strict analogy, there is a connection between poetry and life that deserves exploration. For Shadman's attitudes toward pious Sufis and his pious family were quite similar.

There was no named concept to capture this attitude in the everyday life they shared together. In a sense, the attitude is like the virtue of not asking that appeared in the anecdote about Kak Ehmedî Sheikh: despite not having a name, it has an affective sensibility, a texture in Laugier's sense of a gesture, a manner, or style, and it enables a particular kind of relationship.

Observers must tread carefully when giving names to unnamed virtues. In giving a name to a virtue, one risks assimilating it to an established paradigm and thus losing track of what is distinctive about it. For example, one may be tempted to call this attitude "tolerance." But that evokes a long tradition in liberal thought that obscures the way this attitude works in the ordinary life of Shadman and his family. As Wendy Brown has shown, the idea of tolerance in the liberal tradition has drawn on an assumption that what one tolerates is something—some view or someone—that is essentially repulsive. Liberal tolerance seeks to control what is affectively "revolting, repugnant or vile" about religious difference.[17] But the religious difference in Shadman's family is rarely characterized by its aversions. It is a set of attractions and affective modes of attachment that characterize religious differences. This is the sense in which their engagement constitutes a form of resistance or, rather, *dissent* from the kind of Islamic revival that Mela Krêkar sought. For rather than allow the separation of faith and *kufir* to provide the criteria for evaluating ordinary relations, that criteria shared space with ordinary relations of conviviality and receptivity.

Bearing in mind the difficulty of naming this virtue, let the phrase "ethos of reception" describe the particular attitude toward religious difference that I have sought to describe in Shadman's household. It is an attitude that privileges the capacity to encounter others who have different orientations to Islamic traditions without ignoring or erasing that difference. Shadman's ethos of reception has two main features. First, Shadman's own stance is passive, and others take the active role. He declines an active disavowal of *dîn* in his house, and he goes along with his pious relatives, facilitating through small gestures their efforts to pray and fast. Second, that passive stance is precisely what allows for ongoing action and interactions—ongoing relationships with others in everyday life and in his engagements with poetry. It is thus a passive power in which power is not the ability to dominate but a capacity to accept, absorb, and accommodate. Rather than attempt to subject others to his own approach, he shows that he can accommodate other orientations to Islamic traditions. Through an ethos of reception, Shadman neither accedes to the project of pious self-making nor rejects that project outright (which would incur the isolation of the "dark human"). Rather, he receives and accommodates those projects, acknowledging their attractive force.

This ethos of reception shares much with Amira Mittermaier's description of "modes of religiosity that centre neither on acting against nor on acting within but on being acted upon."[18] When describing the prospect of an encounter with saints or the Prophet Muhammad in one's dreams, Mittermaier's Egyptian interlocutors insisted that while one could invite a visitational dream, one could not produce it. The dream was not the product of self-cultivation and directed striving but came from an "elsewhere" acting on the subject. Yet even those who were most unlikely to receive a dream (for example, if their piety was expressed in seemingly inconsistent ways) shared a pietistic orientation that they affirmed through public performances such as prayer and veiling.[19] And they also shared a desire to welcome dreams that come from "elsewhere." In that context, reception appears to be a theological concept, broadly conceived, that emerges from a community with a shared religious orientation. In contrast, Shadman's ethos of reception worked across lines of difference in his home. Instead of agreement on a desire to become more pious, reception in Shadman's home worked alongside implicit disagreements.

Certainly there is a dimension of obligation at work in this ethos. If I had asked Shadman to make general statements about his relations with his family, I suspect that in replying he would have alluded to duty and obligation. Even when sitting down for dinner during Ramadan and waiting for the call to prayer, his pleasure in sharing those moments with his kin was saturated with a sense that it was the necessary or natural thing to do. But obligation and duty cannot in themselves explain this ethos of reception, most obviously because Shadman exempted himself from the duties and obligations of being a Muslim.

CONFLICTING PROJECTS OF SELF-MAKING

Just as members of the household showed different orientations to the obligations and duties of being a Muslim, they engage in different projects of self-making. That is, the pious seek to strengthen their faith and become better Muslims through the practices of prayer and fasting, and Shadman also seeks to make himself into a good person, respecting and caring for his pious kin without relying on the discourse of piety. Yet as Cheryl Mattingly has shown, projects of self-making inevitably impinge on others: the task of making oneself virtuous often entails taking care of another person, offering support or reproof, or addressing other people in a particular way. Describing "ground projects" of moral self-making, Mattingly writes, "We humans simply would not exist individually or collectively without being, at times in our lives, a central ground project for significant others."[20]

Mattingly described engagement in ground projects as common to "we humans," and that address includes readers of this book as well. Perhaps readers can reflect on how their own effort to be or become a good friend, sibling, parent, student, or neighbor relies on the participation of others. Conversely, readers may also reflect on how they also have been ground projects for others, which may involve receiving advice, encouragement, discouragement, gifts, or rebukes. In both cases, such projects can entail care and support but also conflict and tension.

This was particularly true for Shadman in his home. His own effort to care for and respect his family might intrude on their piety, and their effort to become more pious Muslims might impinge on Shadman in some way. The more deeply enmeshed one is in those relations, the more palpable are the subtle moves through which family members show their power or vulnerability in relation to one another.

When projects of self-making conflict, how did Shadman and his family respond? How did they recalibrate the relations of power among themselves? Such conflicts can create moments of fragility in which pleasure might be overtaken by resentment. One such moment affords insight into how Shadman and his family encounter the limits of reception.

Structures of power and kinship in Kurdistan conferred on Shadman privilege and authority as a father in the home.[21] When describing different orientations to Islam in his family, Shadman had said, "My family was not built on this, that I could say, 'You should believe as I do.'" That seems to imply that it was he, as the father figure, who decided what the family was built on. Yet the question of how he and his family inhabited those structures should be investigated carefully and not taken for granted. One moment that I witnessed reveals how they inhabited various roles in relation to one another while tying together the themes of literature, pleasure, power, and projects of self-making.

A predominant image of fatherhood in Kurdistan presents a man who fears only God and wields authority over a wife and children who fear God first and their father second. In a famous novella written by Sherzad Hesen in 1988, these forms of authority blend into an image of fatherhood that is a caricature ripe for critique.[22] In that image, a merciless father underwrites his authority with threats and violence that instill fear in his children. The father understands his own authority as his power to keep his family—principally wives and daughters—cloistered in his courtyard. In a scene in which he seems almost intoxicated with authoritarian anger, the father declares to his children, "I am your father, and I am the only one who knows what is good for you and what is bad. A servant does not ask his lord why he is left to hunger or thirst."[23] With these words, the father seeks to usurp divine knowledge of good and bad, and he appears as an anxious authority who issues moral decrees and requires silent obedience from his children.

Hesen's image of the father is quite well known in part because it provides traction for critique of broader concerns about fatherly authority in Iraqi Kurdistan. Many fathers and others in Kurdistan disowned that image of fatherhood and sought to remake themselves as open (*krawe*) by making their daughters free (*azad*).[24] Both Shadman and his wife were among these "open" thinkers.

Early one morning, I sat with his wife over breakfast as she spoke nostalgically about going out with her friends late in the evening to visit Baghdad in the 1970s. She then brought the topic of conversation into the present by describing how she and Shadman sought to raise their daughter. "We tell her to go out, to go someplace nice with her friends," she said. The phrase "someplace nice" (*şwênêkî xoş*) clearly referred to the dozens of hotels, malls, and some Euro-American-style cafés that had sprouted up in both Silêmanî and Hewlêr by 2009. Youth of various classes increasingly visited these "nice places" in mixed-gender groups, although some had more money to spend than others. Through their encouragement, Shadman and his wife opened up a mode of self-making to their daughter by which she could become a chic, independent consumer, staying out late at night in commercial spaces and defying an expectation that unmarried girls should be home before dark. They also sought to make themselves into the kind of parents who could prove their acceptance of this new mode of sociality through their daughter's free movement.

But their daughter did not indulge them. As her mother told me that morning, their daughter answered their pleas by saying simply, "The people in this city are immoral." That turn of phrase registered her disgust with the leering and gossip she risked by visiting those places. Thus, projects of self-making in this household were at odds with each other and may not provide a reliable framework for understanding how pleasure thrived in the household. One fleeting moment in the course of the routines and habits that characterized domestic life illustrates how those projects clashed.

One evening, the family had gathered to watch the *American Idol*–style talent show that was popular in Kurdistan. The pleasure afforded by this show had become a nightly routine for the family. As I sat with the family watching television, Shadman shared the idea for a piece of writing he was considering publishing. Its title was a bit risky since it alluded to an aspect of Muslim doctrine that is quite central to Sunni thought in Kurdistan and appears precisely in the hadith of Gabriel described earlier that enumerates what faith is for Muslims. No sooner had the words of the prospective title left his mouth than his daughter shot him a glare and exclaimed, "'Eybe!,'" which in this context means "How dare you!" There followed an awkward but meaningful moment of silence, and then the conversation was quickly rerouted to the television.

Later in the evening, when Shadman and I sat alone in his study, I asked him about his writing, and he said he had given up on that title altogether. His daughter seemed to have heard in the title an expression of doubt or skepticism about one of the central aspects of faith, and putting that out in print was troubling for her.[25] I suggested that his daughter's reaction might be a good predictor of other people's reactions, but he dismissed others' reactions as irrelevant. "It's not important what people say," he said. "What's important is what my daughter says!" And then he added with delight, "Have you ever seen a man so afraid of his own daughter?" The conversation moved on, but the broad smile and tenacious cheer in his voice announced the pleasure he took in describing himself as fearing his daughter this way.

His daughter's rebuke had done its work. Her project of self-making had evoked this response to her father's words. Shadman's project of self-making allowed for the unintended consequence that he might injure his daughter with his words. But faced with that problem, he withdrew quietly and relented. In reflecting on that moment, Shadman did not venture into the sociological register of describing religious norms in Kurdistan to show himself consciously accommodating them. Rather, he foregrounded the affective dimension of his relation to his own daughter, naming it as "fear" while smiling broadly. In contrast to the desperation and anxiety of Hesen's literary father figure and Shadman's effort to forge a "modern family" in which daughters venture out, Shadman showed delight and celebrated the vulnerability of his own authority.[26] So pleasure here is not only the privilege of power but also the form of its vulnerability. In a moment of vulnerability when different religious orientations clashed, Shadman did not seek mastery over others. Rather, he affirmed his vulnerability and showed the ethos of reception.

The affective dynamics of that interaction also shed light on the scene that opened this chapter, which contained a moment of what appears to be ostensive instruction, where a father tells his daughter what to do. But I argued that the words of instruction had a different valence when they appeared in the course of an ordinary conversation. Although those words indexed one of Shadman's own anxieties, they did not constitute a "rule" for his daughter. In contrast, the scene of his daughter's rebuke revolved around a single word that only implies instruction or direction. Yet the authority of her speech, its affective force, was deeply felt by everyone present in the room.

PLEASURE AND RELIGIOUS DIFFERENCE

The scene of his daughter's rebuke demonstrates much of what is at stake in this chapter, and indeed in the book as a whole. When one asks how to describe a religious orientation, abstract claims and doctrinal statements certainly play a crucial role. The text of the hadith that inspired the rebuke has become part of Shadman's daughter's ethical sensibility and her attunement to the world and others. Yet the declaration she made in response to Shadman set that text to work in an ordinary relationship. There it was not merely a question of guiding Shadman to piety, for it was commonly recognized in the household that his aspirations were not directed toward piety. It was instead a question of acknowledging a form of religious difference present in their everyday interactions. This acknowledgment happens through carefully chosen words and gestures (not grand moral claims). It is not merely domestic harmony because it contains the prospect of deep conflict that lurches to the surface of ordinary relationships in interactions such as this scene of rebuke.

Shadman himself also transformed texts of poetry and the stories about Sufi figures. While those texts were produced and began circulating in a world that directed recipients toward piety, Shadman both acknowledged his attraction to Sufi figures and his aversion to taking up their pious practice for himself. And that ethos of reception appeared in his domestic relations when he welcomed and encouraged the pious pursuits of his family members.

With inspiration from Hama's generous offer to think about the pleasure of poetry, this chapter directs attention to how pleasure persists in domestic relationships even in the face of potential conflict. Muslims in Shadman's household orient themselves quite differently toward Islamic traditions yet orient themselves toward *one another* in overlapping ways, sharing an ethos of reception and savoring the pleasures of one another's company. It is precisely by attending to how these Kurdish Muslims are oriented toward one another, acknowledging both their ability to affect others and their vulnerability to others' affects, that one gets a sense of how they relate to Islamic traditions more broadly.

Epilogue

"DEAR READER!"

WHEN THE EDITORS OF THE VOLUMES OF KURDISH POETRY EXPLORED in Chapter 2 write introductions and epilogues for their work, they frequently include a section that begins with a second person address, "xwênerî 'ezîz!," or, "Dear Reader!" The section commonly includes several components. The editors humbly write that they have done the best they could to collect and edit all the manuscripts they could find. They also thank those who have helped them procure documents and prepare the publications. They then likely beg the reader's forgiveness for the errors that inevitably remain in the book. And finally, the reader is often invited to communicate any shortcomings found in the work directly to the editor so that a second edition of the same work might improve.

The address to the reader thus imagines a relationship between the editor and the reader based on critique, mutual affection, and ongoing dialogue. The address assumes a relative intimacy of reader and editor—it assumes that they inhabit the same social world and share similar commitments to the precision and accuracy of texts. There is a project of intellectual production that unites them. Yet it also suggests the possibility that the text will travel beyond that social world, to places the editor could not predict. Indeed, it is the traveling of the text beyond that set of connections that requires the address to the reader in the first place.

These forms of address underline the fact that written texts are not only in dialogue with other written texts. They are also in dialogue with oral conversations about written texts. Chapter 2 describes some of these conversations as contests about interpretation. When a new edition of a *dîwan* appeared in the bazaar, it was often subject to intensive evaluations in the bookshops and cafés that I frequented. Has the editor contributed something new to the *dîwan*? Do the footnotes offer new or insightful interpretations, or do they merely paraphrase existing commentaries? While written evaluations were published in the style of a review, the address to the reader anticipates, even invites, scenes of oral evaluation that are regarded as crucial to the reception of the text.

The address "Dear Reader!" in Kurdish collections of poetry poses several questions that might also frame an approach to other kinds of texts. What religious commitments or ethical orientations does a text assume its readers share? How does a text anticipate its own reception? More generally, how does a text interpolate its reader?

This Epilogue addresses those questions with respect to the preceding chapters. Thinking comparatively about how the anthropology of Islam frames its addressees, these concluding thoughts seek to articulate the assumptions that have guided the writing of these chapters and also to imagine some ways that an ethnographic text such as this book might be received.

RELATING TO READERS IN THE ANTHROPOLOGY OF ISLAM

Much recent work in the anthropology of Islam has shifted attention away from the question of what Islam is to the question of how Islam has become a thing. These studies pivot away from comparing Islam to Christianity or Judaism as if they were two tokens of the same type toward rethinking the framework that renders them into a type to begin with. The framework that does the rendering is secularism: the mode of thinking, feeling, and governing that assumes religion can be quarantined in some way, and by doing so comes to reshape what people experience as religion.

Secularism has profoundly reshaped a wide range of theories and practices for Muslims all over the world, and the anthropology of Islam has set out to identify precisely how secularism accomplishes the work that it does. Thus, the anthropology of Islam has become inseparable in many ways from an anthropology of secularism. Hussein Ali Agrama's book *Questioning Secularism* is especially insightful and influential in this regard. It shows that when observing Egypt's simultaneous claims to be secular and to use Islamic law as a source of law, asking whether Egypt is a secular or an Islamic state is not merely a question of finding a category for a set of facts. Asking that question inspires anxiety and uncertainty about the boundaries between secularism and religion, and precisely that anxiety and uncertainty inspire the Egyptians state's efforts to settle the question through legislation. By asking whether Egypt is secular or Islamic, and investing the question with anxious urgency, observers usually empower the state itself to properly draw the line between religion and politics. Paradoxically, then, observers who privilege the question of whether Egypt is secular or religious show how deeply secular they are (no matter how "religious" they may also be).[1]

At the same time, Agrama draws attention to a set of practices that deflect this question. Looking at the moments shared between a diverse group of activists at the time of the Egyptian revolution in 2011, Agrama describes these moments as *a*secular because they asked about shared governance and the common good without the pressure to decide whether they were secular or religious.[2] If they had sat down and worked out statements of belief, these activists may have held opposing positions on an ideological and doctrinal spectrum. Yet when they deflected these questions through which state power is inevitably expanded, the activists were able to exercise a political sensibility that was cooperative, peaceful, and inclusive. They demonstrated care for one another and a willingness to defend one another against state violence. The ethos of mutual care and responsiveness that emerged was indifferent about whether or how religion might be quarantined in their engagement with one another.

This and many other works show how deeply entrenched secularism is in the contemporary world. They seek to denaturalize secularism both by showing its historical contingencies and by highlighting the moments of exception when the ideas and sensibilities characteristic of secularism are held in abeyance. Returning to the question of how ethnography interpolates its readers, these works seem to address readers who do not yet acknowledge or appreciate the depth at which secularism has shaped their world. The reader is interpolated as implicated in the politics of secularism by virtue of sharing many assumptions and sensibilities about Islamic traditions and the work of the modern state. Yet the reader is too dimly aware of this, and the task of ethnography is to bring readers to a new awareness of their relation to the world around them, a new sensitivity to their entanglement in secular politics, and perhaps their disentanglement as well. This and other works perform that task with argumentative clarity and rigor.[3]

READERS WHO RELATE TO OTHERS

This book shares with these works the task of denaturalizing secular common sense. Secular common sense, if it can be personified, has often looked askance at Islam, asking Muslims to explain themselves, wondering why it is that people are committed to Islam when they need not be. Scholars of the comparative study of religion have long drawn attention to the fact that religious belief or practice has been framed as a problem to be explained. This book seeks to invert the critical gaze by asking why people are not exactly committed to Islam when they might have been. The Introduction begins this work by diverting attention away from "secular" as an adequate description of the religious orientation of the Kurdish Muslims described in the book.

Yet this book also takes up a different methodological sensibility. Instead of describing the depth of secularism's influence in Kurdistan and concluding with the explication of exceptions, it seeks to examine the moments of exception to secular common sense that proliferate in everyday life. Of course, the effect of secular reforms has been visible at many levels, from the Ottoman reforms and the rise of Kurdish nationalism as described in Chapter 2 to the efforts to reform of family relations that appeared in Chapters 3 and 4. Attending to ordinary relations shows the extent to which these efforts have been transformed in everyday life. The relationships described throughout the book have neither assumed nor aspired to make one's orientation to Islam into a matter of private, individual conscience or a matter confined to the walls of domestic family space without being entangled in public debate. Whether engaging the texts of the Quran and hadith, or poetry, or sermons, the book shows how Kurdish Muslims regard the truth of these texts as neither given nor irrelevant. In gauging their attraction or aversion to the kinds of piety that those texts present, Kurdish Muslims in this book have not appealed to any space beyond religion. They have assumed, as Shadman put it, that the world itself is a religious world. To extend that idea, ordinary relationships are inescapably religious relationships as well. And the task of engaging others in everyday life—others who come bearing different orientations to Islamic traditions—cannot be accomplished or avoided through doctrinal statements of any religious or secular kind. In sum, the book attends to the often delicate work of sustaining ordinary relationships when secularism provides no solid grounding for that work.

This method has inspired its own way of addressing readers as well. Each chapter contains a seed of address that interpolates the reader in a different mode.

EPILOGUE

The Introduction begins by tentatively suggesting that readers may approach the text from a set of ordinary relationships that make up their own lives. Chapter 1 interpolates readers as neighbors who live in close proximity to some whose orientations to Islam may be felt, heard, or discerned in different ways. Chapter 2 interpolates readers as coming to have a stake in a debate about Kurdish poetry—either because they bring their own interpretive tools to the texts or because the poetry itself interpolates them as Muslim, Christian, Jewish, Zoroastrian, or other non-Muslims. Chapter 3 interpolates readers as having embodied reactions to Newzad's flirtation and imagination of a polyamorous romance—reactions no doubt grounded in their own experience or imagination of such relations. Chapter 5 assumes that readers are involved in relationships where ground projects of moral self-making impinge on one another—where efforts to shape oneself as a moral being require the participation of others. Throughout the book, the mode of address privileges a mode of relating to others. Readers in this sense are relational: they relate to their own kin or friends, their own neighbors, their own spouses or romantic partners. Rather than make those relations irrelevant to the book, I have invited them to its center.

The arguments also have interpolated readers in other ways. Chapter 1 invites readers to extend the concept of the discursive tradition to allow for an account of Muslims' aversion to Islamic traditions. It assumes that readers may be tempted to regard these Muslims' experiences as irrelevant to Islamic traditions. Chapter 2 argues against the tendency to separate Sufism from Islamic traditions, assuming readers may find it possible to do so. Chapter 3 argues against the idea that a Muslim's attraction to Sufi poetry proves that the individual is finally striving to be pious after all. Chapter 4's argument takes on a set of commonsense ideas about Islamist movements, which it assumes were commonly available to readers. Contrary to the commonsense idea that Islamism is conservative and traditional in regard to family matters and seeks revolutionary upheaval in matters of state and political parties, the chapter argues that in Kurdistan, one such movement has sought a radical transformation of the family and other ordinary relations, turning away from the state and mainstream politics. Finally, Chapter 5 argues that even given the challenges posed by religious difference and the politicization of ordinary relationships, modes of pleasure, receptivity, and conviviality persist in everyday life. Those modes of engagement are more discernible in verbal descriptions, gestures, and affect than in the definition of abstract values or clear statements of belief. It interpolates in readers the temptation to seek clearly articulated claims or prescriptions about how one should behave in the face of religious difference.

So the arguments of this book engage readers who already move within a complex set of attractions and aversions to Islamic traditions. The arguments engage readers who barter in commonsense ideas about Sufism and Islamism, about piety and its absence. But finally, the arguments engage readers who, above all, seek to feel and think more carefully about how they and others relate to Islamic traditions. The book addresses readers who *already* relate to Islamic traditions and already relate to other Muslims in their daily lives. Perhaps readers' engagement with other Muslims is as sparse as encountering images and reports on television or fragments of an Islamic text that appeared fleetingly as a meme on social media. Or perhaps it is as broad and complex as having first encountered the Quran moments after birth when the call to prayer was directed toward their ears (as is common practice among Muslims). In either case, readers approach the ethnographic text equipped with ideas, positions, facts, and statements of belief that relate to Islamic traditions. They are also people who move within relationships with others in ways that may not exactly match statements of belief. Thus, rather than assume that readers are more secular in principle than they know they are, and without assuming that readers are not secular, this book seeks to address readers who are already engaged with Islamic traditions in ways that do not exactly or exclusively fall under the rubric of secularism.

The readers of this ethnography are in this sense not unlike Pexshan, Newzad, and Shadman, or even Mela Krêkar: all relate to Islamic traditions by relating to others. And readers may now include their imagination of those four Kurdish Muslims in their own relation to Islam. This is another reason that I have written about individuals, asking readers to devote careful attention to calibrating a picture of these individual lives in their imagination.[4] These four Kurdish Muslims may become figures of thought for readers. That is, just as the *kafir* was a figure of thought for the Pillar Poets, or as Sufi poets were figures of thought for Shadman, readers may develop imaginary relations with these four Kurdish Muslims. Chapter 2 describes two modes in which the poetic imagination of non-Muslims related to the sociopolitical reality of everyday life: one of relative depoliticization and another of the new politicization of religious identity. As readers imagine these figures, there is a range of ways that that ethnographic imagination can relate to the sociopolitical reality of readers' everyday lives. That relation is subject to all the constraints and creativity that readers summon.

I have tried to imagine that this ethnography is a text that might resemble some of the very texts it describes: texts that are taken up piecemeal, cited and recited creatively in the course of ordinary conversations about religious difference in daily life. I have imagined that its readers will be inspired by the creativity, or the patience, or the receptive attitudes demonstrated by some of the figures the book has sought to bring to life on the page. Conversely, I have also imagined that its readers may be annoyed or frustrated, either with those who insist on turning away from piety or with those who call others to piety. In all cases, I hope that ethnography offers "just two words," as Newzad said poetry offered him, to see things from a different perspective.

If the central claim of this book is that claims about religion appear differently when considered from the point of view of relationships, then the same thing must be said about the claims of this book: they may appear differently when readers look at them from the perspective of their own ordinary relations. I cannot guess how readers' relations to their brother, to their neighbors, to their mother, or to a preacher they found on the internet will inflect their reception of the claims in this book.

Michael Jackson argued against anthropology's recurring impulse to frame its description of human experience with neat and clean models for social life rather than with the messier paradoxes of lived experience. Insisting that the starting point for both the writing and reading of ethnography is lived experience, Jackson wrote that "our understanding of others can *only* proceed from within our own experience."[5] For this book, I have sought to begin precisely from experience: from my own experience in the Introduction and with the assumption that readers will proceed from *their* experiences rather than from mechanical models of social life. And here I would add to Jackson's formulation that our understanding of others can be meaningful only if it is *returned* to our own experience. How, then, might readers return this book to their own lived experience?

Just as neither abstract claims nor carefully calibrated descriptions can secure the future of the ordinary relationships in the lives described in this book, so too the author of a book cannot suppose that its claims and descriptions secure a future conversation with his readers. I cannot be free from uncertainty, even anxiety, about how the book is read, about what sensibility or ethos readers bring to its descriptions. But perhaps uncertainty about how a text will be taken up in everyday life, how large claims will be *returned* to lived experience, is one thing that the reader-author relationship has in common with other ordinary relationships. The uncertainty is not something to overcome but something to bear up with whatever pleasure is available.

Notes

INTRODUCTION

1. For an extended account of "aspiration" in Muslim ethical life, see Naveeda Khan, *Muslim Becoming*, especially 21–54, 203–207.

2. Indeed, such moments of reflexivity about an inability to pray may occur not only within a life span but also within the few minutes of a prayer itself, as practitioners gain or lose concentration. See Haeri, "Private Performance of Salat Prayers."

3. According to Marion Katz, most medieval Muslim scholars recognized that prayer was an obligation for all Muslims and regarded this as an immutable article of faith. At the same time, they recognized that many Muslims did not conduct their prayers. While publicly denying the fact that it was an article of faith could solicit condemnation, simple indifference toward the performance of the prayer was a commonly accepted fact. See Katz, *Prayer in Islamic Thought and Practice*, 162–172.

4. See Katz, 162–172; and Friedmann, *Tolerance and Coercion in Islam*, 121–159.

5. Some may insist that these two norms are not entirely irreconcilable. Others may insist that there are other established modes of responding to Muslims who turn away from piety. Yet others may point out that one may combine elements from each to find a distinctive path between them. All of these points underline the argument in this paragraph that the presence of multiple norms requires debate, contestation, and interpretation.

6. In this sense, "religion" is like "secularism." Both are traditions of debate and contestation that equip humans with inclinations or tendencies to not merely make

a claim in a debate but also to respond to the speech of others with pleasure, disgust, anger, or anxiety. On the relation between thought and affect generally, see Connolly, *Neuropolitics*; on secularism, see Connolly, *Why I Am Not a Secularist*; Asad, *Formations of the Secular*; and Hirschkind, "Is There a Secular Body?"

7. On spirit possession, see especially Boddy, *Wombs and Alien Spirits*; and Bowen, *Muslims Through Discourse*.

8. See Schielke, "Being Good in Ramadan." For an account the different phenomena of "ex-Muslims," see Cottee, *The Apostates*.

9. See Bush, "The Politics of Poetry," 197–203.

10. Gregory Starrett stated this point clearly: "Secularism is ultimately a normative concept, and we make a mistake if we treat it as an analytical one.... The use of 'the secular' as an analytical concept retains only the ability to minimize the complexity of real lives, to obscure our understanding of contemporary history ... and to mislead us into thinking that we might someday experience the luxury of escaping from our interpretive rivals." See Starrett, "The Varieties of Secular Experience," 648, 649.

11. Das, "What Does Ordinary Ethics Look Like?," 71.

12. Khan, *Muslim Becoming*, 6.

13. In 2014, the populations of the provinces of which these two cities are capitals were around two million each. The Kurdistan region of Iraq had a population of just over five million, and the entire population of Iraq was reported to be just over thirty-six million. See Kurdistan Regional Statistics Office, *Demographic Survey*.

14. The Sorani dialect of Kurdish is spoken in these two cities as well as in some parts of Iran. The Kurmanji dialect is spoken in Turkey, Syria, and parts of Iran and Iraq. For information on further dialects and the historical relation of Kurdish languages to regimes of power, see Hassanpour, Sheyholislami, and Skutnabb-Kangas, "Kurdish Linguicide."

15. See Wein, *Iraqi Arab Nationalism*.

16. For most of the war, Iraqi Kurdish martyrs who died fighting for the Iraqi government were recognized as Iraqi martyrs, not as Iraqi *Kurdish* martyrs. See Khoury, *Iraq in Wartime*, 224–225.

17. Hardi, *Gendered Experiences of Genocide*, 13.

18. The broader context for this shift is described at length in Baram, *Saddam Hussayn and Islam*.

19. Hardi, *Gendered Experiences of Genocide*, 13.

20. See Hiltermann, *A Poisonous Affair*, 12–18.

21. See Bengio, *The Kurds of Iraq*, 197–242.

22. On these "minorities," see Omarkhali, *Religious Minorities in Kurdistan*. For a broader historical view of Assyrian Christians and their relations with Kurdish Muslims, see Joseph, *Modern Assyrians of the Middle East*; and Benjamen, "Assyrians and the Iraqi Communist Party," 106–121.

23. Van Bruinessen, "Kurdish Studies in Western and Central Europe," 58.

24. On the development of communist thought and politics in Iraq with reference to its influence among Kurds, see Batatu, *Old Social Classes and the Revolutionary Movements of Iraq*; Bashkin, *The Other Iraq*, especially 52–123; Ismael, *Rise and Fall of the Communist Party of Iraq*; and Bet-Shlimon, *City of Black Gold*, especially 135–164.

25. Schmidinger, *Rojava*, 101.

26. Most prominently, these movements have evolved among Kurds under the leadership or influence of Abdullah Ocalan. See Krajeski, "Kurdistan's Female Fighters," cited in Duzgun, "Jineology."

27. The most insightful passages on these evenings are in Hejar's *Çêştî Micêwer*. See also Mehmudiyan, *Feqê w feqeyetî le Kurdistan*.

28. *Dîwanî Nalî*, 355.

29. *Dîwanî Mehwî*, 343 (quatrain 24).

30. El-Rouayheb, *Islamic Intellectual History in the Seventeenth Century*, 13–59.

31. For example, Mufti Zehawî (Muhemmed Ehmed Hesen Beg) was born in Silêmanî in 1793. He taught in Silêmanî, as well as in Kirkuk and Baghdad. He then held the post of mufti of Baghdad for thirty-eight years until his death in 1890. His biographers report that he taught six thousand students across his career of almost eighty years. See Zekî Beg, *Te'rîxî Silêmanî we welatî*, 183; and Xal, *Muftî Zehawî*, 41.

32. See Derengil, *Conversion and Apostasy in the Late Ottoman Empire*.

33. For a study of the Kurdish militias who were later involved in the Armenian genocide, see Klein, *The Margins of Empire*; for accounts of earlier violence against Assyrian Christians in Bohtan and Hakkari, see Donabed, *Reforging a Forgotten History*, 54.

34. For a firsthand account of Armenian and Kurdish boys together in relocation camps, see Panian, *Goodbye, Antoura*.

35. See Kern, *Imperial Citizenship*.

36. For an account of the similar institution called madrasa in the Northern Kurdish emirates, see Yüksel, "Dengbej, Mullah, Intelligentsia," 150.

37. See Bashkin, *New Babylonians*, especially 141–182; Ismael, *Rise and Fall of the Communist Party of Iraq*; and Benjamen, "Assyrians and the Iraqi Communist Party."

38. Abu-Lughod, *Veiled Sentiments*, 244.

39. For a description of a different context in which the relations enabled by jokes are comparable to the joke I describe here, see Gilsenan, "Joking, Play, and Pressure," in Gilsenan, *Lords of the Lebanese Marches*. In both cases, truth and eros engage with each other in ways that are neither possible beyond the joke nor separable from their lives beyond the joke.

40. As Steve Caton's *Yemen Chronicle* demonstrates, the mere idea that an anthropologist might be a spy can be deployed in creative, useful, and harmful ways in the midst of a political conflict. In Caton's case, holding captive someone who may be a spy was just as useful as holding a spy captive.

41. Soane, *To Mesopotamia and Kurdistan in Disguise*.

42. Edmonds, *Kurds, Turks, Arabs*.

43. Strathern, "Kinship as a Relation," 45.

CHAPTER 1

1. Asad, *The Idea of an Anthropology of Islam*.

2. Asad, 14.

3. Asad, 14.

4. See Mahmood, *Politics of Piety*; Gade, *Perfection Makes Practice*; and Hirschkind, *The Ethical Soundscape*. For an insightful study of how anthropologists have received Asad's idea of a discursive tradition, see Anjum, "Islam as a Discursive Tradition."

5. Surat al-Baqarah 2:183, in Nasr et al., *The Study Quran*.

6. The Egyptian philosopher, poet, and translator Abdulrahman Badawi is one of the most famous of these Arab intellectuals whose work circulates in Kurdistan.

7. The thirteenth-century Kurdish scholar Ibn al-Salah al-Shahrazuri wrote one of the most influential works in the science of the hadith. Eerik Dickinson translated it as *An Introduction to the Science of the Hadith*.

8. For a detailed study of this topic, see Sayeed, *Women and the Transmission of Religious Knowledge in Islam*.

9. Paul Losensky translated this verse in Sells, *Early Islamic Mysticism*, 169. For a comprehensive study of Rabi'a al-'Adawiyya, including her appearance in Western scholarship, see Cornell, *Rabi'a*.

10. Bowen, *Muslims Through Discourse*, 169.

11. The insight afforded by thinking of one's relation to the discursive tradition as always necessarily shaped and mediated by ordinary relations is not limited to those such as Pexshan who "turn away" from piety. For example, Bowen's interlocutor in Gayo, Abang Muhammad, recited the hadith *after* his mother had raised the spectral

possibility—precisely by denying it—of his practice challenging divine unity. Just before the moment of recitation just described, Bowen writes: "His mother, who was deathly afraid of committing the sin of *shirk* or 'duplicating God' (menduei Tuhen) by communication with spirits, intervened at this point to say sharply that the instructions 'came straight from God,' that they were *ilham* (divine inspiration). Abang Muhammad remained silent." Bowen, 169. Thus, as much as Abang Muhammad was offering an account or justification of his practice to an anthropologist, he was offering that account or justification to his mother and sustaining his good relation with her.

12. I later learned that this idea was not a hadith but rather a verse in the Quran, in Surat al-A'raf 7:204: "And when the Quran is recited, harken unto it, and listen, that haply you may receive mercy" (Nasr et al., *The Study Quran*). I had heard it described as a hadith in another context where its recitation was saturated with irony. When a group of men were listening to the music of Egyptian singer Umm Kulthum, others in the room were making distracting noise. One of the men interested in listening to the music recited the phrase, replacing the Quran as the proper object of attention with Umm Kulthum's music.

13. Nelson, *Art of Reciting the Quran*, 89–100.

14. Metin Yüksel skillfully locates Goran's communism within a wider global movement of anticolonial literature in "Solidarity Without Borders."

15. 'Ebdullah Goran, *Dîwanî Goran*, 118.

16. Powers, *Intent in Islamic Law*, 43.

17. Powers, 44.

18. She referred to the following poem:

A simple vessel of wine that sells for a dime,
won't be broken at end of the drink, however drunk you are;
but this sweet vessel with a face and hands,
why make it only to destroy it in the end?

This is my translation from the Kurdish. I used the Kurdish translation from the Persian by Sheikh Selam in *Çwarînekanî Xeyam*, 91.

19. Szanto, "Zoroaster Was a Kurd!"

20. See especially Allison, "Representations of Yezidism and Zoroastrianism," 288–290, cited in Szanto.

21. A translation of Mary Boyce's introductory text *Zoroastrians: Their Religious Beliefs and Practices* was commonly available in the bazaar. Older texts include *Zerdeşt*, a work by Ahmad Shantawi. Shantawi presented Zoroastrianism as a forerunner of Islam by discussing its doctrinal emphasis on divine unity; the ritual practice of re-

quired prayer; and the forbidding of fornication, drunkenness, and magic. Much more recently Baban Seqzî's *Zerdeşt: Hîway Rizgarî* explicitly contested this "Islamicized" Zoroastrianism in an effort to recover a pre-Islamic Zoroastrianism.

22. Najam Haider's account of these events distinguishes between the elements of the narrative commonly acknowledged by Sunni and Shi'i Muslims and the elements that differ between several contesting Shi'i narrative traditions. See Haider, *Shi'i Islam*, 66–81.

23. See *Dîwanî Salim*, 522 (poem N-7, lines 80–85) and 610 (poem N-27); and *Dîwanî Narî*, 37–40 (poem 4).

24. See Aminrazavi, *The Wine of Wisdom*, 134–156.

25. Sheikh Selam, *Çwarînekanî Xeyam*, 27.

26. For an introduction to the pre-Islamic hajj, see Wensinck, "Hadjdj."

27. Hendrickson, "Prohibiting the Pilgrimage," 176.

28. Hendrickson, 196. This is Hendrickson's paraphrase of Muhammad Bello (d. 1837).

29. Ahmed, *What Is Islam?*, 282. For more on collective modes of experimentation in Islamic tradition, see Naveeda Khan, *Muslim Becoming*, especially 21–54, where the risk of violence and exclusion appears as an integral part of experimentation.

30. Lewis, "Sexual Occidentation," 698n14.

31. I did not find this poem in Persian editions of Khayyam's poetry. J. B. Nicols includes the Persian with his French translation in *Les Quatrains de Kheyam*, 123. The last line reads, "dani z cheh chiz, az musalman-i khwish." The word "khwish" is not gendered in Persian, but I have rendered it in English with "she" and "her" because the self is often feminized in accounts that rely on the feminine Arabic word *nafs* for self. Also, it allows the poem to speak more directly to Pexshan's condition.

CHAPTER 2

1. Qeredaxî, *Silêmanî*, 7.

2. "Sufism has an old history that did not require the arrival or development of the Islamic message, but the Sufi front was able to expand at the edges of Islam so that Sufism and Islam worked together to encompass the region." Qeredaxî, 11.

3. Qeredaxî, 12.

4. See also Letîf Helmet's vision in *Sofî w Sofîgerêtî: Karîgerî hizir u îdiyu kilture na-îslamîyekan le ser sofî w sofigerêtî îslamî*. The book's title makes its thesis clear: "Sufis and Sufism: The Influence of Non-Islamic Thought and Culture on Sufis and Islamic Sufism." Early in the book he states, "We should acknowledge that in their thought, speech, and activity, the Sufis behave in way that is openly opposed to sharia" (12).

5. For an account of how European colonial agents contributed Sufism's supposed antinomianism in South Asia, see Ernst, *Sufism*, 1–31.

6. For a full list of *dîwan*s, see the Bibliography. My selection of these *dîwan*s was guided by the advice of my interlocutors. I read the work of poets that my interlocutors cited and recited to me in formal interviews as well as in my conversations in daily life. While these seventeen *dîwan*s make for a wide survey, they are not necessarily representative of all the poetry from this era.

7. Amir Hassanpour describes two bursts of publication in Sorani Kurdish in Iraqi Kurdistan: the first with the arrival of a printing press brought by the British in 1920 and the second following the 1958 revolution. While the manuscript tradition of copying poetry by hand was still vibrant in the early twentieth century, many of the poems composed then were published first in journals. See Hassanpour, *Nationalism and Language in Kurdistan*, 169–220. One of the most prominent of these journals was *Pêşkewtin*, supervised by British officer E. B. Soane.

8. Notably, publication of these *dîwan*s was restricted and censored but not prohibited during the Ba'athist years in Iraq. The collective sense among Kurdish speakers during my fieldwork was that the Ba'athist regime reluctantly accommodated some publication of Kurdish poetry, though in general the memory of Kurdish literature suffered greatly under the Ba'athist effort to produce a pan-Arab historical memory. See Davis, *Memories of State*, especially 200–226.

9. The Kurdish text I have found most useful in the exposition of rhetorical devices is Mela 'Ebdulkerîm Mudarris's *Badi' w 'eruzî Namî*, in which he offers definitions of different terms along with examples from his own poetry. For a concise summary in English of these devices in classical Arabic literature, see Heinrichs, "Rhetorical Figures."

10. While "folk" poetry in Sorani and both classical and folk poetic traditions in the Kurmanji dialect have received more attention, the corpus of English writings on classical Sorani Kurdish poetry is quite small. Landmark works include Atmaca, "Politics of Alliance and Rivalry on the Ottoman-Iranian Frontier"; Shakely, "The Kurdish Qasida"; and most recently, Ghaderi, "Emergence of Modern Kurdish Poetry." For a sociohistorical study in Kurdish, see Ce'fer, *Şarî Silêmanî*.

11. On Mawlana Khalid, see Mudarris, *Yadî Merdan*.

12. Kemal Re'uf Muhemmed offers a careful study of this text in *'Eqîdey Îman*.

13. For a summary of Persian prosody, see Theisen, *Manual of Classical Persian Prosody*; and for an argument about the origins of Arabic prosody, see Frolov, *Classical Arabic Verse*. Ehmed Herdî argues in *'Eruz le şî'irî Kurdîda* that the genealogy of

Kurdish rhyme and meter schemes is not a direct translation of their use in Arabic but rather an adaption of their use in Persian. This genealogy, however, does not invalidate the study of rhyme and meter schemes in Arabic. Indeed, Arabic was the primary reference point for students of Kurdish literature at the University of Silêmanî when I took a course on *'eruz* there in 2009.

14. For a summary of the data from C. J. Rich's observations in 1820, see van Bruinessen, *Agha, Shaikh, and State*, 172.

15. Seccadî, *Mêjuy Edebî Kurdî*, 263.

16. Seccadî, 263.

17. *Dîwanî Salim*, 11.

18. *Dîwanî Nalî*, 24–32.

19. See, for example, Sîweylî, *Nalî*; and Muhemmed, *Çepkêk le Gulzarî Nalî*.

20. There is a lively debate about whether, or to what extent, these figures were themselves actively committed to the Naqshbandi or Qadri Sufi paths in their own daily practices. Whatever the outcome of that debate, there is little room for doubt that their poetic output relies on and contributes to the dimension of the poetic imagination associated with Sufi thought.

21. For a lucid account of these last days, see Atmaca, "Resistance to Centralisation in the Ottoman Periphery."

22. Ce'fer, *Şarî Silêmanî*, 102–104, citing Rich, *Narrative of a Residence in Koordistan*.

23. Lumbard, "Quranic View of Sacred History and Other Religions," 1769.

24. Lumbard, 1766.

25. Lumbard, 1777.

26. See Friedmann, *Tolerance and Coercion in Islam*, 72–76; and Sharkey, *A History of Muslims, Christians, and Jews in the Middle East*, 77.

27. Izutsu, *Structure of Ethical Terms in the Quran*, 113–144.

28. Shabistari, *Garden of Mystery*, 140–141.

29. *Dîwanî Salim*, 79 (poem A-22). Note: Citations in this chapter identify the poems by including the number of the poem and the letter of its rhyme. Most *dîwan*s are organized alphabetically by the last letter of a poem's rhyme: for example, this poem is the twenty-second in this edition's collection of poems ending in the letter *alif*.

30. *Dîwanî Salim*, 79 (poem A-22).

31. *Dîwanî Salim*, 478 (poem M-22).

32. *Dîwanî Salim*, 244 (poem J-1).

33. Najmabadi, *Women with Mustaches and Men Without Beards*.

34. Shabistari, *Garden of Mystery*, 140.

35. *Dîwanî Ehmed Muxtar Caf*, 82 (poem 30).

36. *Dîwanî Wefayî*, 115 (poem 37).

37. Lewis, "Sexual Occidentation," 658n14. For an account of the sexualization of Christians in certain strands of classical Arabic literature, see also Montgomery, "For Love of a Christian Boy."

38. 'Attar, *Conference of the Birds*, 65.

39. *Dîwanî Mehwî*, 231 (poem M-10).

40. *Dîwanî Salim*, 452 (poem M-12).

41. 'Attar, *Conference of the Birds*, 74.

42. Here again I disagree with popular readings of this story as I heard them in many conversations during fieldwork in Silêmanî. The overwhelming majority of my interlocutors who described this story emphasized the sheikh's conversion to Christianity, insisting that it was a tale of love transcending religious boundaries.

43. *Dîwanî Salim*, 229 (poem T-23).

44. *Dîwanî Salim*, 86 (poem A-25).

45. Some readers may recognize the image of "grabbing by the beard" as a trope derived from the Quran. See Surat Ta-ha 20:94, where Harun (Aaron) pleads with Musa (Moses) that Musa not direct his rage at him by grabbing Harun's beard because he allowed the idolatry of the people who bowed in worship to a golden calf.

46. The idea is most clearly expressed in a poem by Mawlana Rumi. A. J. Arberry translates two couplets in that poem as follows: "Die now, die now, in this Love die; / when you have died this Love, you will all receive new life. // . . . Die now, die now, and break away from this carnal soul, / for this carnal soul is as a chain and you are as prisoners." Rumi, *Mystical Poems of Rumi*, 106. See also Rumi, *The Mathnawi of Jalaluddin Rumi*, 6:754–758.

47. *Dîwanî Salim*, 274 (poem R-1).

48. *Dîwanî Kurdî*, 14.

49. Two cautionary notes are necessary here. First, this claim is confined to the living archive that I encountered during fieldwork—which is limited to a set of *dîwan*s that the twentieth-century editors have preserved and presented. Further research on the history of Kurdish poetry may reveal female authors and/or a distinctive gendering of the poetic voice in the *ghazal*. Second, while this claim holds for the genre of "romantic" poetry (the *ghazal*), it is not true for poetry as such. Most famously, the genre of *hecu*, or lampoon, is one in which the poetic self is usually masculine. The paradigmatic lampoon poet in Kurdish is not only male but one who flouts power by penetrating either males or females. (The exception to the masculine voice is a short

exchange that Masture Erdelan held with Nalî, in which the two poets impugn one another with extensive reference to their pudenda.)

50. Dominic Parviz Brookshaw argues that the use of a feminine name does not require the assumption of a distinctively feminine poetic voice: "It is perhaps not possible to argue for a distinctly *feminine* voice in the poetry penned by women that has survived from early nineteenth-century Iran, but there is evidence of a *female* voice." Brookshaw, "Qajar Confection," 133.

51. For an efficient summary of the intertwined history of these Christians, including nomenclature and doctrinal matters, see Murre-van den Berg, "Chaldeans and Assyrians"; on Hakkari, see Klein, *The Margins of Empire*; on Urmia, see Becker, *Revival and Awakening*; on Assyrians in Iraq, see Donabed, *Reforging a Forgotten History*.

52. See Gavish, *Unwitting Zionists*; and Zaken, *Jewish Subjects and Their Tribal Chieftains in Kurdistan*.

53. This is no doubt partly because Mosul had been the center of Chaldean intellectual and social life for many centuries, but in the mid-twentieth century it shifted to Baghdad, as reported in Girling, *The Chaldean Catholic Church*, 74.

54. Metin Atmaca's inaugural study makes this argument persuasively in part by comparing the two emirates. See Atmaca, "Politics of Alliance and Rivalry on the Ottoman-Iranian Frontier."

55. Rich, *Narrative of a Residence in Koordistan*, 1:120. Rich reports a roughly similar proportion for Sine, which in the nineteenth century was the most important sibling city to Silêmanî in regard to poetic production and social life. There were four to five thousand families, which included two hundred Jewish families and fifty Chaldean households. Rich, 209.

56. Zaken, *Jewish Subjects and Their Tribal Chieftains in Kurdistan*, 108.

57. There is ample evidence in several traditions of Sunni legal interpretation to support the view that marriage between a Muslim man and a Christian woman is permissible. See Friedmann, *Tolerance and Coercion in Islam*, 179–181. While oral reports of this marriage insist that the woman remained Christian, 'Ebdulkerîm Mudarris claimed that she converted. See Mudarris, *Binemaley Zanayan*, 351. I thank Bushra Kasnazani for this reference.

58. For a judicious summary of these events, see Jwaideh, *The Kurdish National Movement*, 160–202.

59. Exemplary of this reliance on stereotypes is Lyon, *Kurds, Arabs, and Britons*, 154.

60. Edmonds names the minister as the father of two of his own clerks but neglects

to mention what the minister's former role had been. See Edmonds, *Kurds, Turks, and Arabs*, 82.

61. See Hawar, *Şêx Mehmudî Qareman u dewletekey xwaruy Kurdistan*, 2:318–319. I thank Shenah Abdullah for this published reference.

62. Edmonds, *Kurds, Turks and Arabs*, 80.

63. Donabed, *Reforging a Forgotten History*, 54–92.

64. Robson, "Refugee Camps and the Spatialization of Assyrian Nationalism in Iraq," 244.

65. Bet-Shlimon, *City of Black Gold*, 65.

66. Laura Robson also highlights the role of the British in separating the Assyrians and consolidating their religious and ethnic difference by recruiting Assyrians as an armed force, then using the violent reactions against these forces as evidence of primordial prejudice against Christians. She concludes that "the widening gap between refugees and local Arab and Kurdish populations as Assyrians were drawn into service with the colonial military apparatus proved useful to a narrative of Assyrian 'minority' persecution emerging in British diplomatic and military discourse." See Robson, "Peripheries of Belonging," 32.

67. Derengil, *Conversion and Apostasy in the Late Ottoman Empire*, 29–66.

68. *Dîwanî Ehmed Muxtar Caf*, 7.

69. *Dîwanî Ehmed Muxtar Caf*, 106 (poem 50).

70. *Dîwanî Muftî Pêncwênî*, 31–33.

71. *Dîwanî Muftî Pêncwênî*, 76. Qani' composed a *texmîs* on this poem (adding three lines of his own to each couplet of Mufti's). See *Dîwanî Qani'*, 322. (Wolfhart Heinrichs translates the Arabic *takhmis* as "fiver gloss" in his article "Allusion and Intertextuality," 82.)

72. *Dîwanî Muftî Pêncwênî*, 40.

73. For the wider Iraqi context, see Bashkin, "When Mu'awiya Entered the Curriculum," for a description of some of the critiques and contradictions that emerged in the reception of Iraqi public education in the classroom. For a description of the ways that gender difference was contested and preserved in Iraqi education, see Pursley, *Familiar Futures*, 57–126.

74. Umed Ashna described Mufti Pêncwênî in these terms in his contribution to the preface in Mufti's *Dîwan*, 19–26.

75. *Dîwanî Muftî Pêncwênî*, 61–62.

76. See also the poem in which Qani' explicitly calls for the transformation of *'ilm*: away from Quran and hadith and toward *sen'et*/industry. *Dîwanî Qani'*, 269.

77. *Dîwanî Muftî Pêncwênî*, 118.

78. Another advantage of the notion of "tendency" is that is allows for recognition of the work of Hacî Qadrî Koyî (1817–1897), which I did not include in my survey for this chapter. See Hacî Qadrî Koyî, *Dîwanî Hacî Qadrî Koyî*. Hacî was a little younger than the Pillar Poets, yet much of his poetic production anticipates the nationalist vision of the later generations. Farangis Ghaderi makes this case persuasively in "The Emergence of Modern Kurdish Poetry," 73–120.

79. *Dîwanî Narî*, 60 (poem 18).

80. Sluglett, *Britain in Iraq*, 267n42.

81. Haj, *The Making of Iraq*, 55–75.

82. Haj, 55–75; see also Sluglett, *Britain in Iraq*, 135–140.

83. *Dîwanî Narî*, 92 (poem 39).

84. *Dîwanî Narî*, 92 (poem 39).

85. *Dîwanî Narî*, 92 (poem 39).

86. *Dîwanî Qani'*, 77.

87. Seccadî, *Mêjuy Edebî Kurdî*, 538–541.

88. *Dîwanî Bêkes*, 109.

89. *Dîwanî Qani'*, 197.

CHAPTER 3

An earlier version of this chapter was published as J. Andrew Bush, "How 'God Becomes a Lover': Sufi Poetry and the Finitude of Desire in Kurdistan," *Journal of Middle East Women's Studies* 12, no. 1 (2016): 68–85.

1. Strathern, *Partial Connections*, 76.

2. Olszewska, *The Pearl of Dari*, 148–149, 164–165.

3. Najmabadi, *Women with Mustaches and Men Without Beards*, 97–131.

4. Sells, "The Infinity of Desire," 206.

5. Laugier, "The Ethics of Care," 223.

6. Jackson, *As Wide as the World Is Wise*, 63.

7. Jackson, 81.

8. For a lucid introduction, see Barnard Haykel's essay "On the Nature of Salafi Thought and Action."

9. For a detailed account of how the Saudi state has mobilized Wahhabi activists, and vice versa, see Al-Rasheed, *Kingdom Without Borders*, pt. 2.

10. See Chapter 4 for another version of this story.

11. Qutbuddin, "Piety and Virtue in Early Islam," 132.

12. The book was Shams al-Din Muhammad ibn Ahmad al-Safarini al-Hanbali, *Al-Qawl al-'ali li-sharh athar al Imam 'Ali*.

13. For more on Alevi thought and practice in Kurdistan, see van Bruinessen, "Dersim and Delahu."

14. *Dîwanî Narî*, 95.

15. Hejar, *Çwarînekanî Xeyam*, 47.

16. This approach to analyzing Newzad's reference to poetic texts in light of his relationships resembles Stefania Pandolfo's description of dream interpretation: it is not a matter of decoding the meaning of a text but of finding the openings and connections between subjects that the text allows. See Pandolfo, *Impasse of the Angels*, 176.

17. Najmabadi, *Women with Mustaches and Men Without Beards*, 174. For a study of similar shifts in Egypt, see Cuno, *Modernizing Marriage*, 77–122.

18. See Bashkin, "Representations of Women in the Writings of Intelligentsia in Hashemite Iraq," 60; Efrati, "Negotiation Rights in Iraq," 581–592; and Efrati, *Women in Iraq*, 60–65, 116.

19. Pursley, "Daughters of the Right Path," 67–73.

20. Efrati, *Women in Iraq*, 115.

21. Motlagh, *Burying the Beloved*, 21–31.

22. For a genealogy of the term *mal*, see Fischer-Tahir, *Brave Men and Pretty Women?*, 48–50.

23. *Dîwanî Mehwî*, 231. Chapter 2 contains an alternative translation of this couplet.

24. I am not aware of any legal case in Kurdistan in which third parties sought to produce a judicial separation between a husband and wife on the grounds of one party's apostasy. However, the lack of a precedent within Kurdistan did not make it any less possible for Newzad to imagine. And there is a famous precedent for such a case beyond Kurdistan—the case of Nasr Abu Zayd in Egypt. See Agrama, *Questioning Secularism*, 42–68.

25. See Shahid, "The *Sura* of the Poets, Quran XXVI."

26. Jackson, *As Wide As the World Is Wise*, 81.

27. *Dîwanî Mehwî*, 220.

CHAPTER 4

1. "Jiyanname 3," 15–18. Note: Citations in this chapter identify the title of the audio file downloaded from the website didinwe.net followed by the minute mark of the

cited speech. For multiple files of the same title, the website itself added letters to distinguish the files (thus, "Hukm be Gheyri Xwa C"), and when there were multiple files of the same title, I have added numbers (thus, "Jiyanname 3"). I have unified variant spellings of file titles but retained the transliteration pattern on the website.

2. For a biography of Abdallah Azzam, see Hegghammer, "Abdallah Azzam," 81–101. For further details on Azzam's relation to Osama bin Laden, see Miller, *The Audacious Ascetic*, 84–91. While I have not heard Krêkar mention Abu Muhammad al-Maqdisi, the terms of debate and the positions Krêkar holds suggest that he is quite close to many of al-Maqdisi's positions as presented in Wagemakers, *A Quietist Jihadi*, especially 165–179.

3. For different accounts, see Salomon, *For Love of the Prophet*; and Wickham, *The Muslim Brotherhood*.

4. See Hirschkind, *The Ethical Soundscape*; Mahmood, *The Politics of Piety*; and more recently, see Arsalan Khan, "Islam and Pious Sociality."

5. For a brief overview, see Leezenberg, "Political Islam Among the Kurds," 213–224.

6. See Idrîs Sîweylî, *Rewtî Islamî le başurî Kurdistan*.

7. These parties are the Kurdistan Islamic Union (Yekgirtuy Islamiy Kurdistan), the Kurdistan Islamic Group (Komeli Islami Kurdistan), and the Kurdistan Islamic Movement (Bizutnewey Islami Kurdistan).

8. See Hirschkind, *The Ethical Soundscape*, for the paradigmatic study of this phenomenon.

9. "Bnemakani Rabwn," 3.

10. In his use of this term, Krêkar borrows key concepts of the founders of the Muslim Brotherhood in Egypt, Sayyid Qutb and Hassan Al-Bana. See Khatab, *Political Thought of Sayyid Qutb*. While tracing the development of the concept in Qutb's writings, Khatab translates one definition of *jahiliyyah* (Ar.) that appears closest to Krêkar's usage of the term: "a typical attitude of mind [that] comes to the forefront when those standards and norms of behavior sanctioned by Allah give way to those inspired merely by sophisticated and debased appetites" (150). As Toshihiko Izutsu explains, the term *jahiliyet* is not only opposed to *'ilm* (knowledge), but it is also opposed to *hilm* (Ar.), a fundamentally moral concept that encompasses a sense of nobility as well as "patience and freedom from blind passion." See Izutsu, *Ethico-Religious Concepts in the Quran*, 28.

11. See Abu Dawud, *Sunan Abu Dawud*, 5:156 (*Kitab al-Sunnah, Bab Sharh al-Sunnah*); Nasiruddin al-Khattab translated the hadith there as, "This *ummah* will split

into seventy-three sects, seventy-two of which will be in the Fire, and one in Paradise. That is the Jama'ah (main group of Muslims)."

12. See "Hukm be Gheyri Xwa C." Around the fifteen-minute mark, he emphasizes that the forms of governance here are the ones not only related to "prayer and worship" but to all aspects of life—that is, not only the sphere of "privacy" reserved by secular thought for religious life but all aspects of public conduct, including commerce, politics, and crime.

13. "Bnemakani Rabwn," 22.

14. "Bnemakani Rabwn," 22–24.

15. Friedmann, *Tolerance and Coercion*, 161.

16. "Rabuni Islam: Roli Lawan," 51–52.

17. "Rabuni Islam: Roli Lawan," 53–54.

18. Krêkar commonly offers the phrase "becoming an Islamic human" (*dariştinî însanî Islamî*) to describe the long and slow process of transformation by which Kurdish Muslims can recover their humanity—a process that requires extensive engagement with others in everyday life. This long process offers a stark contrast with the vision of recovering humanity through the dramatic act of martyrdom that Minoo Moallem describes in revolutionary Iran, where "the Muslim man had to reject his humanity in order to regain it." See Moallem, *Between Warrior Brother and Veiled Sister*, 109.

19. Devji, *The Terrorist in Search of Humanity*, 25–56. Krêkar's views on the usefulness of violence to achieve these ends shifted across his career. His association with the violence of the civil war has delegitimized him in the eyes of many observers in Kurdistan. (Some observers hold the secular parties to the same standard and condemn for the same reasons; others condemn Krêkar all the more strongly because he saw the violence as authorized by Islamic traditions.) Yet rather than follow the more sensational analytic of violence in Krêkar's career, this chapter focuses on the thread that connects his vision of a total transformation that is consistent throughout his career.

20. Ahmed, *What Is Islam?*, 282.

21. In his discussion of the youth as a vanguard, Krêkar draws on a recognizable social psychology of teenagers in Iraq, which assumes teenagers are passing through a distinctive stage of psychological development. See Pursley, "The Stage of Adolescence." For a contrasting case in which a modernizing state emphasized the role of fathers in producing (or failing to produce) "healthy" youth within a patriarchal family, see Menoret, *Joyriding in Riyadh*, 182–184.

22. "Rabuni Islam: Rabuni Kurdistan," 17.

23. "Rabuni Islam: Rabuni Kurdistan," 17–18.

24. "Rabuni Islam: Rabuni Kurdistan," 19.

25. "Rabuni Islam: Rabuni Kurdistan," 20.

26. See the translation by Nasr et al. in *The Study Quran*, Surat Luqman 31:15: "But if they strive to make thee ascribe as a partner unto Me that of which thou hast no knowledge, then obey them not. Consort with them in the world in a kindly manner, and follow the path of those who turn in repentance unto Me." Krêkar repeats this message again with reference to the same verse in "Gishty: Regai Peghemberan," 9.

27. This practice of supplication of saints often happens at their graves. While Mela Krêkar denies responsibility for the act ("Jiyanname 6," 55), it is worth mentioning that during the time his movement had wide influence in Hewraman, the graves of several saints there were desecrated to condemn these practices.

28. "Rabuni Islam: Rabuni Kurdistan," 20.

29. "Jiyanname 3," 26.

30. "Gishty: Axlaq," 5.

31. "Chezhy Hawsariaty 1," 61.

32. Pursley, *Familiar Futures*, 118–126. For another study of companionate marriage in Egypt, see Kholoussy, *For Better, for Worse*; and Cuno, *Modernizing Marriage*.

33. "Chezhy Hawsariaty 2," 22.

34. "Jiyanname," 77.

35. Their marriage contract was not based on the transfer of material wealth, as is common, but on the exchange of knowledge. That is, instead of paying a dower (Ar. *mihr*), he gave knowledge to his bride: the knowledge of how to interpret and recite the Quran (*tejwîd u tefsîr*). "Jiyanname," 77.

36. "Jiyanname," 77.

37. As Sara Pursley has shown, the idea that women have a natural inclination to domestic life and child rearing informed the efforts of Iraqi and American reformists to craft a public education system that properly prepared women to raise children at home. See Pursley, *Familiar Futures*, 79–123.

38. "Jiyanname," 78.

39. "Jiyanname," 79.

40. McLarney, *Soft Force*, 231–253.

41. "Gishty: Zina," 13.

42. "Chezhy Hawsariyati 1," 32.

43. See Leezenberg, "Political Islam Among the Kurds," 217.

44. "Gishty: Zina," 52.

45. "Ometi Islam 7: Wryabunewe," 8.

46. "Ometi Islam 7: Wryabunewe," 8–38.

47. Asad, *Genealogies of Religion*, 204–236.

48. "Ometi Islam 3: Komelgey Nmuney Peghember," 11; the reference is to the Kuwaiti group Ahli Turath.

49. "Gishty: Rewshti Muselmanan," 43.

50. "Gishty: Rewshti Muselmanan," 44.

51. *Dîwanî Narî*, 60 (poem 18), 92 (poem 39).

52. "Reweshti Muselmanan," 15.

53. "Ometi Islam: Lawazi Islam," 26. Nasiruddin al-Khattab translates the hadith as "Whoever kills a man from among the Ahl al-Dhimmah, he will not smell the fragrance of Paradise, and its fragrance may be detected from a distance of seventy years." An-Nasa'i, *English Translation of "Sunan An-Nisa'i,"* 5: 398 (Kitab al-Qasamah, Bab al-Ta'dzim Qatal al-Ma'ahad).

54. "Jiyanname 8," 20.

55. "Jiyanname Peghemberan: Eisa B," 2.

56. "Jiyanname Peghemberan: Eisa B," 2–3.

57. Marsden, *Living Islam*, 252.

CHAPTER 5

An earlier version of this chapter was published as J. Andrew Bush, "An Offer of Pleasure: Islam, Poetry, and the Ethics of Religious Difference in a Kurdish Home," *American Ethnologist* 44, no. 3 (2017): 516–527.

1. Robbins, "Cultural Values," 120.

2. Das, "Ordinary Ethics," 140. For other work on the place of the ordinary in the anthropology of ethics, see Das, "Engaging the Life of the Other"; Al-Mohammed, "Poverty Beyond Disaster in Postinvasion Iraq"; and Lambek, *The Ethical Condition*.

3. Laugier, "The Ethics of Care," 223.

4. See Murata and Chittick, *The Vision of Islam*, 37, where they discuss the distinction between faith and belief. For the full hadith, see also Muhammad Khan, *Translation of the Meanings of Sahih al-Bukhari*, 1:81.

5. Murata and Chittick, *The Vision of Islam*, xxv.

6. See the prominent nineteenth-century poet Mewlewî's masterful doctrinal creed written in verse that he composed in Kurdish, Arabic, and Farsi. This formu-

lation about the presence and expression of faith appears in the Kurdish version, *'Eqîdey Merziye*, 37–45. Murata and Chittick also translate a hadith that grounds this definition: "Faith is a knowledge in the heart, a voicing with the tongue, and an activity with the limbs." See Murata and Chittick, *The Vision of Islam*, 37.

7. For a recent account that compares various approaches, see the biographical account of a prominent Islamist figure from Iranian Kurdistan in 'Ebdulkerîm, *Kak Ehmed Muftîzade*.

8. *Dîwanî Mehwî*, 226.

9. Caton, *Peaks of Yemen I Summon*, 223.

10. Neqşbendî, *Tesewuf çiye?*, 208, 221.

11. Brinkley Messick describes hand kissing in Yemen as double-edged because it can be either a mode of demonstrating deference or a gesture of ostensive respect that conceals "silent hostility." See Messick, *The Calligraphic State*, 165–166.

12. See Metin Yüksel's analysis of a poem by the Kurdish poet Cegerxwîn titled "I Do Not Kiss Your Hand," which connects the poet's spite for religious authority with the demand for intellectual awakening akin to developments in Europe. Yüksel, "Dengbej, Mullah, Intelligentsia," 224.

13. See Mudarris, *Mektûbatî Kak Ehmedî Şêx*.

14. A nearly identical anecdote appears in Farid al-Din 'Attar's twelfth- to thirteenth-century compendium on the lives of Sufi saints in which the famous Persian mystic Bayazid Bistami plays the role of Kak Ehmedî Sheikh and a Zoroastrian plays the role of the Jewish merchant. See 'Attar, *Memorial of God's Friends*, 205. In Shadman's version, though, the event was part of the more recent history of Sufism in nineteenth-century Kurdistan.

15. Hallisey, "Between Intuition and Judgment," 145.

16. Rodrigue, "Difference and Tolerance in the Ottoman Empire."

17. Brown, *Regulating Aversion*, 25.

18. Mittermaier, "Dreams from Elsewhere," 252.

19. Mittermaier, 254–255.

20. Mattingly, *Moral Laboratories*, 204.

21. In the urban context of Iraqi Kurdistan, see Fischer-Tahir, *Brave Men and Pretty Women?*; for the rural dimension, see King, "The Personal Is Patrilineal"; for comparison with Kurdish societies in and beyond Iraqi Kurdistan, see Mojab, *Women of a Non-state Nation*.

22. Hesen, *Hesar u segekanî bawkim*.

23. Hesen, 30.

24. This mode of self-making was not limited or determined by class, since many fathers of the lower classes embraced it, while many wealthy or middle-class fathers resisted it.

25. Shadman's daughter's desire not to see those words in print is one reason I have not included them in this chapter.

26. This scene echoes one dimension of interactions between men and women that Farha Ghannam describes in Egypt: "Women are judges of normality who monitor how men conform to norms that define a proper man, evaluate shortcomings, and exert pressure to modify conduct." Ghannam, *Live and Die like a Man*, 104.

EPILOGUE

1. Agrama, *Questioning Secularism*, especially 1–41.

2. Agrama, 224–235.

3. The effort to historicize the work of secularism and then identify the persistence of an asecular, nonsecular, or otherwise not-quite-secular sensibility also describes the general approach in Furani, *Silencing the Sea*.

4. In this regard, my mode of address resembles that taken by Amira Mittermaier at the conclusion of her book *Dreams That Matter*. Having written extensively about the political conditions that are made and transformed by her Egyptian interlocutors through their imagination, Mittermaier suggests that her *readers'* imagination can be just as important: "At this particular historical juncture, I believe, thinking—or rather imagining—one's way beyond dichotomous distinctions between us/them, real/imagined, subjective/objective, and either/or is not only an ethical and epistemological but also a political exercise. And an urgent one at that" (239).

5. Jackson, *Paths Toward a Clearing*, 17.

Bibliography

Abu Dawud Sulaiman bin Ash'ath, Imam Hafiz. *Sunan Abu Dawud*. Translated by Nasiruddin al-Khattab. Riyadh: Darussalam, 2008.

Abu-Lughod, Lila. *Veiled Sentiments: Honor and Poetry in a Bedouin Society*. Berkeley: University of California Press, 1999.

Agrama, Hussein Ali. *Questioning Secularism: Islam, Law and Sovereignty in Egypt*. Chicago: University of Chicago Press, 2012.

Ahmed, Shahab. *What Is Islam? The Importance of Being Islamic*. Princeton, NJ: Princeton University Press, 2015.

Al-Hanbali, Shams al-Din Muhammad ibn Ahmad al-Safarini, ed. *Al-Qawl al-'alili-sharh athar al-Imam 'Ali*. Beirut: Dar al-Bisharah al-Islamiyah, 2008.

Allison, Christine. "Representations of Yezidism and Zoroastrianism in the Kurdish Newspapers *Hawar* and *Roja Nu*." In *From Daena to Din: Religion, Kultur, und Sprache in der iranischen Welt*, edited by Christine Allison, Anke Joisten-Pruschke, and Antje Wendtland, 285–291. Wiesbaden: Harrassowitz, 2009.

Al-Mohammed, Hayder. "Poverty Beyond Disaster in Postinvasion Iraq: Ethics and the 'Rough Ground' of the Everyday." *Current Anthropology* 56, no. 11 (2015): 108–115.

Al-Rasheed, Madawi, ed. *Kingdom without Borders: Saudi Arabia's Political, Religious, and Media Frontiers*. New York: Columbia University Press, 2008.

Al-Shahrazuri, Ibn al-Salah. *An Introduction to the Science of the Hadith*. Translated by Eerik Dickinson. Reading, UK: Garnet, 2005.

Aminrazavi, Mehdi. *The Wine of Wisdom: The Life, Poetry and Philosophy of Omar Khayyam*. Oxford: Oneworld, 2005.

Anjum, Ovamir. "Islam as a Discursive Tradition: Talal Asad and His Interlocutors." *Comparative Studies of South Asia, Africa and the Middle East* 27, no. 3 (2007): 656–672.

An-Nasa'i, Imam Hafız Abu Abdur Rahman Ahmad bin Shu'aib bin 'Ali. *English Translation of "Sunan An-Nasa'i."* Translated by Nasiruddin al-Khattab. Riyadh: Darussalam, 2008.

Asad, Talal. *Formations of the Secular: Islam, Christianity, Modernity*. Stanford, CA: Stanford University Press, 2003.

———. *Genealogies of Religion: Discipline and Reasons of Power in Christianity and Islam*. Baltimore: Johns Hopkins University Press, 1993.

———. *The Idea of an Anthropology of Islam*. Occasional Papers Series. Washington, DC: Georgetown University Press, 1986.

Atmaca, Metin. "Politics of Alliance and Rivalry on the Ottoman-Iranian Frontier: The Babans (1500–1851)." PhD diss., Albert Ludwig University of Freiburg, 2012.

———. "Resistance to Centralisation in the Ottoman Periphery: The Kurdish Baban and Bohtan Emirates." *Middle Eastern Studies* 55, no. 4 (2019): 519–539.

'Attar, Farid al-Din. *Conference of the Birds*. Translated by Afkham Darbandi and Dick Davis. London: Penguin Books, 1984.

———. *Memorial of God's Friends: Lives and Sayings of Sufis*. Translated by Paul Losensky. New York: Paulist, 2009.

Baram, Amatzia. *Saddam Hussayn and Islam, 1968–2003: Ba'athi Iraq from Secularism to Faith*. Washington, DC: Woodrow Wilson Center, 2014.

Bashkin, Orit. *New Babylonians: A History of Jews in Modern Iraq*. Stanford, CA: Stanford University Press, 2012.

———. *The Other Iraq: Pluralism and Culture in Hashemite Iraq*. Stanford, CA: Stanford University Press, 2009.

———. "Representations of Women in the Writings of the Intelligentsia in Hashemite Iraq, 1921–1958." *Journal of Middle East Women's Studies* 4, no. 1 (2008): 53–82.

———. "'When Mu'awiya Entered the Curriculum': Some Comments on the Iraqi Education System in the Interwar Period." *Comparative Education Review* 50, no. 3 (2006): 346–366.

Batatu, Hanna. *The Old Social Classes and the Revolutionary Movements of Iraq*. Princeton, NJ: Princeton University Press, 1978.

Becker, Adam. *Revival and Awakening: American Evangelical Missionaries in Iran and the Origins of Assyrian Nationalism*. Chicago: University of Chicago Press, 2015.

Bengio, Ofra. *The Kurds of Iraq: Building a State Within a State*. Boulder, CO: Lynne Rienner, 2007.

Benjamen, Alda. "Assyrians and the Iraqi Communist Party." In *Minorities in the Arab World*, edited by Laura Robson, 106–121. Syracuse, NY: Syracuse University Press, 2016.

Bet-Shlimon, Arbella. *City of Black Gold: Oil, Ethnicity, and the Making of Modern Kirkuk*. Stanford, CA: Stanford University Press, 2019.

Boddy, Janice. *Wombs and Alien Spirits: Women, Men, and the Zar Cult in Northern Sudan*. Madison: University of Wisconsin Press, 1989.

Bowen, John. *Muslims Through Discourse: Religion and Ritual in Gayo Society*. Princeton, NJ: Princeton University Press, 1993.

Boyce, Mary. *Zoroastrians: Their Religious Beliefs and Practices*. London: Routledge, 1979.

Brookshaw, Dominic Parviz. "Qajar Confection: The Production and Dissemination of Women's Poetry in Early Nineteenth-Century Iran." *Middle Eastern Literatures* 17, no. 2 (2014): 113–146.

Brown, Wendy. *Regulating Aversion: Tolerance in the Age of Identity and Empire*. Princeton, NJ: Princeton University Press, 2006.

Bush, J. Andrew. "How 'God Becomes a Lover': Sufi Poetry and the Finitude of Desire in Kurdistan." *Journal of Middle East Women's Studies* 12, no. 1 (2016): 68–85.

———. "An Offer of Pleasure: Islam, Poetry, and the Ethics of Religious Difference in a Kurdish Home." *American Ethnologist* 44, no. 3 (2017): 516–527.

———. "The Politics of Poetry." In *Companion to the Anthropology of the Middle East*, edited by Soraya Altorki, 188–204. Walden, MA: Wiley-Blackwell, 2015.

Caton, Steven C. *Peaks of Yemen I Summon: Poetry as Cultural Practice in a North Yemeni Tribe*. Berkeley: University of California Press, 1990.

———. *Yemen Chronicle: An Anthropology of War and Mediation*. New York: Hill and Wang, 2005.

Ce'fer, Mamosta. *Şarî Silêmanî: Milmilanêy grupe komelayetîyekan 1820–1920*. Silêmanî, Iraq: Binkey Jîn, 2006.

Connolly, William. *Neuropolitics: Thinking, Culture, Speed*. Minneapolis: University of Minnesota Press, 2002.

———. *Why I Am Not a Secularist*. Minneapolis: University of Minnesota Press, 1999.

Cornell, Rkia Elaroui. *Rabi'a: From Narrative to Myth*. London: Oneworld, 2019.

Cottee, Simon. *The Apostates: When Muslims Leave Islam*. London: Hurst, 2015.

Cuno, Kenneth M. *Modernizing Marriage: Family, Ideology, and Law in Nineteenth- and Early Twentieth-Century Egypt*. Syracuse, NY: Syracuse University Press, 2015.

Das, Veena. "Engaging the Life of the Other: Love and Everyday Life." In *Ordinary Ethics*, edited by M. Lambek, 376–399. Fordham, NY: Fordham University Press, 2010.

———. "Ordinary Ethics." In *A Companion to Moral Anthropology*, edited by Didier Fassin, 133–149. Chichester, West Sussex, UK: Wiley and Blackwell, 2012.

———. "What Does Ordinary Ethics Look Like?" In *Four Lectures on Ethics: Anthropological Perspectives*, edited by Michael Lambek, Veena Das, Didier Fassin, and Webb Keane, 53–125. Chicago: Hau Books, 2015.

Davis, Eric. *Memories of State: Politics, History, and Collective Identity in Modern Iraq*. Berkeley: University of California Press, 2005.

Derengil, Selim. *Conversion and Apostasy in the Late Ottoman Empire*. Cambridge: Cambridge University Press, 2012.

Devji, Faisal. *The Terrorist in Search of Humanity*. London: Hurst, 2008.

Donabed, Sargon George. *Reforging a Forgotten History: Iraq and the Assyrians in the Twentieth Century*. Edinburgh: Edinburgh University Press, 2016.

Duzgun, Meral. "Jineology: The Kurdish Women's Movement." *Journal of Middle East Women's Studies* 12, no. 2 (2016): 284–287.

'Ebdulkerîm, Sebur. *Kak Ehmed Muftîzade*. Silêmanî, Iraq: Çapxaney Kurdistan, 2014.

Edmonds, Cecil J. *Kurds, Turks and Arabs: Politics, Travel and Research in North-Eastern Iraq, 1919–1925*. Oxford: Oxford University Press, 1957.

Efrati, Noga. "Negotiation Rights in Iraq: Women and the Personal Status Law." *Middle East Journal* 59, no. 4 (2005): 577–595.

———. *Women in Iraq: Past Meets Present*. New York: Columbia University Press, 2012.

El-Rouayheb, Khaled. *Islamic Intellectual History in the Seventeenth Century: Scholarly Currents in the Ottoman Empire and the Maghreb*. Cambridge: Cambridge University Press, 2015.

Ernst, Carl. *Sufism: An Introduction to the Mystical Tradition of Islam*. Boston: Shambhala, 1997.

Fischer-Tahir, Andrea. *Brave Men and Pretty Women? Gender and Symbolic Violence in Iraqi Kurdish Urban Society*. Berlin: Europäisches Zentrum für Kurdische Studien, 2009.

Friedmann, Yohanan. *Tolerance and Coercion in Islam*. Cambridge: Cambridge University Press, 2003.

Frolov, Dimitry. *Classical Arabic Verse: History and Theory of 'Arud*. Leiden, Netherlands: Brill, 2000.

Furani, Khaled. *Silencing the Sea: Secular Rhythms in Palestinian Poetry*. Stanford, CA: Stanford University Press, 2012.

Gade, Anna M. *Perfection Makes Practice: Learning, Emotion, and the Recited Quran in Indonesia*. Honolulu: University of Hawai'i Press, 2004.

Gavish, Haya. *Unwitting Zionists: The Jewish Community of Zakho in Iraqi Kurdistan*. Detroit, MI: Wayne State University Press, 2010.

Ghaderi, Farangis. "The Emergence of Modern Kurdish Poetry." PhD diss., University of Exeter, 2016.

Ghannam, Farha. *Live and Die like a Man: Gender Dynamics in Urban Egypt*. Stanford, CA: Stanford University Press, 2013.

Gilsenan, Michael. *Lords of the Lebanese Marches: Violence and Narrative in an Arab Society*. London: I. B. Tauris, 1996.

Girling, Kristian. *The Chaldean Catholic Church: Modern History, Ecclesiology and Church-State Relations*. New York: Routledge, 2017.

Hacî Qadrî Koyî. *Dîwanî Hacî Qadrî Koyî*. Edited by Serdar Hamîd Mîran and Kerîm Mustefa Şareza. Sine, Iran: Intisharat Kurdistan, 2007.

Haeri, Niloofar. "The Private Performance of Salat Prayers: Repetition, Time, and Meaning." *Anthropological Quarterly* 86, no. 1 (2013): 5–34.

Haider, Najam. *Shi'i Islam: An Introduction*. Cambridge: Cambridge University Press, 2014.

Haj, Samira. *The Making of Iraq: 1900–1963: Capital, Power, and Ideology*. Albany: State University of New York Press, 1997.

Hallisey, Charles. "Between Intuition and Judgment: Moral Creativity in Theravada Buddhist Ethics." In *Ethical Life in South Asia*, edited by Anand Pandian and Daud Ali, 141–152. Bloomington: Indiana University Press, 2010.

Hardi, Choman. *Gendered Experiences of Genocide: Anfal Survivors in Kurdistan-Iraq*. Farnham, Surrey, UK: Ashgate, 2011.

Hassanpour, Amir. *Nationalism and Language in Kurdistan, 1918–1985*. San Francisco: Mellen Research University Press, 1992.

Hassanpour, Amir, Jaffer Sheyholislami, and Tove Skutnabb-Kangas. "Introduction: Kurdish: Linguicide Resistance and Hope." *International Journal of the Sociology of Language* 217 (2012): 1–18.

Hawar, Muhemmed R. *Şêx Mehmudî Qareman u dewletekey xwaruy Kurdistan*. London: Jaf Press, 1991.

Haykel, Bernard. "On the Nature of Salafi Thought and Action." In *Global Salafism: Islam's New Religious Movement*, edited by Roel Meijer, 33–57. New York: Oxford, 2009.

Hegghammer, Thomas. "Abdallah Azzam: Imam of Jihad." In *Al Qaeda in Its Own Words*, edited by Gilles Kepel and Jean-Pierre Milelli, 81–101. Cambridge, MA: Belknap, 2009.

Heinrichs, Wolfhart. P. "Allusion and Intertextuality." In *Encyclopedia of Arabic Literature*, edited by Julie Scott Meisami and Paul Starkey, 1:81–83. London: Routledge, 1998.

———. "Rhetorical Figures." In *Encyclopedia of Arabic Literature*, edited by Julie Scott Meisami and Paul Starkey, 2:656–662. London: Routledge, 1998.

Hejar. *Çêştî Micêwer*. N.p.: Kitêbî Mîhregan, 2009.

———. *Çwarînekanî Xeyam*. Tehran: Suroush, 1370Sh./1991.

Helmet, Letîf. *Sofî w Sofîgerêtî: Karîgerîy hizir u îdiyu kilture na-îslamîyekan le ser sofî w sofîgerêtî îslamî*. Silêmanî, Iraq: Blawkrawekanî Paşkoy Rexney Çawdêr, 2009.

Hendrickson, Jocelyn. "Prohibiting the Pilgrimage: Politics and Fiction in Maliki Fatwas." *Islamic Law and Society* 23 (2016): 161–238.

Herdî, Ehmed. *'Eruz le şî'irî Kurdîda*. Translated by Asos Herdî. Silêmanî, Iraq: Serdem, 2009.

Hesen, Shêrzad. *Hesar u segekanî bawkim*. 1988. Reprint, Silêmanî, Iraq: Ghezelnus, 2014.

Hiltermann, Joost. *A Poisonous Affair: America, Iraq, and the Gassing of Halabja*. Cambridge: Cambridge University Press, 2007.

Hirschkind, Charles. *The Ethical Soundscape: Cassette Sermons and Islamic Counterpublics*. New York: Columbia University Press, 2005.

———. "Is There a Secular Body?" *Cultural Anthropology* 26, no. 4 (2011): 633–647.

Ismael, Tarek. *The Rise and Fall of the Communist Party in Iraq*. Cambridge: Cambridge University Press, 2008.

Izutsu, Toshihiko. *Ethico-Religious Concepts in the Quran*. Montreal: McGill-Queen's University Press, 2002.

———. *The Structure of Ethical Terms in the Quran*. Chicago: ABC International, 2000.

Jackson, Michael. *As Wide as the World Is Wise*. New York: Columbia University Press, 2016.

———. *Paths Toward a Clearing: Radical Empiricism and Ethnographic Inquiry*. Bloomington: Indiana University Press, 1989.

Joseph, John. *The Modern Assyrians of the Middle East*. Leiden, Netherlands: Brill, 2000.

Jwaideh, Wadie. *The Kurdish National Movement: Its Origins and Development*. Syracuse, NY: Syracuse University Press, 2006.

Katz, Marion. *Prayer in Islamic Thought and Practice*. Cambridge: Cambridge University Press, 2013.

Kern, Karen. *Imperial Citizenship: Marriage and Citizenship in the Ottoman Frontier Provinces of Iraq*. Syracuse, NY: Syracuse University Press, 2011.

Khan, Arsalan. "Islam and Pious Sociality: The Ethics of Hierarchy in the Tablighi Jamaat in Pakistan." *Social Analysis* 60, no. 4 (2016): 96–113.

Khan, Muhammad Muhsin Khan. *The Translation of the Meanings of Sahih al-Bukhari*. Riyadh: Darussalam, 1997.

Khan, Naveeda. *Muslim Becoming: Aspiration and Skepticism in Pakistan*. Durham, NC: Duke University Press, 2012.

Khatab, Sayed. *The Political Thought of Sayyid Qutb: The Theory of Jahiliyyah*. New York: Routledge, 2006.

Kholoussy, Hanan. *For Better, for Worse: The Marriage Crisis That Made Modern Egypt*. Stanford, CA: Stanford University Press, 2010.

Khour, Dina Rizk. *Iraq in Wartime: Soldiering, Martyrdom, and Remembrance*. Cambridge: Cambridge University Press, 2013.

King, Diane. "The Personal Is Patrilineal: Namus as Sovereignty." *Identities* 15, no. 3 (2008): 317–342.

Klein, Janet. *The Margins of Empire*. Stanford, CA: Stanford University Press, 2011.

Krajeski, Jenna. "Kurdistan's Female Fighters." *The Atlantic*, January 30, 2013. https://www.theatlantic.com/international/archive/2013/01/kurdistans-female-fighters/272677/.

Kurdistan Regional Statistics Office. *Demographic Survey: Kurdistan Region of Iraq, July 2018*. 2018. Formerly available at http://www.krso.net.

Lambek, Michael. *The Ethical Condition: Essays on Action, Person, and Value*. Chicago: University of Chicago Press, 2015.

Laugier, Sandra. "The Ethics of Care as a Politics of the Ordinary." *New Literary History* 46 (2015): 217–240.

Leezenberg, Michiel. "Political Islam among the Kurds." In *The Kurds: Nationalism and Politics*, edited by Faleh Jabar and Hosham Dawod, 203–227. London: Saqi, 2006.

Lewis, Franklin. "Sexual Occidentation: The Politics of Boy-Love and Christian-Love in Attar." *Journal of Iranian Studies* 42, no. 5 (2009): 693–723.

Lumbard, Joseph. "The Quranic View of Sacred History and Other Religions." In *The Study Quran: A New Translation and Commentary*, edited by Seyyed Hossein Nasr,

Caner K. Dagli, Maria Massi Dakake, Joseph Lumbard, and Mohammed Rustom, 1765–1784. New York: Harper One, 2015.

Lyon, Wallace. *Kurds, Arabs, and Britons: The Memoir of Wallace Lyon in Iraq, 1918–44.* Edited by David K. Fieldhouse. London: I. B. Tauris, 2002.

Mahmood, Saba. *Politics of Piety: The Islamic Revival and the Feminist Subject.* Princeton, NJ: Princeton University Press, 2004.

Marsden, Magnus. *Living Islam: Muslim Religious Experience in Pakistan's North-West Frontier.* Cambridge: Cambridge University Press, 2005.

Mattingly, Cheryl. *Moral Laboratories: Family Peril and the Struggle for a Good Life.* Berkeley: University of California Press, 2014.

McLarney, Ellen. *Soft Force: Women in Egypt's Islamic Awakening.* Princeton, NJ: Princeton University Press, 2015.

Mehmudiyan, Se'îd Mustefa. *Feqê w feqeyetî le Kurdistan.* Tehran: Ihsan, 1382Sh./2003.

Menoret, Pascal. *Joyriding in Riyadh: Oil, Urbanism and Road Revolt.* Cambridge: Cambridge University Press, 2014.

Messick, Brinkley. *The Calligraphic State: Textual Domination in a Muslim Society.* Berkeley: University of California Press, 1993.

Mewlewî. *'Eqîdey Merziye, dananî Siyid 'Ebdulrehîmî Mewlewî.* Edited by Mela 'Ebdulkerîm Mudarris. Baghdad: Hatif, 1988.

Miller, Flagg. *The Audacious Ascetic: What the Bin Laden Tapes Reveal About Al-Qa'ida.* Oxford: Oxford University Press, 2015.

Mittermaier, Amira. "Dreams from Elsewhere: Muslim Subjectivities Beyond the Trope of Self-Cultivation." *Journal of the Royal Anthropological Institute* 18 (2012): 247–265.

———. *Dreams That Matter: Egyptian Landscapes of the Imagination.* Berkeley: University of California Press, 2011.

Moallem, Minoo. *Between Warrior Brother and Veiled Sister: Islamic Fundamentalism and the Politics of Patriarchy in Iran.* Berkeley: University of California Press, 2005.

Mojab, Shahrzad, ed. *Women of a Non-state Nation: The Kurds.* Costa Mesa, CA: Mazda Publishers, 2001.

Montgomery, James. "For Love of a Christian Boy: A Song by Abu Nuwas." *Journal of Arabic Literature* 27, no. 2 (1996): 115–124.

Motlagh, Amy. *Burying the Beloved: Marriage, Realism, and Reform in Modern Iran.* Stanford, CA: Stanford University Press, 2012.

Mudarris, Mela 'Ebdulkerîm. *Badi' w 'eruzî Namî.* Baghdad: Dar al-Jahiz, 1991.

———. *Binemaley Zanayan.* Edited by Muhemmed 'Elî Qeredaxî. Baghdad: Shafıq, 1984.

———. *Mektûbatî Kak Ehmedî Şêx*. Hewlêr, Iraq: Aras, 2008.

———. *Yadî Merdan*. 2 vols. Baghdad: Korî Zanyarî Kurd, 1979.

Muhemmed, Kemal Re'uf. *'Eqîdey Îman: 'Eqîdey Kurdî*. Hewlêr, Iraq: Aras, 2004.

Muhemmed, Mes'ud. *Çepkêk le Gulzarî Nalî*. Hewlêr, Iraq: Aras, 2004.

Murata, Sachiko, and William Chittick. *The Vision of Islam*. St. Paul, MN: Paragon House, 1994.

Murre-van den Berg, Heleen. "Chaldeans and Assyrians: The Church of the East in the Ottoman Period." In *Christian Heritage of Iraq*, edited by Erica Hunter, 146–164. Piscataway, NJ: Gorgias Press, 2009.

Najmabadi, Afsaneh. *Women with Mustaches and Men Without Beards*. Berkeley: University of California Press, 2005.

Nasr, Seyyed Hossein, Caner K. Dagli, Maria Massi Dakake, Joseph Lumbard, and Mohammed Rustom, ed. and trans. *The Study Quran: A New Translation and Commentary*. New York: Harper One, 2015.

Nelson, Kristina. *The Art of Reciting the Quran*. Austin: University of Texas Press, 1985.

Neqşbendî, Sheikh Emîn Sheikh 'Ila'aldîn. *Tesewuf çiye?* 3rd ed. N.p.: Kitêbxaney Bêxud, 2015. Originally published in 1985.

Nicols, Jean Baptiste, ed. and trans. *Les Quatrains de Kheyam*. Paris: L'Imprimerie Impériale, 1867.

Olszewska, Zuzanna. *The Pearl of Dari: Poetry and Personhood among Young Afghans in Iran*. Bloomington: Indiana University Press, 2015.

Omarkhali, Khanna, ed. *Religious Minorities in Kurdistan: Beyond the Mainstream*. Wiesbaden, Germany: Harrassowitz Verlag, 2014.

Pandolfo, Stefania. *Impasse of the Angels: Scenes from a Moroccan Space of Memory*. Chicago: University of Chicago Press, 1997.

Panian, Karnig. *Goodbye, Antoura: A Memoir of the Armenian Genocide*. Stanford, CA: Stanford University Press, 2015.

Powers, Paul. *Intent in Islamic Law: Motive and Meaning in Medieval Sunni Fiqh*. Leiden, Netherlands: Brill, 2006.

Pursley, Sara. "Daughters of the Right Path: Family Law, Homosocial Publics, and the Ethics of Intimacy in the Works of Shi'i Revivalist Bint Al-Huda." *Journal of Middle East Women's Studies* 8, no. 2 (2012): 51–77.

———. *Familiar Futures: Time, Selfhood, and Sovereignty in Iraq*. Stanford, CA: Stanford University Press, 2018.

———. "The Stage of Adolescence: Anticolonial Time, Youth Insurgency, and the Marriage Crisis in Hashimite Iraq." *History of the Present* 3, no. 2 (2013): 160–197.

Qeredaxî, 'Eta. *Silêmanî: Zemîney Peresendin u milmilanêy tesewuf.* Silêmanî, Iraq: Blawkrawekanî Heftenamey Kurdistanî Nwê, 2003.

Qutbuddin, Tahera. "Piety and Virtue in Early Islam: Two Sermons by Imam Ali." In *Self-Transcendence and Virtue: Perspectives from Philosophy, Psychology, and Theology*, edited by Jennifer A. Frey and Candace Vogler, 125–153. London: Routledge, 2019.

Rich, Claudius James. *Narrative of a Residence in Koordistan, and on the Site of Ancient Nineveh.* London: James Duncan, 1836.

Robbins, Joel. "Cultural Values." In *A Companion to Moral Anthropology*, edited by Didier Fassin, 117–312. Malden, MA: Wiley-Blackwell, 2012.

Robson, Laura. "Peripheries of Belonging: Military Recruitment and the Making of a 'Minority' in Wartime Iraq." *First World War Studies* 7, no. 1 (2016): 23–42.

———. "Refugee Camps and the Spatialization of Assyrian Nationalism in Iraq." In *Modernity, Minority, and the Public Sphere: Jews and Christians in the Middle East*, edited by Sasha Goldstein-Sabbah and Hendrika Lena Murre-van den Berg, 237–257. Leiden, Netherlands: Brill, 2016.

Rodrigue, Aron. "Difference and Tolerance in the Ottoman Empire." Interview by Nancy Reynolds. *Stanford Humanities Review* 5, no. 1 (1996). https://web.stanford.edu/group/SHR/5-1/text/rodrigue.html.

Rumi, Mawlana Jalaluddin. *The Mathnawi of Jalaluddin Rumi.* Edited and translated by Reynold Nicholson. Cambridge, UK: E. J. W. Gibb Memorial, 1926.

———. *Mystical Poems of Rumi.* Edited by Franklin Lewis. Translated by Arthur J. Arberry. Chicago: University of Chicago Press, 2009.

Salomon, Noah. *For Love of the Prophet: An Ethnography of Sudan's Islamic State.* Princeton, NJ: Princeton University Press, 2016.

Sayeed, Asma. *Women and the Transmission of Religious Knowledge in Islam.* Cambridge: Cambridge University Press, 2013.

Schielke, Samuli. "Being Good in Ramadan: Ambivalence, Fragmentation, and the Moral Self in the Lives of Young Egyptians." *Journal of the Royal Anthropological Institute* 15, no. 1 (2009): 24–40.

Schmidinger, Thomas. *Rojava: Revolution, War, and the Future of Syria's Kurds.* Translated by Michael Schiffmann. London: Pluto, 2018.

Seccadî, 'Eleddîn. *Mêjuy Edebî Kurdî.* Edited by Se'îd Keremî. Sine, Iran: Blawkirdinewey Kurdistan, 1389Sh./2010.

Sells, Michael. *Early Islamic Mysticism.* New York: Paulist Press, 2006.

———. "The Infinity of Desire: Love, Mystical Union, and Ethics in Sufism." In *Crossing*

Boundaries: Essays on the Ethical Status of Mysticism, edited by G. William Bernard and Jeffrey Kripal, 184–229. New York: Seven Bridges, 2002.

Seqzî, Baban. *Zerdeşt: Hîway Rizgarzî*. Silêmanî, Iraq: Kurdistan Regional Government's Ministry of Culture, 2006.

Shabistari, Mahmud. *Garden of Mystery: The Gulshan-i Raz of Shabistari*. Translated by Robert Darr. London: Archetype, 2007.

Shahid, Irfan. "The *Sura* of the Poets, Quran XXVI: Final Conclusions." *Journal of Arabic Literature* 35, no. 2 (2004): 175–220.

Shakely, Ferhad. "The Kurdish Qasida." In *Qasida Poetry in Islamic Asia and Africa*, vol. 1, *Classical Traditions and Modern Meanings*, edited by Stefan Sperl and Christopher Shackle, 327–338. Leiden, Netherlands: Brill, 1996.

Shantawi, Ahmed. *Zerdeşt*. Translated by Shakir Fatih. Baghdad: Çapxaney Salman al-I'zamî, 1967.

Sharkey, Heather. *A History of Muslims, Christians and Jews in the Middle East*. Cambridge: Cambridge University Press, 2017.

Sheikh Selam, trans. *Çwarînekanî Xeyam*. Silêmanî, Iraq: Çapxaney Şiqan, 2007.

Sîweylî, Idrîs. *Rewtî Islamî le başurî Kurdistan, 1946–1991*. N.p.: n.p., 2009.

Sîweylî, Rêbwar. *Nalî: Le belaxewe bo Modêrnîtî*. Hewlêr, Iraq: Akadîmyay Kurdî, 2018.

Sluglett, Peter. *Britain in Iraq: Contriving King and Country*. New York: Columbia University Press, 2007.

Soane, Ely Bannister. *To Mesopotamia and Kurdistan in Disguise*. London: John Murray, 1912.

Starrett, Gregory. "The Varieties of Secular Experience." *Comparative Studies in Society and History* 52, no. 3 (2010): 626–651.

Strathern, Marilyn. "Kinship as a Relation." *L'Homme* 210 (2014): 43–61.

———. *Partial Connections*. Walnut Creek, CA: AltaMira Press, 2004.

Szanto, Edith. "'Zoroaster was a Kurd!': Neo-Zoroastrianism among the Iraqi Kurds." *Iran and the Caucasus* 22 (2018): 96–110.

Theisen, Finn. *A Manual of Classical Persian Prosody*. Wiesbaden, Germany: Otto Harrassowitz, 1982.

Van Bruinessen, Martin. *Agha, Shaikh, and State: The Social and Political Structures of Kurdistan*. London: Zed, 1992.

———. "Dersim and Delahu: Some Reflections on Kurdish Alevism and the Ahl-i Haqq Religion." In *Pursuit of the Others: Festschrift in Honor of Ahmet Yasar Ocak*, edited by Mehmet Oz and Fatih Yesil, 577–594. Istanbul: Timas, 2015.

———. "Kurdish Studies in Western and Central Europe." *Wiener Jahrbuch für Kurdische Studien* 2 (2015): 18–96.

Wagemakers, Joas. *A Quietist Jihadi: The Ideology and Influence of Abu Muhammad al-Maqdisi*. Cambridge: Cambridge University Press, 2012.

Wein, Peter. *Iraqi Arab Nationalism: Authoritarian, Totalitarian, and Pro-fascist Inclinations, 1932–1941*. London: Routledge, 2006.

Wensinck, Arent J. "Hadjdj." In *Encyclopaedia of Islam*, 2nd ed. Leiden, Netherlands: Brill, 1986.

Wickham, Carrie. *The Muslim Brotherhood: Evolution of an Islamist Movement*. Princeton, NJ: Princeton University Press, 2013.

Xal, Mamosta Şêx Muhemmedî. *Muftî Zehawî*. Edited by 'Ebdulhemîd Mela Muhemmedemîn Kanî Mîranî. Silêmanî, Iraq: Senterî Zehawî, 2018.

Yüksel, Metin. "Dengbej, Mullah, Intelligentsia: The Survival and Revival of the Kurdish-Kurmanji Language in the Middle East, 1925–1960." PhD diss., University of Chicago, 2011.

———. "Solidarity Without Borders: Poetic Tributes to Paul Robeson of Goran and Cegerxwîn." *Journal of Postcolonial Writing* 51, no. 5 (2015): 556–573.

Zaken, Mordechai. *Jewish Subjects and Their Tribal Chieftains in Kurdistan: A Study in Survival*. Leiden, Netherlands: Brill, 2007.

Zekî Beg, Muhemmedemîn. *Te'rîxî Silêmanî we welatî*. Edited by Refîq Salih. 1918. Reprint, Silêmanî, Iraq: Binkey Jîn, 2006.

COLLECTED WORKS OF POETRY IN SORANI KURDISH

Dîwanî Bêkes. Edited by Muhemmedî Mela Kerîm. Silêmanî, Iraq: Çapxaney Şivan, 2009.

Dîwanî Bêxud. Edited by Muhemmedî Mela Kerîm. Sine, Iran: Blawkirdinewey Kurdistan, 1386Sh./2008.

Dîwanî Ehmed Muxtar Caf. Edited by 'Izedîn Mustafa Rasul. Baghdad: Al-Adeeb, 1986.

Dîwanî Goran. Tehran: Nashre Paniz, 2003.

Dîwanî Hejar. Edited by Majid Murdox Ruhani. Tehran: Çapxaney Paniz, 2012.

Dîwanî Hêmin. Edited by Wirya Zirarî. N.p.: Çapxaney Azad, 2012.

Dîwanî Kurdî. Edited by Gîw Mukriyanî. Hewlêr, Iraq: Çapxaney Kurdistan, 1973.

Dîwanî Mehwî: Mela Muhemmedî Kurî Mela 'Uthmanî Balxî. Edited by Muhemmedî Mela Kerîm. Baghdad: Korî Zanyarî Kurd, 1984.

Dîwanî Mesture Erdalan. Edited by Majid Murdokh Rohani. Sine, Iran: Nashrana, 2009.

Dîwanî Muftî Pêncwênî. Edited by Mela 'Ebdullay Tutinçî. N.p.: Iraqi Technical Printing, 1990.

Dîwanî Nalî: Mela Xidrî Ehmedî Şaweysî Mikayelî. Edited by Mela 'Ebdulkerîm Mudarris, Fatih 'Ebdulkerîm, and Muhemmedî Mela Kerîm. Baghdad: Korî Zanyarî Kurd, 1976.

Dîwanî Narî. Edited by Kakey Falah. Sanandaj, Iran: Intisharat Kurdistan, 2003.

Dîwanî Natîq. Edited by Hakîm Mela Salih. Silêmanî, Iraq: Kitêbxaney Şêx Reza, 2009.

Dîwanî Qani'. Edited by Burhan Qani'. Tehran: Nashre Paniz, 2014.

Dîwanî Salim: 'Ebdurrehman begî Sahibqiran. Edited by Mela 'Ebdulkerîm Mudarris, Fatih 'Ebdulkerîm, and Muhemmedî Mela Kerîm. Silêmanî, Iraq: Binkey Jîn, 2015.

Dîwanî Şêx Reza Talebanî. Edited by Şêx Muhemmedî Xal. Hewlêr, Iraq: Aras, 2003.

Dîwanî Wefayî: Mîrza 'Ebdurrehîmî Seblaxî. Edited by Muhemmed 'Elî Qeredaxî. Sanandaj, Iran: Intisharat Kurdistan, 1379Sh./2001.

RECORDINGS FROM MELA KRÊKAR'S INTERNET ARCHIVE (DIDINWE.NET)

Bnemakani Rabwn [Foundations of the awakening]

Chezhy Hawsariaty 1 [The sense of marriage]

Chezhy Hawsariaty 2

Gishty: Axlaq [General: Ethics/morals]

Gishty: Hawelani Peghember [General: Companions of the Prophet]

Gishty: Juleke [General: Jews]

Gishty: Regai Peghemberan [General: The way of the prophets]

Gishty: Rewshti Muselmanan [General: Muslim ethics]

Gishty: Zina [General: Illicit sex]

Hukm be Gheyri Xwa C [Governance by any other than God]

Jiyanname [Life story/autobiography]

Jiyanname 3

Jiyanname 6

Jiyanname 8

Jiyanname Peghemberan: Eisa B [Lives of the prophets: 'Isa/Jesus]

Ometi Islam: Lawazi Islam [Islam's *ummah*: The weakness of Islam]

Ometi Islam 3: Komelgey Nmuney Peghember [Islam's *ummah* 3: Society modeled on the Prophet]

Ometi Islam 7: Wryabunewe [Islam's *ummah*: Coming to consciousness]

Rabuni Islam: Rabuni Kurdistan [Islamic awakening: Kurdistan's awakening]

Rabuni Islam: Roli Lawan [Islamic awakening: Youth's role]

Index

Abu-Lughod, Lila, 22
accommodation, 53, 93, 150, 156, 158–60. *See also* reception
advice. See *nesîhet*
Afghanistan, 112, 116
Agrama, Hussein Ali, 168–69
Ahmed, Shahab, 51, 123
Al-'Adawiyya, Rabi'a, 34
alcohol, 88, 96–97, 101, 104, 125–26, 179n18
Al-Hallaj, Mansur, 153
Ali, (Imam Ali ibn Talib), 45; love of, 94–96; as warrior, 70, 83, 137
Anfal Campaign, 14, 113
analogy, 66; of lover and beloved, 87–90, 97, 110–11; of poetry and life, 158–59, 110–11
anxiety: of authority, 161–64; about conversion, 103; about illicit sex, 132; in nationalist poetry, 84; as productive power, 168–69; about Shi'ism, 95
apostasy. See *kufir*
Arabs, 13–14, 16–17, 44, 99–100

archive, 57–59, 117–18
Armenians, 20, 73, 83, 137, 177n33
Asad, Talal, 29–32, 50–53, 134. *See also* discursive tradition
ascendance of Islam, 68, 86, 136, 156
Assyrians, 14, 15, 20, 73–76
atheists, 24
Atmaca, Metin, 73
'Attar, Farid al-Din, 67. *See also* Sheikh San'an
attraction: to beloved, 64–66, 80–81; and aversion as concepts, 50–53, 72; to fasting, 36, 39, 42; to heresy, 95–96; to Islam, 155–56; to non-Islamic traditions, 68–72, 76, 84; to Quran, 107; to Shi'ism, 94–96; to Sufism, 154–56; to Zoroastrianism, 44
authority: attraction and, 35–36; critique of, 39–40; in Islam, 29–30, 50–53; of men, 102, 121, 129, 141, 161–64; of norms, 4–6; of political parties, 105, 122–23; Salafism and, 123–25; Sufism and, 56

aversion: and attraction as concepts, 50–53, 72; inspired by Islamism, 114; to Islam, 44–45, 89; to isolation, 149; to piety, 31, 164–65; to prayer, 36; to Quranic audition, 38–39; tolerance and, 159

awakening (*rabun*), 118–122; youth as vanguard of, 124–28. See also *nesîhet*

Azzam, Abdallah, 113

Baban Emirate, 61–63, 73–76
Badr, battle of, 94–95, 137
Baghdad, 20, 45, 49, 77, 162, 177n31
Bashkin, Orit, 185n73
beauty, 65; of Zoroastrianism, 44; of Quran, 38, 107–8; of humans, 96–98; of poetry 151–54
bêdîn (irreligious), 7–8, 145
Bêkes, 85
belief (*bawer*), 4; like an apple, 146; in Christianity, 23–24; in Islam, 145–50, 169; readers and, 172; seeming belief, 93–94;
beloved, 64–66, 80–83, 112
Berzencî, Sheikh Mehmud, 73–74
Bet-Schlimon, Arbella, 74–75
Bistami, Bayazid, 192n14
Bowen, John, 35, 178n11
British Mandate, 21, 74–77, 82–85
Brookshaw, Dominic Parviz, 184n50
Brown, Wendy, 159

Caf, Ehmed Muxtar, 66, 77–78, 80
cassette audition, 117–18, 124
Caton, Steve, 154
Ce'fer, Mamosta, 62
Chaldeans, 14, 15, 73–76. See also Christians
children, 133. See also youth
Christians, 14; author as, 23; colonizers as, 81–85; churches of, 64, 82; conversion of, 67, 136–37; holidays of, 138–39; as *kafir*s, 55; in Kurdistan, 20; Muslims becoming, 66–67, 102–3; in poetry, 64–69; in Quran, 63–64 in Silêmanî, 72–76; marriage and, 102, 120; Krêkar's view of, 136–39. See also Armenian; Chaldean; Assyrian; Church; Jesus

civil war, in Kurdistan, 14, 46, 92, 116, 145, 189n19
class, 32, 100, 143, 193n24
claims: description and, 1–2, 27–28, 142–43, 173; sufficiency of, 111, 127, 146–50, 156, 164, 173
colonialism. See British Mandate
communism, 21, 40, 85, 127–28
conservatism, 115, 128–129
conversion, 23, 43–44, 66–68, 82–84, 101–4, 137, 184n57
critique, 32; of gender roles, 162; of God, 96; of Islam, 33; of melas, 40; of others 37–39; of Salafism, 93; of Sufi paradigm, 77–84. See also *nesîhet*

Das, Veena, 8, 143
daughters, 33–39, 53, 120, 128, 135, 141–42, 148–150, 162–64
death, 45–46, 69–70, 153
debate: avoided, 93–94, 98; constituting Islam, 5–7, 18–22, 29–32, 45, 48; Islamists and, 46, 127–28, 145; outside of, 46, 48; about poetic meaning, 59–60; scenes of, in poetry, 68–69
description: of beloved, 64–68, 81–84, 96–97; claims and 1–8, 27–28, 142–43, 146–51; as ethnographic task, 1–8, 27–28, 159, 173; gestures and, 90, 142, 158, 164; of *kafir*s, 64–71; of piety and its absence, 30–31, 36, 144; poetry as,

53–54, 109–11; of relations as religious orientation, 1–2, 23–24, 98, 148–49; scholar's, of religion, 44; of small acts, 142; as task in everyday life, 36, 92–94, 104–5, 141, 144–45, 148

desire, 88–90, 99–104, 106–11, 134, 155

Devji, Faisal, 123

dîn, 7–8, 67, 85, 146–49, 159

discipline, 2, 133–34, 144, 153–53. *See also* prayer; fasting

discursive tradition, 29–32; as broader than piety, 50–53, 58; in poetry, 60; in Islamism, 117

divine unity (*tewhîd*), 64–66, 92, 97, 126, 134

divorce, 100–106, 126, 129

doctrine. *See* '*eqîde*

domestic space, 32, 58, 100, 112, 124–26, 129–34, 141–44, 157–64

doubt, 47–48, 163

editors, 58–59, 82, 85, 167–68

Edmonds, Cecil J., 25, 74, 184n60

Ehmed Muxtar Caf, 66, 77–78, 81

'Eleke, Kerîmî, 74

eloquence, 116–17, 133

'*eqîde* (doctrine in action), 119–120, 126, 137–38, 191n6

ethics, 3–6, 29–54, 142–43, 156–57, 164, 168; affect and, 36–39; body and, 146–148; *exlaq* as, 79–80, 90–95, 101, 127, 132–33; *dîn* as, 7, 85; learning, 33–36, 38; obligation and, 160; as system, 92–98; 146; as vision, 109. *See also* immorality; self-formation; virtue

ethnicity, 16

ethnography, 111; focus on individuals in, 51, 91, 116, 142, 172

experience: as teacher, 33, 94–95; description of, 51–52; ordinary, xiii, 113; as shared, 51–52, 90–91; of ethnography, 171–173

faith (*îman*), 4, 191n6; attraction and, 64–68; ritual worship and, 34–35; growth of, 33–34, 89; in hadith of Gabriel, 147; *kufir* and, 113–114, 118–123; Muslim, and Christian, 138–39; as nationalist, 81–86; in Quran, 63–64; in speech and action 146–48; theology and, 27

face, of beloved, 64–71, 78–80, 96–97, 179n18

family, *kufir* within, 120–21; gender roles within, 128–31, 161–64; Islamist conceptions of, 124–34; liberal conceptions of, 131; readers and, 27; state reform of, 98–100; religious difference within, 33–36, 48–50, 92–98, 104–8, 124–28, 148–50, 158–65

fasting, 3, 33, 40–48; advice about, 104–6, 135–36; health and, 41–43; in Quran, 30; as neglected, 3, 33–37, 144; as practiced, 3, 40–48, 148–150, 151; as required, 3, 30, 33–37, 153

fathers, 33–36, 93–94, 120, 126, 129, 141, 161–64

fear, 33–34, 38, 82, 132, 162–64

fieldwork: conditions of, 22–27; reading texts in/as, 19, 32, 39–40, 57

figures of thought, 12, 40, 88, 100, 122–23, 163–64; *kafir* as, 55–60, 63–72, 81–86, 136; for readers, 172–73; Sufis as, 48, 152–57

finitude, 89, 104, 106

friendship, 27, 108–11, 127, 130, 151–52

Gaylani, Abdul Qader, 126

gender, 65, 71, 80, 128–31. *See also* men; women

generational difference, 33, 125
gesture, 26, 90, 145, 146, 155, 157, 159, 192n11
Ghaderi, Farangis, 181n10, 186n78
Ghannam, Farha, 193n26
Goran, 'Ebdullah, 39–41
gratitude, 34, 63–64
guerillas, 14, 17, 112
gwê nedan (not listening), 31, 101, 144–45

hadith, 2, 33–37, 119, 125, 178n7; discursive tradition and, 29–32; of faithful and neglectful Muslims, 34; of Gabriel, 147, 163; of killing a *dhimma*, 137; of medicine and illness, 35; of seventy-three sects, 119
Hafız, 61
Haj, Samira, 82
hajj, 48–50, 62
Hallisey, Charles, 156
Hassanpour, Amir, 181n7
Hedayet, Sadegh, 100
Hejar, 96
Helmet, Letîf, 180n4
Hendrickson, Jocelyn, 49
heresy, 95–96
Hesen, Sherzad, 162
Hewraman, 39, 46–47, 113, 133, 190n27
hierarchy of religions, 56, 68, 72, 76, 85–86, 136
Hindu, 64
hospitality, 25, 153
hucre (religious seminary), 18–22, 79–84, 121, 151
humanity, 96, 107, 122–23, 189n18
humility, 68–69, 72, 137, 156–67
humor, 25–26, 47, 101, 107, 158
Hussein, Saddam, 13–15
Hussein ibn Ali, 45–46, 70
hypocrisy, 8, 26, 102–3

intention, 41–42
iltîzam (binding/commitment), 31, 138
imagination, 46–47, 55–72, 76–86, 88, 103, 136; readers and, 60, 167–68, 170–73. See also *xeyal*
immorality, 101, 113, 132, 162–63
in-laws, 120, 128, 130–32
Iraqi state, 13–15, 21, 46, 80, 82, 99–100; relation with Kurds, 13, 112–13
Islam: Christianity and, 62–68, 72–76, 81–85, 136–39; as discursive tradition, 29–32, 50–53; early history of, 45–46, 94–95; history in Kurdistan, 16–22; orientations to, 2–8; persists in the bones/blood, 146; Sufism and, 55–56, 152–57; Zoroastrianism and, 43–45, 50–53
Islamism, 112–40; behind secularism, 105; communism and, 21, 127–28; families and, 91–98, 104–8, 124–28, 141; history in Kurdistan 115–17; influence on piety, 18, 114; Kurdish nationalism and, 116; Salafism and, 92, 115–17
'îşq (love/desire), 108–11
Izutsu, Toshihiko, 182n27, 188n10

Jackson, Michael, 91, 108, 173
jahiliyet (crass ignorance), 118
Jesus, 63, 68, 97, 101, 138
Jews, in "Islamic society," 136–39; Kak Ehmedî Sheikh and, 155–56; in poetry, 97; in Quran, 63; in Silêmanî, 73–74
jihad, 74–75, 112, 117, 119, 130, 134, 137
jokes, 25–27, 101–2, 178n39
Judgement Day, 34, 66, 109, 132, 147, 152–53

kafir (Ar. *kafr*, apostate): accusation within families, 48–50, 106, 114, 120–21; beloved as, 63–69; colonizer as, 81–86; deserves execution, 69–71; as figure of

thought, 55–60, 63–86, 172; identifying, 119–120, 139; jihad against, 74, 137; within self, 63–71, 110; traitor to nation as, 86. See also *kufir*
Kak Ehmedî Sheikh, 73–74, 155–56
Khan, Naveeda, 10
Khayyam, Omar, 43, 47–48, 53–54, 96–98, 108
kidnapping, 26
kindness, 5, 99, 126–28, 134, 137, 157
Kirkuk, 75, 82
kissing hands, 155
knowledge, 12, 79–82, 118–27, 134
Krêkar, Mela (Necmedîn Ferec Ehmed), background and influences, 112–13, 133, 188n10; communism and, 127–28; *nesîhet* and, 134–36; as political theorist, 114; position in Islamism, 116–17; view of Christians and Jews, 136–39; view of marriage, 128–31, 190n35; view of political parties, 122–24
KRG (Kurdistan Regional Government), 14–15, 105, 113, 116, 117, 158
Kurdî (Mustafa Begî Sahibqiran), 62, 70, 71
Kurdish studies, 15, 44, 55–60, 73
Kurdistan: background, 13–17; regional connections, 20; as geographic referent, 13; Islam in, 18–22; Islamism in, 112–40; nationalism in 15, 77–86, 153; response to US-led invasion, 25
kufir (Ar. *kufr*, apostasy): betraying nation as, 77, 85; Christian holidays and, 138–39; faith and, 63, 89, 113–14, 118–122, 159; within families, 48–50, 120–21; as grounds for divorce, 187n24; as internal to the self, 69–71; public accusations of, 145, 187n24; in Quran, 63–64; vigilance against, 113–14, 120–21, 135–36. See also *kafir*

Laugier, Sandra, 90, 143, 159
Lewis, Franklin, 53, 183n37
liberalism, 21–22, 131–134, 159
listening. See *gwê nedan*
Lumbard, Joseph, 63

madrasa. See *hucre*
marriage, 98–104; between Muslims and non-Muslims, 120; Krêkar and, 127–28; gender roles in, 128–31; as worship, 129; role of in-laws in, 130–31; proposal for, 136
Marsden, Magnus, 140
masculinity, 71–72, 79–80, 99, 183n49
Masture Erdelan, 71, 183n49
Mattingly, Cheryl, 161
Mehwî, 21, 67, 87, 101–2, 108–111, 151–53
mela (religious scholar), 18–22, 39–40, 58, 125, 155. See also *hucre*
men: as brothers, 48–50, 92–94, 98, 104–8, 127, 130–31; as friends, 99, 110–11; as husbands, 99, 102–6, 121, 129–32, 135–36; as sons, 93; as uncles, 104–5. See also fathers
Mewlewî, 154, 191n6
Mittermaier, Amira, 160, 193n4
Moallem, Minoo, 189n18
mosque, 18–19, 88, 112, 117, 144
Motlagh, Amy, 100
Mudarris, Mela 'Ebdulkerîm, 181n9
Mufti Pêncwênî, 78–81
Muhammad (Prophet), 2, 45–49, 63, 66, 92–96, 119–22, 141, 147. See also hadith

Najmabadi, Afsaneh, 88
Nalî (Mela Xidr Ehmed Şaweysî Mikayelî), 19, 62, 71, 151–52, 182n19, 183n49
Naqshbandi, Mawlana Khalid, 60–61, 81
Narî (Mela Kake Hemey Bêlu), 180n23, 81–84, 96–97, 137

nationalism, Kurdish, 15–16, 21–22, 44, 77–86
neighbors, 41–42
nesîhet (advice), 93, 104, 111, 113–14, 132–36

oil, 82
Olszewska, Zuzanna, 88
ordinary relationships: 8–13; activism and, 105–6, 114–15; betrayal and, 108–111; labor of sustaining, 93–94, 150, 170; mysticism and, 87–91; politics of, 105–6, 114–15, 120–22, 124–28, 134–136; small acts and, 142; social structures and, 26–27; texture of, 27, 90, 110–111, 142. *See also* family; marriage; public
orientation, religious, 1–8; belief and, 24, 93, 148–50; causes of, 18; as combining discourses, 98; expressed in comparison, 98; expressed in poetry, 63, 72, 96–98; expressed in small gestures, 142–43, 159; within families, 35–36, 48–49, 93–98, 104–8, 125–28, 139, 148–50, 160–65; nationalism and, 77–86; "non-religious" as, 89; as paradoxical, 63–71; as a system, 93–94
Ottoman Empire, 19–22, 61–62, 74–76, 156

Pandolfo, Stefania, 187n16
paradox, 1–8, 93–94; dichotomy and, 114; of faith, 34; of piety, 112; in poetry, 22, 52–54, 64, 111; productivity of, 56–57, 69–72, 81
patience, 5, 125–28, 134, 173; readers and, 12, 173
pedagogy, 33–36, 124–28, 131–36
Persian literature, 19, 53, 59–61, 65, 71–72, 100, 153
persuasion, 126–27, 136, 154
piety, xiv, 1–8; in anthropology of Islam, 3–6; as collective, 81–82; leftist politics and, 17–18; paradoxes of 81, 89, 112; passage beyond Islam and, 56, 81; pedagogies of, 33–36, 124–28, 131–36; pleasures of, 158; plurality of self and, 72; of poets, 64–72, 81; turning away from, 3–4, 31, 50–54, 107–8, 114, 142–45
Pillar Poets (*sê koçkey Baban*), 61–77, 89, 113–114, 127, 136, 139, 172
pleasure, 12, 65, 143, 151–60, 164–65
poetry: as description, 53–54, 96–98, 109–111; editing *dîwan* of, 58–59; as expressing paradox, 22, 53–54; history in Kurdish language, 60–61; *hucre* and, 18–22, 79–80; *kafir* in, 55–86; non-didactic functions of, 109–10; as philosophy or cosmology, 22; pleasure of 151–57; Quran and, 107, 179n12; recitation in everyday life, 103, 152; tradition of interpreting, 59–60, 108
political parties, 14–15, 17, 25, 92, 115–117; rejection of, 92–93, 114, 122–24; secularism and, 7, 105–6. *See also* civil war
polygamy, 99, 102–3, 127–28
polytheism (*şirk*), 64–65, 97, 134
prayer, xiv, 2–4, 33–34, 144, 175n2; advise about, 93, 110, 125–128; aversion to 34–36, 145, 148–49, 157; in Christianity, 23, 31, 65; as marking piety, 45, 65–66, 126, 127, 144, 151, 158
public, 37–39, 131, 134–36
public education, 79
Pursley, Sara, 100, 189n21, 190n37

Qajar dynasty, 61
Qani', 84–85, 185n71, 185n76
Qeredaxî, 'Eta, 56
Quran, 2, 18; audition in public 36–39; beauty of, 37–38, 107–8; discursive tradition and,

29–32; non-Muslims in, 63–64; poetry and, 58–59, 69, 107; religious difference in, 63–64; Salafi view of, 119–22, 132–33, 138–39; verse on conduct with parents (31:15), 126; verse on fasting (2:183), 30; verse on listening to Quran (7:204), 179n12; verse on Musa's anger (20:94), 183n45

Qutb, Sayyid, 188n10

Qutbuddin, Tahera, 94–95

Ramadan, 36–49, 101, 104, 135, 144, 158, 160

readers, xv, 27, 42, 60, 102, 111, 161, 167–73

reception, 98, 158–60. *See also* accommodation

relationships, 5, 8–13; analogies in, 88; activism in, 112–14, 120, 124–28, 136; describing religious orientation in, 23–28, 42–43, 51–52, 90–91, 98, 148–50; uncertainty in, 104–6, 108–11, 142–43

religious difference: accommodation of, 106, 159–60; within families, 33–36, 48–50, 92–98, 104–8, 124–28, 148–50, 158–65; Islamist movements and, 124–28, 136–39; internal to Islam, 6, 52, 92–98; internal to self, 66–68, 70; in Kurdish studies, 15; in nationalist discourse, 81–86; in Ottoman era, 20, 74–76, 156; in Quran, 63–64; tolerance and, 159

resurrection. *See* Judgement Day

revolution, 88, 116, 122–24

rhetorical devices, 181n9, 185n71

Rich, Claudius J., 73, 83

Robson, Laura, 185n64, 185n66

Rumi, Mawlana, 183n46

Salafism, 92–95, 112–140; principles of, 118–122

Salim ('Ebdulrehman Muhemmed Begî Sahibiran), 180n23, 61–62, 65, 68–70

sectarianism, xiii, 48

secular: education as, 79; as insult, 145; Muslims as, 1, 6–7; readers as, 12, 169–73; political parties as, 46, 105–6, 113

secularism: anthropology of, 32, 168–69; communism and, 21; as disguise for Islam, 105–6; *hucre* and, 21; Islamist view of, 113; liberalism and, 131; governance and, 6–7, 21, 100

self-fashioning, 146–148, 160–64

Sells, Michael, 89

sensibility, 22, 32, 53, 57, 98, 159

Sepehri, Sohrab, 152

şer' (divine law), 4, 41, 55–56, 69–70, 102, 117, 133, 135

sermons, 118–23, 133–36, 138–40

Shabistari, Mahmud, 64

Sheikh San'an, 66–67

Sheikh Selam, 48, 179n18

Shi'ism: as attractive heresy, 94–96, 119; Krêkar's view of, 119; in sectarian Iraq, xiii; veneration of Hussein, 45–46, 94; veneration of Imam Ali, 95–96

shukr (Ar., gratitude), 64

Silêmanî (Ar., Sulaimaniyah): history of, 61–63, 73–75; as immoral, 101, 162; Islamism in, 132; links to Baghdad, 20, 61–62, 77, 162, 177n31; name, 13; population profile, 176n13; Sufism in, 56, 155

spy, 25

Strathern, Marilyn, 27, 88

Sufis/Sufism: as anti-Islamic, 56, 180n4; critique of, 77–81, 126; descriptions of, 34, 49–50, 53–55; in *hucre*, 19–20; as interpretive paradigm, 60, 88–90, 110–111; as model of paradoxical subjectivity, 57, 72, 81; in poetry, 53–55, 60, 63–71; as figures of thought, 152–57

Sunnism, 45, 46; as defined by Krêkar,

119–21; Imam Ali and, 95–96, 137; Kurdish identity and, 94–95; as neglected in Kurdish studies, 15; in sectarian Iraq, xiii

surprises, 92, 146, 150

sympathy, 98

Szanto, Edith, 44

Taher Beg, 97–98

television, 45, 107, 144

tendency, 50, 70–72, 80–81, 85–86, 186n78

texts: absorbed in life, 9–10, 13, 90, 164, 168, 173; oral dialogue and, 59, 167–68; circulation of, 57–59, 173. *See also* fieldwork; discursive tradition

tolerance, 93–94, 156, 159

tradition: orientation toward, 4; non-Islamic, 53–57, 68–72, 85–86; outside of, 35; *sunna* as, 119. *See also* discursive tradition; Islam; poetry; Persian literature

translation: for ethnography, 7, 53–54, 89, 118–19, 141, 144; to and from claims, 145; in Kurdistan, 44; of poetry, 48, 53–54, 58, 61, 96

tresses, 64–66, 69, 77–79, 97, 102

'ulama'. *See* mela

Umm Kulthum, 179n12

United States of America, 25–27, 47, 113, 116

Van Bruinessen, Martin, 15

veiling, 37, 135–36

vigilance, against *kufir*, 113, 119, 135

violence: as analytic, 11; colonial, 26, 74–75; in domestic space, 100, 162; of early Islam, 45–47; in Iraq, xiii, 13–15; Krêkar and, 189n19; in poetry, 69–71, 152–54; religious difference and, 75. *See also* civil war

virtue, 2, 31, 121; as absent, 109; humanitarian 94–95; of Jesus, 68–69; nationalism and, 76–82; of not asking, 156–59; skepticism toward, 48; unnamed virtues, 156. *See also* fear; patience; kindness; gratitude; humility; sympathy

vulnerability, 10, 99; of authority, 162–64; to beauty, 96–98, 107; home as space of, 131; to others, 96–98, 110–11, 160–65

women, as daughters, 33–39, 53, 120, 128, 141, 148–50, 161–64; as jihadis, 130; as mothers, 36–37, 144, 162, 178n11; *nesîhet* and, 38–39, 132, 135–36; as poets, 183n49, 184n50; in poetry, 78, 83, 96, 153; as wives, 67, 99–103, 105, 120, 127–31, 158

world: beauty of, 99, 151–52; as corrupt, 82, 154–55; as religious, 146, 170; suffering in, 87–90, 109–11, 151

writing, ethnographic, 1–2, 8–12, 27–28, 173

xeyal (imagination), 47, 97

youth, 23, 33–36, 124–28, 141, 162

zîne (illicit sex), 132

Zoroaster/ Zoroastrianism, 39–40, 43–46, 63, 65, 192n14

zunnar (P., girdle/belt for non-Muslims), 53, 66–67

Stanford Studies in Middle Eastern
and Islamic Societies and Cultures

Joel Beinin and Laleh Khalili, editors

EDITORIAL BOARD

Asef Bayat, Marilyn Booth, Laurie Brand, Timothy Mitchell,
Jillian Schwedler, Rebecca L. Stein, Max Weiss

Showpiece: The Building of Dubai 2020
TODD REISZ

Archive Wars: The Politics of History in Saudi Arabia 2020
ROSIE BSHEER

The Optimist: A Social Biography of Tawfiq Zayyad 2020
TAMIR SOREK

Graveyard of Clerics: Everyday Activism in Saudi Arabia 2020
PASCAL MENORET

Cleft Capitalism: The Social Origins of Failed Market Making in Egypt 2020
AMR ADLY

The Universal Enemy: Jihad, Empire, and the Challenge of Solidarity 2019
DARRYL LI

Waste Siege: The Life of Infrastructure in Palestine 2019
SOPHIA STAMATOPOULOU-ROBBINS

Heritage and the Cultural Struggle for Palestine 2019
  CHIARA DE CESARI

Iran Reframed: Anxieties of Power in the Islamic Republic 2019
  NARGES BAJOGHLI

Banking on the State: The Financial Foundations of Lebanon 2019
  HICHAM SAFIEDDINE

Familiar Futures: Time, Selfhood, and Sovereignty in Iraq 2019
  SARA PURSLEY

Hamas Contained: The Rise and Pacification of Palestinian Resistance 2018
  TAREQ BACONI

Hotels and Highways: The Construction of Modernization Theory in Cold War Turkey 2018
  BEGÜM ADALET

Bureaucratic Intimacies: Human Rights in Turkey 2017
  ELIF M. BABÜL

Impossible Exodus: Iraqi Jews in Israel 2017
  ORIT BASHKIN

Brothers Apart: Palestinian Citizens of Israel and the Arab World 2017
  MAHA NASSAR

Revolution without Revolutionaries: Making Sense of the Arab Spring 2017
  ASEF BAYAT

Soundtrack of the Revolution: The Politics of Music in Iran 2017
  NAHID SIAMDOUST

Copts and the Security State: Violence, Coercion, and Sectarianism in Contemporary Egypt 2016
  LAURE GUIRGUIS

The authorized representative in the EU for product safety and compliance is:
Mare Nostrum Group
B.V Doelen 72
4831 GR Breda
The Netherlands

www.ingramcontent.com/pod-product-compliance
Lightning Source LLC
Chambersburg PA
CBHW020836160426
43192CB00007B/674